On
This Day

On
This Day

RANDOM HOUSE
NEW YORK

Published in the United States by
Random House, Inc., New York.
No part of this publication may be reproduced in
any form or by any means, electronic or mechanical,
including photocopying, without permission in writing
from the publisher. All inquiries should be addressed to
Reference & Information Publishing, Random House, Inc.,
201 East 50th Street, New York, NY 10022-7703.
This edition has been completely updated and retypeset,
based on a version originally published in Great Britain in
different form by Helicon Publishing Ltd, Oxford, in 1994.

Library of Congress Cataloging-in-Publication Data
ISBN 0-679-76972-2

Printed in the United States of America
First US Edition

9 8 7 6 5 4 3 2 1

New York   Toronto   London   Sydney   Auckland

Introduction

Every day should be passed as if it were to be our last.
PUBLILIUS SYRUS, *1st century BC*

Today is a significant anniversary! Don't let it pass without finding out why. Look through these pages and see the notable events throughout time for every day of the year.

On This Day is packed full of dates of important events, achievements of the famous and infamous, quotes, births, and deaths. Use it to discover what else happened on the special anniversaries of you or your loved ones, to provide a wealth of ideas for speeches or presentations—or just browse and enjoy the serendipity.

Every day of the year is allocated a page, showing national days, past events, and births and deaths of significant people on this day. In addition every day has a quotation—be it light-hearted, provoking, or illuminating—usually relating to one of the events on the page. Space is left on every page for the addition of personal anniversaries and important dates. And at the back of the book you will find further information about dates, including important religious festivals, a list of the materials associated with wedding anniversaries, and birthstones.

Editors and Contributors

MANAGING EDITOR
Hilary McGlynn

CONTRIBUTORS
Jane Anson
Sam Cridlan
Anna Farkas
John Wright

PROJECT EDITOR
Avril Cridlan

PRODUCTION
Tony Ballsdon

PAGE MAKEUP
TechType

On This Day

January 1

New Year's Day, and the national days of Cuba, Sudan, and Haiti.

EVENTS

1863 President Lincoln issued the Emancipation Proclamation, ordering the freeing of the slaves. **1901** The Commonwealth of Australia was formed. **1958** The European Community (now European Union) came into existence. **1959** Fidel Castro overthrew the government of Fulgencio Batista and seized power in Cuba. **1993** Czechoslovakia split into two separate states, the Czech Republic and Slovakia; the peaceful division had been engineered in 1992. **1994** The North American Free Trade Agreement (NAFTA) came into effect for the US, Canada, and Mexico.

BIRTHS

Lorenzo de' Medici (the Magnificent), Florentine ruler, **1449**; Paul Revere, US patriot, **1735**; E.M. Forster, English novelist, **1879**; William Fox, US movie mogul, **1879**; J. Edgar Hoover, director of the FBI, **1895**; J.D. Salinger, US author, **1919**; Terry Moore, US film actress, **1929**; Madonna (Ciccone), US pop singer, **1961**.

DEATHS

William Wycherley, English dramatist, **1716**; Maurice Chevalier, French actor and singer, **1972**; Julius "Groucho" Marx, US film comedian, **1977**; Ron Hubbard, US science-fiction writer and founder of Scientology, **1986**.

NOTES

_____

_____

_____

_____

January 2

"Time the devourer of everything."
—OVID, Metamorphoses

EVENTS

1635 Cardinal Richelieu established the Académie Française. **1788** Georgia became the 4th state. **1839** French photographer Louis Daguerre took the first photograph of the Moon. **1905** Russians surrendered Port Arthur, a humiliating defeat in the Russo-Japanese War. **1946** King Zog of Albania, who had been residing in England since 1939, was deposed. **1959** The Russian unmanned spacecraft *Luna I*, the first rocket to pass near the Moon, was launched.

BIRTHS

Michael Tippett, English composer, **1905**; Isaac Asimov, US biochemist and science-fiction writer, **1920**; Roger Miller, US singer and composer, **1936**; David Bailey, English photographer, **1938**.

DEATHS

Ovid, Roman poet, **17**; Livy, Roman historian, **17**; George Airy, English astronomer royal, **1892**; Emil Janning, German film actor, **1950**; Tex Ritter, US stage and screen singing cowboy, **1974**.

NOTES

January 3

"Laws are silent in time of war."
—MARCUS TULLIUS CICERO, *"Pro Milone"*

EVENTS

1521 Pope Leo X excommunicated German church reformer Martin Luther. **1777** The Continental Congress adopted the Stars and Stripes as the official national flag. **1777** The Battle of Princeton took place in the American Revolution, in which George Washington defeated British forces led by Cornwallis. **1924** English explorer Howard Carter discovered the sarcophagus of Tutankhamen in the Valley of the Kings, near Luxor, Egypt. **1959** Alaska became the 49th state. **1962** Pope John XXIII excommunicated Cuban Prime Minister Fidel Castro. **1963** The US broke off diplomatic relations with Castro's Cuba. **1993** President George Bush and Russian President Boris Yeltsin signed the second Strategic Arms Reduction Treaty (START) in Moscow.

BIRTHS

Marcus Tullius Cicero, Roman orator and statesman, **106 BC**; Clement Attlee, British prime minister, **1883**; J.R.R. Tolkien, English writer, **1892**; Ray Milland, US film actor, **1907**; Victor Borge, Danish musician and comedian, **1909**; Mel Gibson, US film actor, **1956**.

DEATHS

Josiah Wedgwood, English potter, **1795**; Pierre Larousse, French editor and encyclopedist, **1875**; Jaroslav Hasek, Czech novelist, **1923**; Dick Powell, US film actor, **1963**; Conrad Hilton, US hotel magnate, **1979**; Joy Adamson, British naturalist and author, **1980**.

NOTES

January 4

*"I grow old ... I grow old ... I shall wear
the bottoms of my trousers rolled."*
—T.S. ELIOT, Love Song of J. Alfred Prufrock

The national day of Myanmar.

EVENTS

1884 The socialist Fabian Society was founded in London. **1885** The first successful surgical removal of an appendix was performed, in Iowa. **1896** Utah became the 45th state. **1944** The attack on Monte Cassino was launched by the British Fifth Army in Italy. **1980** President Carter imposed grain and technology embargos on the USSR after it invaded Afghanistan. **1981** The Broadway show *Frankenstein* lost an estimated $2 million, when it opened and closed on the same night. **1991** The UN Security Council voted unanimously to condemn Israel's treatment of the Palestinians in the occupied territories.

BIRTHS

Louis Braille, French deviser of an alphabet for the blind, **1809**; Augustus John, Welsh painter, **1878**; Jane Wyman, US film actress, **1914**; Floyd Patterson, US boxer, **1935**; Grace Bumbry, US opera singer, **1937**; Dyan Cannon, US film actress, **1937**.

DEATHS

Ralph Vaughan Williams, English composer, **1958**; Albert Camus, French novelist and dramatist, **1960**; T.S. Eliot, US-born British poet and critic, **1965**; Christopher Isherwood, English novelist and dramatist, **1986**.

NOTES

January 5

"How could they tell?"
—DOROTHY PARKER, *on being told of President Coolidge's death*

EVENTS

1896 German physicist Röntgen gave the first demonstration of X-rays. **1938** Billie Holiday recorded "When You're Smiling (the Whole World Smiles with You)" in New York. **1964** On his tour of the Holy Land, Pope Paul VI met Patriarch Athenagoras I, the first meeting between the heads of the Roman Catholic and Orthodox Churches in over 500 years. **1976** French premier Giscard d'Estaing promulgated a law making French the only language permitted in advertising in France. **1987** The US recorded its first trillion-dollar budget. **1994** The US announced that North Korea had agreed to allow inspection of its nuclear facilities.

BIRTHS

King Camp Gilette, US safety-razor inventor, **1855**; Konrad Adenauer, German statesman, **1876**; Stella Gibbons, English poet and novelist, **1902**; Walter Mondale, US vice president, **1928**; Alfred Brendel, Austrian concert pianist, **1931**; Robert Duvall, US film actor, **1931**; Juan Carlos, king of Spain, **1938**; Diane Keaton, US film actress, **1946**.

DEATHS

Edward the Confessor, king of England, **1066**; Catherine de' Medici, queen of France, **1589**; Calvin Coolidge, 30th US president, **1933**; George Washington Carver, US agricultural scientist, **1943**; Charlie Mingus, US jazz bassist and composer, **1979**; Harold Clayton Urey, US chemist, **1981**; Thomas "Tip" O'Neill, US politician, **1994**.

NOTES

January 6

Epiphany.

EVENTS

871 England's King Alfred defeated the Danes at the Battle of Ashdown. **1540** England's King Henry VIII was married to Anne of Cleves, his fourth wife. **1838** Inventor Samuel Morse gave the first public demonstration of the electric telegraph. **1912** New Mexico became the 47th state. **1941** President Franklin Roosevelt announced the "Four Freedoms" as speech, religion and freedom from want and fear. **1945** The Battle of the Bulge, or Ardennes offensive, ended in an Allied victory over the Germans. **1988** La Coupole, the Parisian brasserie made famous by generations of notable artists and writers who frequented it, was sold for over $9 million to be converted into an office block.

BIRTHS

Richard II, king of England, **1367**; St. Joan of Arc, French military leader, **1412**; Gustave Doré, French artist and illustrator, **1833**; Carl Sandburg, US poet, **1878**; Loretta Young, US film actress, **1913**.

DEATHS

Fanny Burney, English novelist and diarist, **1840**; Gregor Mendel, Austrian monk and biologist, **1884**; Theodore Roosevelt, 26th US president, **1919**; Rudolf Nureyev, Russian dancer, **1993**; Dizzy Gillespie, US jazz trumpeter, **1993**.

NOTES

_____

_____

_____

_____

January 7

Christmas Day in the Greek Orthodox Church.

EVENTS

1610 Italian astronomer Galileo discovered Jupiter's four satellites, naming them Io, Europa, Ganymede, and Callisto. **1785** The first aerial crossing of the English Channel was made by the Frenchman Jean Pierre Blanchard and American Dr. John Jeffries, in a hot-air balloon. **1927** The New York–London telephone service began operating, a three-minute call costing around $20. **1983** The US lifted its arms embargo against Guatemala. **1990** The Leaning Tower of Pisa was closed, as its accelerated rate of leaning raised fears for the safety of its many visitors.

BIRTHS

Joseph Bonaparte, king of Naples and Spain, **1768**; Millard Fillmore, 13th US president, **1800**; Carl Laemmle, US film producer, founder of Universal Pictures, **1867**; Adolph Zukor, US film magnate, **1873**; Charles Péguy, French poet, **1873**; Francis Poulenc, French composer, **1899**.

DEATHS

Catherine of Aragon, first wife of Henry VIII of England, **1536**; Nicholas Hilliard, English miniaturist painter, **1619**; André Maginot, French politician, **1932**; John Berryman, US poet, **1972**; Trevor Howard, British actor, **1988**; Hirohito, emperor of Japan, **1989**.

NOTES

January 8

"I can't sing very well but I'd like to try."
—ELVIS PRESLEY, *on first entering a studio*

EVENTS

1815 In the war of 1812, American forces under Andrew Jackson defeated the British at the Battle of New Orleans. **1889** US inventor Herman Hollerith patented his tabulator, the first device for data processing; his firm would later become one of IBM's founding companies. **1916** The final withdrawal of Allied troops from Gallipoli took place in World War I. **1918** President Wilson announced his "Fourteen Points" for ending World War I. **1959** French General Charles de Gaulle became the first president of the Fifth Republic. **1982** The American Telephone & Telegraph Company agreed to sell 22 local companies after losing a seven-year antitrust suit. **1993** Bosnian President Izetbegovic visited the US to plead his government's case for Western military aid and intervention to halt Serbian aggression.

BIRTHS

Wilkie Collins, English novelist, **1824**; Elvis Presley, US rock 'n' roll legend, **1935**; Shirley Bassey, Welsh singer, **1937**; Stephen Hawking, English physicist and mathematician, **1942**; David Bowie, English rock singer and actor, **1947**; Calvin Smith, US athlete, **1961**.

DEATHS

Galileo Galilei, Italian astronomer, **1642**; Eli Whitney, US inventor of the cotton gin, **1825**; Paul Verlaine, French poet, **1895**; Zhou Enlai, Chinese leader, **1976**; Gregori Maximilianovich Malenkov, Soviet leader, **1988**.

NOTES

January 9

"God wants us to be rich and comfortable."
—WALTER HOVING, *chairman of Tiffany's,*
reported on Jan. 9, 1983

EVENTS

1788 Connecticut became the 5th state. **1799** British Prime Minister William Pitt the Younger introduced income tax to raise funds for the Napoleonic Wars. **1902** New York State introduced a bill to outlaw flirting in public. **1969** The supersonic airplane *Concorde* made its first trial flight, at Bristol, England. **1972** The ocean liner *Queen Elizabeth* was destroyed by fire in Hong Kong harbor. **1991** US Secretary of State Baker and Iraqi foreign minister Aziz met for $6\frac{1}{2}$ hours in Geneva, but failed to reach any agreement that would forestall war in the Persian Gulf.

BIRTHS

George Balanchine, Russian-born US choreographer, **1904**; Simone de Beauvoir, French novelist and critic, **1908**; Richard Nixon, 37th US president, **1913**; Gypsy Rose Lee, US striptease artist and actress, **1914**; Judith Krantz, US writer, **1928**; Joan Baez, US singer, **1941**.

DEATHS

Caroline Lucretia Herschel, English astronomer, **1848**; Napoleon III, French emperor, **1873**; Victor Emmanuel, first king of Italy, **1878**; Katherine Mansfield, New Zealand writer, **1984**.

NOTES

January 10

---

*"Our American professors like their literature clear and cold and pure
and very dead."*
—SINCLAIR LEWIS, *Nobel Prize Address, 1930*

EVENTS

1776 Thomas Paine published his pamphlet *Common Sense.* **1901**
Texas recorded its first major oil strike (near Beaumont.) **1920**
The Treaty of Versailles was ratified, officially ending World War
I with Germany. **1920** The League of Nations held its first meet-
ing in Geneva. **1926** Fritz Lang's film *Metropolis* was first shown,
in Berlin. **1946** The first meeting of the United Nations General
Assembly took place in London. **1949** Vinyl records were
launched by RCA (45 r.p.m.) and Columbia (33.3 r.p.m.).

BIRTHS

Ethan Allen, US patriot, **1738**; Michel Ney, French marshal, **1769**;
Barbara Hepworth, English sculptor, **1903**; Paul Henreid, Austrian
actor, **1908**; Galina Ulanova, Russian ballerina, **1910**; Johnny Ray,
US singer, **1927**; Rod Stewart, English rock singer, **1945**.

DEATHS

Carolus Linnaeus, Swedish botanist, **1778**; Samuel Colt, US gun-
smith, **1862**; Sinclair Lewis, US novelist, **1951**; Dashiell Hammett,
US detective-story writer, **1961**; Coco (Gabrielle) Chanel, French
fashion designer, **1971**; Anton Karas, Austrian composer, **1985**.

NOTES

January 11

"That man's silence is wonderful to listen to."
—THOMAS HARDY, Under the Greenwood Tree

EVENTS

1867 Benito Juarez returned to the Mexican presidency, following the withdrawal of French troops and the execution of Emperor Maximilian. **1922** Leonard Thompson became the first person to be successfully treated with insulin, at Toronto General Hospital. **1963** The first disco, called the Whiskey-a-go-go, opened in Los Angeles. **1991** An auction of silver and paintings that had been acquired by the late Ferdinand Marcos, Philippine president, and his wife, Imelda, brought in a total of $20.29 million at Christie's in New York.

BIRTHS

Alexander Hamilton, US statesman, **1757**; Ezra Cornell, US philanthropist, **1807**; Sir John Alexander, first Canadian prime minister, **1815**; Naomi Judd, US country singer, **1946**.

DEATHS

Francis Scott Key, US lawyer and poet who wrote "The Star-Spangled Banner," **1814**; Thomas Hardy, English poet and novelist, **1928**; Alberto Giacometti, Swiss sculptor and painter, **1966**; Richmal Crompton, English author, **1969**; Padraic Colum, Irish poet, **1972**; Isidor Rabi, US physicist, **1988**.

NOTES

January 12

"Every murderer is probably somebody's old friend."
—AGATHA CHRISTIE, The Mysterious Affair at Styles

EVENTS

1875 Kwang-su became emperor of China. **1904** Henry Ford set a new land-speed record of 91.37 mph in his "999" automobile on frozen Lake St. Clair, near Detroit. **1964** The Sultan of Zanzibar was overthrown and a republic proclaimed. **1970** The Boeing 747 aircraft landed in London at the end of its first transatlantic flight. **1991** Congress passed a resolution authorizing President Bush to use military power to force Iraq out of Kuwait. **1993** Sectarian violence continued for the eighth day in Bombay, India; 200 people died in nationwide clashes.

BIRTHS

John Hancock, US statesman, **1737**; Johann Pestalozzi, Swiss educational reformer, **1746**; John Singer Sargent, US painter, **1856**; Jack London, US author, **1876**; Hermann Goering, German Nazi leader, **1893**; P.W. Botha, South African politician, **1916**; Kirstie Alley, US film actress, **1955**.

DEATHS

Maximilian I, Holy Roman Emperor, **1519**; Jan Brueghel the Elder, Flemish painter, **1625**; Pierre de Fermat, French mathematician, **1665**; Isaac Pitman, English teacher and inventor of shorthand, **1897**; Nevil Shute, English novelist, **1960**; Agatha Christie, English detective-story writer, **1976**; Samuel Bronston, US filmmaker, **1994**.

NOTES

January 13

"From birth to 18, a girl needs good parents. From 18 to 35, she needs good looks. From 35 to 55, good personality. From 55 on, she needs good cash. I'm saving my money."
—SOPHIE TUCKER

EVENTS

1898 French novelist Emile Zola published *J'accuse* (*I Accuse*), a pamphlet indicting the persecutors of Alfred Dreyfus. **1910** Opera was broadcast on the radio for the first time, with Enrico Caruso singing from the stage of New York's Metropolitan Opera House. **1964** Capitol records released the Beatles' first single in the US; "I Wanna Hold Your Hand" sold one million copies in the first three weeks. **1978** NASA selected its first women astronauts, 15 years after the USSR had a female astronaut orbit the Earth. **1984** Christine Craft, US broadcaster who had been demoted for being "Too old, unattractive, and not deferential enough to men" was awarded $325,000 in damages.

BIRTHS

Sophie Tucker, US singer and vaudeville star, **1884**; Johannes Bjelke-Petersen, Australian politician, **1911**; Robert Stack, US film actor, **1919**; Michael Bond, English creator of the Paddington Bear stories for children, **1926**.

DEATHS

Edmund Spenser, English poet, **1599**; George Fox, English founder of the Society of Friends, **1691**; Stephen Foster, US songwriter, **1864**; James Joyce, Irish novelist, **1941**; Hubert Humphrey, US politician, **1978**.

NOTES

_____

_____

_____

_____

January 14

*"What is the use of a book, thought Alice,
without pictures or conversations?"*
—LEWIS CARROLL, Alice's Adventures in Wonderland

EVENTS

1900 Puccini's opera *Tosca* was first performed, in Rome. **1907** An earthquake killed over 1,000 people in Kingston, Jamaica, virtually destroying the capital. **1938** Walt Disney's *Snow White and the Seven Dwarfs*, his first full-length Technicolor movie, was released in the US. **1943** President Roosevelt and British Prime Minister Churchill met at Casablanca during World War II and agreed to seek Germany's unconditional surrender. **1954** Baseball hero Joe DiMaggio married film star Marilyn Monroe.

BIRTHS

Henri Fantin-Latour, French painter, **1836**; Albert Schweitzer, French missionary surgeon, **1875**; Cecil Beaton, British photographer and stage designer, **1904**; Joseph Losey, US film director, **1909**; Jack Jones, US singer, **1938**; Faye Dunaway, US film actress, **1941**; Anthony Eden, British prime minister, **1977**

DEATHS

Sir Edmond Halley, English astronomer, **1742**; Jean Auguste Dominique Ingres, French painter, **1867**; Lewis Carroll, English mathematician and author, **1898**; Humphrey Bogart, US film actor, **1957**; Peter Finch, English actor, **1977**; Anaïs Nin, US novelist and diarist, **1977**; Kurt Gödel, US mathematician and philosopher, **1978**; Ray Kroc, US founder of McDonald's, **1984**.

NOTES

January 15

*"If A is success in life, then A equals X plus Y plus Z.
Work is X; Y is play; and Z is keeping your mouth shut."*
—ALBERT EINSTEIN, *reported on Jan. 15, 1950*

EVENTS

1559 The coronation of England's Queen Elizabeth I took place.
1797 London haberdasher James Hetherington was fined £50 for
wearing his new creation, the top hat. **1865** In the Civil War, the
last Confederate port, at Wilmington, North Carolina, was closed
by Union forces. **1971** The Aswan High Dam, on the Nile,
financed by the USSR, was opened. **1973** President Nixon halted
US offensive operations in Vietnam as peace agreement neared.

BIRTHS

Molière, French dramatist, **1622**; Mazo de la Roche, Canadian
novelist, **1885**; Aristotle Onassis, Greek shipowner, **1906**; Edward
Teller, Hungarian-born US nuclear physicist called "the father of
the hydogen bomb," **1908**; Lloyd Bridges, US film actor, **1913**;
Gamal Abdel Nasser, Egyptian statesman, **1918**; Martin Luther
King, US civil-rights campaigner, **1929**; Margaret O'Brien, US
film actress, **1937**.

DEATHS

Emma Hamilton, English mistress to Lord Nelson, **1815**; Matthew
B. Brady, US Civil War photographer, **1896**; Rosa Luxemburg,
German socialist, **1919**; Jack Teagarden, US jazz musician, **1964**;
Sean MacBride, Irish politician, **1988**; Sammy Cahn, US lyricist,
1993; Harry Nilsson, US singer and songwriter, **1994**.

NOTES

January 16

*"God tells me how he wants this music played
and you get in his way."*
—ARTURO TOSCANINI

EVENTS

1547 Ivan the Terrible was crowned first czar of Russia. **1809** The British defeated the French at the Battle of Corunna, in the Peninsular War. **1919** The 18th Amendment to the US Constitution was ratified, prohibiting the sale of alcoholic beverages. **1925** Leon Trotsky was dismissed as chairman of the Revolutionary Council of the USSR. **1932** Duke Ellington and his Orchestra recorded "It Don't Mean a Thing" in New York. **1944** General Eisenhower was appointed Supreme Commander of the Allied Forces in Europe. **1970** Colonel Qaddafi became virtual president of Libya. **1991** A US-led international force launched Operation Desert Storm on Iraq and Iraqi-occupied Kuwait less than 17 hours after the expiration of the UN deadline for Iraqi withdrawal.

BIRTHS

Franz Brentano, German philosopher, **1838**; André Michelin, French tire-maker, **1853**; Alexander Knox, Canadian film actor, **1907**; Ethel Merman, US singer and actress, **1909**.

DEATHS

Léo Delibes, French composer, **1891**; Carole Lombard, US film actress, **1942**; Arturo Toscanini, Italian conductor, **1957**; Robert Van de Graff, US nuclear physicist, **1967**; Mohammed Reza Pahlavi, former shah of Iran, **1979**; Florence Desmond, British actress, **1993**

NOTES

January 17

EVENTS

1377 The Papal See was transferred from Avignon back to Rome. **1773** Captain Cook's *Resolution* became the first ship to cross the Antarctic Circle. **1912** English explorer Robert Falcon Scott reached the South Pole; Norwegian Roald Amundsen had beaten him there by one month. **1950** Robbers stole $2.8 million from Brink's in Boston (apprehended in 1956). **1959** Senegal and the French Sudan joined to form the Federal State of Mali. **1966** A B-52 carrying four H-bombs collided with a refueling tanker, killing eight of the crew and releasing the bombs. **1977** Double-murderer Gary Gilmore became the first person to be executed in the US in a decade; he chose to be executed by firing squad. **1994** An earthquake registering 6.6 on the Richter Scale hit southern California, causing 57 deaths and estimated damage of up to $20 billion.

BIRTHS

Benjamin Franklin, US statesman and scientist, **1706**; David Lloyd George, English statesman, **1863**; Nevil Shute, English novelist, **1899**; Al Capone, US gangster, **1899**; James Earl Jones, US actor, **1931**; Muhammed Ali (Cassius Clay), US heavyweight boxing champion, **1942**.

DEATHS

Tomaso Giovanni Albinoni, Italian composer, **1751**; Rutherford B. Hayes, 19th US president, **1893**; Francis Galton, English anthropologist and explorer, **1911**; T.H. White, English writer, **1964**.

NOTES

January 18

"If you can talk with crowds and keep your virtue,
Or walk with Kings—nor lose the common touch."
—RUDYARD KIPLING, *"If"*

EVENTS

1778 England's Captain Cook discovered the Sandwich Islands, now known as Hawaii. **1871** King Wilhelm of Prussia was proclaimed the first German emperor. **1911** The first landing of an aircraft on a ship's deck was made by US pilot Eugene Ely, in San Francisco Bay. **1919** The Versailles Peace Conference opened. **1944** The German siege of Leningrad, which began September 1941, was relieved. **1994** US Special Counsel Lawrence Walsh published a report on the Iran-Contra scandal saying President Ronald Reagan had knowledge of the covert operation.

BIRTHS

Peter Mark Roget, English lexicographer, **1779**; A.A. Milne, English author and creator of Winnie-the-Pooh, **1882**; Oliver Hardy, US film comedian, **1892**; Cary Grant, US film actor, **1904**; Danny Kaye, US film actor and comedian, **1913**; David Bellamy, English botanist, **1933**; Kevin Costner, US film actor, **1955**.

DEATHS

John Tyler, 10th US president, **1862**; Rudyard Kipling, English poet and novelist, **1936**; Sydney Greenstreet, English actor, **1954**; Cecil Beaton, English photographer and designer, **1980**.

NOTES

January 19

*"All that we see or seem
Is but a dream within a dream."*
—EDGAR ALLAN POE, *"A Dream within a Dream"*

EVENTS

1853 Verdi's opera *Il Trovatore* was first staged in Rome. **1915** More than 20 people were killed when German zeppelins bombed England for the first time during World War I. **1942** The Japanese invaded Burma (now Myanmar). **1966** Indira Gandhi became prime minister of India. **1969** In protest against the Russian invasion of 1968, Czech student Jan Palach set himself afire in Prague's Wenceslas Square. **1993** IBM announced a loss of $4.97 billion for 1992, the largest single-year loss in US corporate history

BIRTHS

James Watt, Scottish inventor, **1736**; General Robert E. Lee, Confederate commander-in-chief; Edgar Allan Poe, US author and poet, **1809**; Paul Cézanne, French painter, **1839**; Patricia Highsmith, US crime writer, **1921**; Phil Everly, US pop-country singer, **1938**; Janis Joplin, US rock singer, **1943**; Dolly Parton, US country singer **1946**, Stefan Edberg, Swedish tennis player, **1966**.

DEATHS

Hans Sachs, German poet and composer, **1576**; William Congreve, English dramatist, **1729**; Louis Hérold, French composer, **1833**; Pierre-Joseph Proudhon, French journalist and anarchist, **1865**; Bhagwan Shree Rajneesh, Indian guru, **1990**.

NOTES

January 20

"Too bad all the people who know how to run the country are busy driving cabs and cutting hair."
—GEORGE BURNS

EVENTS

1265 The first English parliament met in Westminster Hall, convened by the earl of Leicester, Simon de Montfort. **1841** Hong Kong was ceded by China and occupied by the British. **1892** The game of basketball was first played at the YMCA in Springfield, Massachusetts. **1944** The RAF dropped 2,300 tons of bombs on Berlin. **1961** John F. Kennedy was inaugurated as the 35th US president, and the first Roman Catholic to hold this office. **1981** Fifty-two Americans, held hostage in the US embassy in Teheran for 444 days by followers of the Ayatollah Khomeini, were released. **1986** Martin Luther King Day became an official US holiday. **1987** Terry Waite, the archbishop of Canterbury's special envoy in the Middle East, disappeared on a peace mission in Beirut, Lebanon.

BIRTHS

John Moses Browning, US firearm inventor, **1855**; George Burns, US comedian and actor, **1896**; Federico Fellini, Italian film director, **1920**; Slim Whitman, US country singer, **1924**; Patricia Neal, US film actress, **1926**; Edwin "Buzz" Aldrin, US astronaut, **1930**.

DEATHS

John Ruskin, English art critic and writer, **1900**; George V, king of Britain, **1936**; Johnny Weissmuller, US film actor and swimmer, **1984**; Barbara Stanwyck, US film actress, **1990**; Audrey Hepburn, Dutch-born US film actress, **1993**.

NOTES

January 21

"I believe that my pictures have had an obvious effect upon American life. I have brought a certain sense of beauty and luxury into everyday existence."
—CECIL B. DE MILLE, *in 1924*

EVENTS

1793 King Louis XVI of France was guillotined in the Place de la Révolution. **1911** The first Monte Carlo car rally began; it was won by French racer Henri Rougier. **1954** The world's first nuclear submarine, the USS *Nautilus*, was launched. **1976** The supersonic airplane *Concorde* inaugurated its commercial service with simultaneous take-offs, from Paris to Rio de Janeiro, and from London to Bahrain. **1977** President Carter pardoned some 10,000 Vietnam War draft-resisters.

BIRTHS

John Charles Fremont, US explorer, **1813**; Thomas Jonathan "Stonewall" Jackson, Confederate general, **1824**; Christian Dior, French couturier, **1905**; Benny Hill, English comedian, **1924**; Telly Savalas, US actor, **1925**; Jack Nicklaus, US golfer, **1940**; Placido Domingo, Spanish operatic tenor, **1941**; Robby Benson, US film actor, **1956**.

DEATHS

Elisha Gray, US inventor, **1901**; V.I. Lenin, Russian leader, **1924**; Lytton Strachey, English critic and biographer, **1932**; George Orwell, British novelist, **1950**; Cecil B. De Mille, US film director, **1959**.

NOTES

_____

_____

_____

_____

January 22

EVENTS

1905 Insurgent workers were fired on in St. Petersburg, resulting in "Bloody Sunday." **1924** Ramsay MacDonald took office as Britain's first Labour prime minister. **1932** US unemployment reached 12 million as the depression worsened. **1972** The United Kingdom, the Irish Republic, and Denmark joined the European Community (now the European Union.) **1973** The US Supreme Court case *Roe v. Wade* overturned state anti-abortion laws. **1973** George Foreman knocked out Joe Frazier in Kingston, Jamaica, becoming the world heavyweight boxing champion.

BIRTHS

Ivan III (the Great), grand duke of Muscovy, **1440**; Francis Bacon, English politician and philosopher, **1561**; George Gordon, Lord Byron, English poet, **1788**; D.W. Griffith, US film producer and director, **1875**; Piper Laurie, US film actress, **1932**; Joseph Wambaugh, US writer, **1937**; John Hurt, English actor, **1940**; George Foreman, US heavyweight boxing champion, **1948**; Linda Blair, US film actress, **1959**.

DEATHS

Shah Jahan, Indian emperor who built the Taj Mahal, **1666**; William Paterson, Scottish financier, **1719**; David Edward Hughes, English inventor, **1900**; Victoria, queen of Britain, **1901**; Lyndon B. Johnson, 36th US president, **1973**.

NOTES

_____

_____

_____

_____

January 23

*"No one is entirely useless. Even the worst of
us can serve as horrible examples."*
EDITOR, STATE PRISON NEWSPAPER,
Salt Lake City, Jan. 23, 1949

EVENTS

1556 An earthquake in Shanxi Province, China, is thought to
have killed some 830,000 people. **1849** Elizabeth Blackwell, first
woman doctor, graduated from a New York medical school. **1924**
The first Labour government was formed in Britain under
Ramsay MacDonald. **1960** The US Navy bathyscaphe *Trieste*,
designed by Dr. Auguste Piccard, descended to a record depth of
35,820 ft/10,750 m in the Pacific Ocean. **1968** North Korea seized
the USS *Pueblo* and its 83 crewmen (released December 22). **1985**
The proceedings of Britain's House of Lords were televised for
the first time.

BIRTHS

Stendhal, French novelist, **1783**; Edouard Manet, French painter,
1832; Sergei Mikhailovich Eisenstein, Russian film director, **1898**;
Jeanne Moreau, French actress, **1928**; Caroline, princess of
Monaco, **1957**.

DEATHS

William Pitt the Younger, British prime minister, **1806**; Anna
Pavlova, Russian ballerina, **1931**; Edvard Munch, Norwegian
painter, **1944**; Pierre Bonnard, French painter, **1947**; Paul
Robeson, US actor and singer, **1976**; Salvador Dali, Spanish
painter and sculptor, **1989**.

NOTES

January 24

"Never in the field of human conflict was so much owed by so many to so few."
—WINSTON CHURCHILL, *of the airmen in the Battle of Britain*, Hansard, *June 18, 1940*

EVENTS

1848 James Marshall was the first to discover gold in California, at Sutter's Mill near Coloma. **1916** The US Supreme Court ruled the income tax unconstitutional. **1935** Beer in cans was first sold, in Virginia, by the Kreuger Brewing Company. **1962** French film director François Truffaut's *Jules et Jim* premiered in Paris. **1978** A Russian satellite fell to earth near Yellow Knife in Canada's Northwest Territory. **1991** More than 15,000 Allied air sorties were reported flown in the Gulf War, with 23 aircraft lost.

BIRTHS

Hadrian, Roman emperor, **76**; Frederick II (the Great), king of Prussia, **1712**; Edith Wharton, US novelist, **1862**; Ernest Borgnine, US film actor, **1917**; Maria Tallchief, US ballerina, **1925**; Desmond Morris, English zoologist and writer, **1928**; Neil Diamond, US singer and songwriter, **1941**; Nastassja Kinski, German film actress, **1961**.

DEATHS

Caligula, Roman emperor, assassinated, **41**; Randolph Churchill, British politician, **1895**; Amadeo Modigliani, Italian artist, **1920**; Winston Churchill, British prime minister, **1965**; George Cukor, US film director, **1983**; Thurgood Marshall, first black US Supreme Court justice, **1993**.

NOTES

January 25

*"I've been accused of every death except the
casualty list of the World War."*
—AL CAPONE

EVENTS

1533 England's King Henry VIII and Anne Boleyn were secretly married. **1837** Michigan became the 26th state. **1915** Alexander Graham Bell and Thomas A. Watson conducted the first transcontinental telephone call, from New York to San Francisco. **1917** The US purchased the Danish West Indies (now the Virgin Islands) from Holland for $25 million. **1924** The first Winter Olympic Games began in Chamonix in the French Alps. **1971** Idi Amin led a coup that deposed Milton Obote and became president of Uganda. **1971** Cult leader Charles Manson was found guilty of murdering actress Sharon Tate and four others. **1993** Sears Roebuck announced it was discontinuing its famous catalog, first printed in 1896.

BIRTHS

Robert Boyle, Irish physicist and chemist, **1627**; Robert Burns, Scottish poet, **1759**; William Somerset Maugham, English author, **1874**; Virginia Woolf, English author, **1882**; Wilhelm Furtwängler, German conductor, **1886**; Edvard Shevardnadze, Russian politician, **1928**.

DEATHS

Marcus Cocceius Nerva, Roman emperor, **98**; Lucas Cranach the Younger, German painter, **1586**; Dorothy Wordsworth, English writer, **1855**; Al Capone, US gangster, **1947**; Ava Gardner, US film actress, **1990**.

NOTES

January 26

*"In war, you win or lose, live or die—and the
difference is just an eyelash."*
—DOUGLAS MACARTHUR

The national days of Australia and of India.

EVENTS

1500 Vincente Yanez Pinzon discovered Brazil and claimed it for
Portugal. **1837** Michigan became the 26th state. **1905** The
Cullinan diamond, weighing 11¼ lbs, was found by Captain Wells
at the Premier Mine, near Pretoria, South Africa. **1939** In the
Spanish Civil War, Franco's forces, with Italian aid, took
Barcelona. **1950** India became a republic within the British
Commonwealth. **1965** Hindi was made the official language of
India. **1992** Russian President Boris Yeltsin announced that his
country would stop targeting US cities with nuclear weapons.

BIRTHS

Douglas MacArthur, US general, **1880**; Stephane Grappelli,
French jazz violinist, **1908**; Jimmy Van Heusen, US popular composer, **1913**; Paul Newman, US film actor, **1925**; Eartha Kitt, US
singer, **1928**; Roger Vadim, French film director, **1928**.

DEATHS

Edward Jenner, English physician who discovered smallpox vaccine, **1823**; Charles George Gordon, British general, **1885**;
Nikolaus August Otto, German engineer, **1891**; Edward G.
Robinson, US film actor, **1973**; Nelson Rockefeller, US statesman,
1979; José Ferrer, US actor, **1992**.

NOTES

_____

_____

_____

_____

January 27

"Love, love, love, that is the soul of genius."
—WOLFGANG AMADEUS MOZART

EVENTS

1879 Thomas Edison patented the electric lamp. **1926** The first public demonstration of television was given by John Logie Baird, at his workshop in London. **1943** In World War II, the US Air Force carried out its first bombing raid on Germany. **1967** Three astronauts died in a fire which broke out aboard the spacecraft *Apollo I* during tests at Cape Kennedy. **1973** The Vietnam ceasefire agreement was signed by North Vietnam and the US, and the end of the military draft was announced.

BIRTHS

Wolfgang Amadeus Mozart, Austrian composer, **1756**; Wilhelm II, emperor of Germany, **1859**; Jerome Kern, US composer, **1885**; John Eccles, Australian physiologist, **1903**; Mordecai Richler, Canadian novelist and dramatist, **1931**.

DEATHS

John Audubon, French-born US artist and naturalist, **1851**; Giuseppe Verdi, Italian composer, **1901**; Giovanni Verga, Italian novelist and dramatist, **1922**; Carl Mannerheim, Finnish soldier and statesman, **1951**; Mahalia Jackson, US gospel singer, **1972**; Thomas Sopwith, British aircraft designer, **1989**.

NOTES

January 28

"I have spread my dreams under your feet;
Tread softly, because you tread on my dreams."
—W.B. YEATS, *"He Wishes for the Cloths of Heaven"*

EVENTS

1521 The Diet of Worms began, at which Protestant reformer Martin Luther was declared an outlaw by the Roman Catholic church. **1807** London became the world's first city to be illuminated by gas light. **1871** In the Franco-Prussian War, Paris fell to the Prussians after a five-month siege. **1878** The first telephone exchange was opened, at New Haven, Connecticut. **1935** Iceland became the first country to introduce legalized abortion. **1986** The US space shuttle *Challenger* exploded shortly after lift-off from Cape Canaveral, killing the five men and two women on board.

BIRTHS

Henry Morton Stanley, British-American journalist and explorer, **1841**; Auguste Piccard, Swiss balloonist and deep-sea explorer, **1884**; Ernst Lubitsch, German-born US film director, **1892**; Jackson Pollock, US artist, **1921**; Alan Alda, German-borne US film actor and director, **1936**; Mikhail Baryshnikov, Russian ballet dancer, **1948**.

DEATHS

Charlemagne, Holy Roman Emperor, **814**; Francis Drake, English buccaneer and explorer, **1596**; Vicente Blasco Ibáñez, Spanish writer and politician, **1928**; W.B. Yeats, Irish poet, **1939**; Klaus Fuchs, German spy, **1988**.

NOTES

January 29

"I am free of all prejudice. I hate everyone equally."
—W.C. FIELDS

EVENTS

1728 John Gay's *The Beggar's Opera* was first performed. **1861** Kansas became the 34th state. **1886** The first successful gasoline-driven automobile, built by Karl Benz, was patented. **1916** In World War I, Paris was bombed by German zeppelins for the first time. **1978** The use of environmentally damaging aerosol sprays was banned in Sweden. **1991** In the Gulf War, Iraq began its first major ground offensive into Saudi Arabia.

BIRTHS

Thomas Paine, English-born American political writer, **1737**; William McKinley, 25th US president, **1843**; W.C. Fields, US film actor and comedian, **1880**; Victor Mature, US film actor, **1916**; John Forsythe, US TV and film actor, **1918**; Paddy Chayefsky, US writer, **1923**; Germaine Greer, Australian feminist and author, **1939**; Katharine Ross, US film actress, **1943**; Tom Selleck, US TV and film actor, **1945**.

DEATHS

George III, king of Britain and Ireland, **1820**; Douglas Haig, British field-marshal, **1928**; Fritz Kreisler, Austrian-born US violinist, **1962**; Alan Ladd, US film actor, **1964**; Jimmy Durante, US comedian, **1980**; Robert Frost, US poet, **1988**.

NOTES

January 30

*"Non-violence is the first article of my faith.
It is also the last article of my creed."*
—MOHANDAS KARAMCHAND GANDHI, *speech, March 18, 1922*

EVENTS

1649 The Commonwealth of England was established upon the execution of Charles I. **1933** Adolf Hitler was appointed chancellor of Germany. **1958** Yves Saint Laurent held his first major fashion show in Paris. **1968** US troops were pushed back in Vietnam by the communists' "Tet offensive." **1972** In Londonderry, Northern Ireland, 13 civilians were shot by British troops during riots known as "Bloody Sunday." **1994** Gerry Adams, leader of Northern Ireland's Sinn Fein party, arrived in the US, being admitted after his party, the political arm of the Irish Republican Army (IRA), had renounced violence.

BIRTHS

Anton Chekhov, Russian dramatist and short-story writer, **1860**; Franklin D. Roosevelt, 32nd US president, **1882**; Dorothy Malone, US film actress, **1925**; Gene Hackman, US film actor, **1930**; Tammy Grimes, US film actress, **1934**; Vanessa Redgrave, English actress, **1937**; Boris Spassky, Russian chess champion, **1938**.

DEATHS

Charles I, king of Britain and Ireland, executed, **1649**; Frank Doubleday, US publisher and editor, **1934**; Orville Wright, US aviation pioneer, **1948**; Mohandas Karamchand Gandhi, Indian nationalist leader, assassinated, **1948**; Francis Poulenc, French composer, **1963**.

NOTES

_____

_____

_____

_____

January 31

EVENTS

1876 All Native Americans were ordered to move into reservations. **1929** The USSR exiled Leon Trotsky; he found asylum in Mexico. **1950** President Truman approved production of the H-bomb. **1955** RCA introduced the first musical synthesizer. **1958** *Explorer I*, the first US Earth satellite, was launched from Cape Canaveral.

BIRTHS

Franz Schubert, Austrian composer, **1797**; Zane Grey, US novelist, **1872**; Anna Pavlova, Russian ballerina, **1882**; Eddie Cantor, US actor and entertainer, **1892**; Mario Lanza, US tenor, **1921**; Norman Mailer, US novelist, **1923**; Carol Channing, US actress and singer, **1923**; Jean Simmons, English film actress, **1929**; Suzanne Pleshette, US film actress, **1937**.

DEATHS

Charles Edward Stuart, the "Young Pretender" to the British throne, **1788**; John Galsworthy, English novelist, **1933**; Jean Giraudoux, French novelist and dramatist, **1944**; A.A. Milne, English author who created Winnie-the-Pooh, **1956**; Samuel Goldwyn, US film producer, **1974**.

NOTES

February 1

EVENTS

1790 The US Supreme Court held its first session. **1884** The first edition of the *Oxford English Dictionary* was published. **1893** Thomas Edison opened the first film studio to produce films for peepshow machines in West Orange, New Jersey. **1896** Puccini's opera *La Bohème* was first staged, in Turin. **1958** The United Arab Republic was formed by a union of Egypt and Syria (it was dissolved in 1961). **1960** Black sit-ins began at a Woolworth's lunch counter in Greensboro, North Carolina. **1979** Ayatollah Khomeini returned to Iran after 16 years of exile.

BIRTHS

Victor Herbert, US composer, **1859**; John Ford, US film director, **1895**; Clark Gable, US film actor, **1901**; Renata Tebaldi, Italian operatic soprano, **1922**; Don Everly, US pop-country singer, **1937**; Princess Stéphanie of Monaco, **1966**; Laura Dern, US film actress, **1967**.

DEATHS

René Descartes, French scientist and philosopher, **1650**; Mary Wollstonecraft Shelley, English novelist, **1851**; Carlos I, king of Portugal, **1908**; Aritomo Yamagata, Japanese soldier and politician, **1922**; Piet Mondrian, Swiss painter, **1944**; Buster Keaton, US silent-film comedian, **1966**.

NOTES

_____

_____

_____

_____

February 2

*"Three passions, simple but overwhelmingly strong, have governed
my life: the longing for love, the search for knowledge, and
unbearable pity for the suffering of mankind."*
—BERTRAND RUSSELL, Autobiography

EVENTS

1665 New Amsterdam was renamed New York by the British,
after the duke of York. **1876** Eight US baseball teams joined to
form the National League. **1878** Greece declared war on Turkey.
1943 The German army surrendered to the Soviet army at
Stalingrad. **1986** Women in Liechtenstein went to the polls for the
first time. **1989** The USSR's military occupation of Afghanistan
ended after nine years.

BIRTHS

Nell Gwyn, English actress and mistress of Charles II, **1650**;
Charles Maurice de Talleyrand-Périgord, French statesman and
diplomat, **1754**; Fritz Kreisler, Austrian-born US violinist, **1875**;
James Joyce, Irish author, **1882**; Jascha Heifetz, Russian-born US
violinist, **1901**; Jussi Björling, Swedish operatic tenor, **1911**; Elaine
Stritch, US actress, **1926**; Stan Getz, US jazz saxophonist, **1927**;
Tom Smothers, US comedian and musician, **1937**; Farrah
Fawcett, US TV actress, **1947**.

DEATHS

Pope Clement XIII, **1769**; Dmitri Ivanovich Mendeleyev, Russian
chemist, **1907**; Boris Karloff, US film actor, **1969**; Bertrand
Russell, English philosopher, **1970**; Alistair Maclean, Scottish
novelist, **1987**.

NOTES

February 3

"In the United States, there is more space where nobody is, than where anybody is. That is what makes America what it is."
—GERTRUDE STEIN

EVENTS

1488 The Portuguese navigator Bartholomeu Diaz landed at Mossal Bay in the Cape. **1913** The 16th Amendment to the US Constitution, authorizing the power to impose and collect income tax, was ratified. **1919** The League of Nations held its first meeting in Paris, with US President Wilson chairing. **1966** The first rocket-assisted controlled landing on the Moon was made by the Soviet space vehicle *Luna IX*. **1969** At the Palestinian National Congress in Cairo, Yassir Arafat was appointed leader of the PLO. **1994** The US space shuttle *Discovery* was launched, with the first Russian cosmonaut (Sergei Krikalev) ever to fly as a crewman in an American spacecraft. **1994** The US ended its 19-year trade embargo on Vietnam.

BIRTHS

Felix Mendelssohn, German composer, **1809**; Horace Greeley, US founder of the *New York Tribune* and Republican politician, **1811**; Gertrude Stein, US author, **1874**; Alvar Aalto, Finnish architect, **1898**; James Michener, US novelist, **1907**.

DEATHS

John of Gaunt, English politician, **1399**; **1762**; Woodrow Wilson, 28th US president, **1924**; Buddy Holly, US singer and guitarist, **1959**; Boris Karloff, US film actor, **1969**; John Cassavetes, US film actor and director, **1989**.

NOTES

February 4

*"It is our true policy to steer clear of permanent alliance
with any portion of the foreign world."*
—GEORGE WASHINGTON, *farewell address, Sept. 17, 1796*

The national day of Sri Lanka.

EVENTS

1784 George Washington was elected first US president and John Adams vice president by 69 electors. **1904** The Russo-Japanese War began after Japan laid seige to Port Arthur. **1945** Allied leaders Roosevelt, Churchill, and Stalin met at Yalta, in the Crimea. **1968** The world's largest hovercraft was launched at Cowes, Isle of Wight, England. **1987** The US *Stars and Stripes* won the America's Cup back from Australia. **1993** Russian scientists unfurled a giant mirror in orbit and flashed a beam of sunlight across Europe during the night; observers saw it only as an instantaneous flash.

BIRTHS

Fernand Léger, French painter, **1881**; Jacques Prévert, French poet and novelist, **1900**; Charles Lindbergh, US aviator, **1902**; Ida Lupino, English-born US actress, **1918**; Dan Quayle, US vice president, **1947**; Alice Cooper, US rock singer, **1948**.

DEATHS

Lucius Septimius Severus, Roman emperor, **211**; Giambattista della Porta, Italian natural philosopher, **1615**; Oliver Heaviside, English physicist, **1925**; Karen Carpenter, US singer and musician, **1983**; Liberace, US pianist and entertainer, **1987**.

NOTES

February 5

---

*"In America any boy may become president,
and I suppose it's just one of the risks he takes!"*
—ADLAI STEVENSON, *in a speech, Sept. 26, 1952*

EVENTS

1862 The US issued first "greenback" bills. **1922** *The Reader's Digest* was launched in New York. **1940** Glenn Miller recorded "Tuxedo Junction" with his orchestra. **1974** Patricia Hearst, granddaughter of US newspaper tycoon William Randolph Hearst, was kidnapped by the Symbionese Liberation Army. **1983** Expelled from Bolivia, Nazi war criminal Klaus Barbie flew to France to be tried for crimes against humanity. **1988** The US indicted General Manuel Noriega, Panama's president, for smuggling drugs.

BIRTHS

Robert Peel, British politician, **1788**; Dwight Lyman Moody, US evangelist, **1837**; Adlai Stevenson, US presidential candidate and UN ambassador, **1900**; John Carradine, US film actor, **1906**; William Burroughs, US novelist, **1914**; Red Buttons, US comedian and film actor, **1919**; Bob Marley, Jamaican reggae singer, **1945**; Charlotte Rampling, British actress, **1946**.

DEATHS

Joost van den Vondel, Dutch poet and dramatist, **1679**; Thomas Carlyle, English author and historian, **1881**; George Aliss, English actor, **1946**; Marianne Moore, US poet, **1972**; Joseph Mankiewicz, US director and author, **1993**.

NOTES

February 6

"Of the four wars in my lifetime none came about because the United States was too strong."
—RONALD REAGAN

The national day of New Zealand.

EVENTS

1508 Maximilian I assumed the title of Holy Roman Emperor. **1778** France signed a treaty with the US to assist the American Revolution; Britain declared war on France. **1788** Massachusetts became the 6th state. **1840** The Treaty of Waitangi was signed by Great Britain and the Maori chiefs of New Zealand. **1918** Women over 30 were granted the right to vote in Britain. **1964** Britain and France reached an agreement on the construction of a channel tunnel. **1968** The 10th Winter Olympic games opened in Grenoble, France. **1991** Debris from *Salyut 7*, a Soviet space station abandoned in 1986, reentered the Earth's atmosphere.

BIRTHS

Christopher Marlowe, English dramatist, **1564**; Anne, queen of Britain and Ireland, **1665**; Ronald Reagan, 40th US president, **1911**; Zsa Zsa Gabor, Hungarian-born US actress, **1920**; François Truffaut, French film director, **1932**; Tom Brokaw, US TV anchorman, **1940**; Natalie Cole, US singer, **1950**.

DEATHS

Carlo Goldoni, Italian dramatist, **1793**; Joseph Priestley, English chemist, **1804**; Gustav Klimt, Austrian painter, **1918**; Arthur Ashe, US tennis player, **1993**; Joseph Cotton, US film actor, **1994**.

February 7

*"There are strings ... in the human heart that
had better not be wibrated."*
—CHARLES DICKENS, Barnaby Rudge

EVENTS

1792 Austria and Prussia formed an alliance against France. **1827** The first US ballet company performed at the Bowery Theater in New York. **1947** The main group of the Dead Sea Scrolls, dating to about 150 BC–AD 68, was found in caves on the west side of the Jordan River. **1986** The Haitian dictator Jean-Claude "Baby Doc" Duvalier was forced to flee to France following national antigovernment demonstrations.

BIRTHS

Thomas More, English statesman and author, **1478**; Philippe Buache, French cartographer, **1700**; Charles Dickens, English novelist, **1812**; Alfred Adler, Austrian psychoanalyst, **1870**; James Hubert "Eubie" Blake, US pianist and songwriter, **1883**; Sinclair Lewis, US novelist, **1885**; George Herman "Babe" Ruth, US baseball player, **1895**; Garth Brooks, US country singer, **1962**.

DEATHS

Sheridan Le Fanu, Irish writer, **1873**; Adolphe Sax, Belgian inventor of the saxophone, **1894**; Daniel Malan, South African statesman, **1959**; Igor Vasilevich Kuchatov, Russian nuclear physicist, **1960**; Jimmy Van Heusen, US composer, **1990**.

NOTES

February 8

"When we build, let us think that we build for ever."
—JOHN RUSKIN, The Seven Lamps of Architecture

EVENTS

1725 Catherine I succeeded her husband, Peter the Great, to become empress of Russia. **1861** Seven secessionist southern states formed the Confederate States of America, in Montgomery, Alabama. **1910** The Boy Scouts of America organization was founded. **1920** Odessa, in the Ukraine, was taken by Bolshevik forces. **1969** The Boeing 747, the world's largest commercial plane, made its first flight. **1974** After 85 days in space, the US *Skylab* station returned to Earth.

BIRTHS

John Ruskin, English writer, artist, and art critic, **1819**; William Tecumseh Sherman, US general, **1820**; Jules Verne, French novelist, **1828**; Lana Turner, US film actress, **1920**; Jack Lemmon, US film actor, **1925**; James Dean, US film actor, **1931**; Nick Nolte, US film actor, **1940**; Mary Steenburgen, US film actress, **1953**.

DEATHS

Mary, Queen of Scots, beheaded, **1587**; Peter Alexeivich Kropotkin, Russian anarchist, **1921**; William Bateson, English biologist, **1926**; Max Liebermann, German painter and etcher, **1935**; Del Shannon, US pop singer, **1990**.

NOTES

February 9

"In the long course of history, having people who understand your thought is much greater security than another submarine."
—J. WILLIAM FULBRIGHT

EVENTS

1801 The Holy Roman Empire came to an end with the signing of the Peace of Luneville between Austria and France. **1964** A record audience of 73 million watched The Beatles on the *Ed Sullivan Show*. **1972** The British government declared a state of emergency due to the miners' strike, which was in its third month. **1991** The republic of Lithuania held a plebiscite on independence which showed overwhelming support for secession from the USSR. **1994** The US recognized Macedonia, part of the former Yugoslavian republic.

BIRTHS

Daniel Bernoulli, Swiss mathematician, **1700**; William Henry Harrison, 9th US president, **1773**; Alban Berg, Austrian composer, **1885**; Ronald Colman, English-born US film actor, **1891**; Kathryn Grayson, US film actress and singer, **1922**; Carole King, US singer and songwriter, **1941**; Mia Farrow, US film actress, **1945**.

DEATHS

Nevil Maskelyne, English astronomer royal, **1811**; Fyodor Mikhailovich Dostoevsky, Russian novelist, **1881**; Sergei Vladimirovich Ilyushin, Russian aircraft designer, **1977**; Bill Haley, US rock 'n' roll pioneer, **1981**; Yuri Andropov, Russian leader, **1984**; J. William Fulbright, Arkansas senator, **1995**

NOTES

_____

_____

_____

_____

February 10

"Most people experience love without noticing that there is anything remarkable about it."
—BORIS PASTERNAK, Dr. Zhivago

EVENTS

1763 The Treaty of Paris was signed, ending the Seven Years' War. **1840** Queen Victoria and Prince Albert, both aged 20, were married. **1931** New Delhi became the capital of India. **1942** The first disc sprayed with gold by the record company RCA Victor was presented to Glenn Miller for "Chattanooga Choo Choo."

BIRTHS

Harold Macmillan, British prime minister and publisher, **1894**; Bertolt Brecht, German dramatist and poet, **1898**; Robert Wagner, US film actor, **1930**; Boris Pasternak, Russian novelist, **1890**; Roberta Flack, US singer, **1939**; Mark Spitz, US swimmer, **1950**; Greg Norman, Australian golfer, **1955**; John Grisham, US novelist, **1955**.

DEATHS

Luca della Robbia, Italian sculptor, **1482**; Aleksandr Sergeyevich Pushkin, Russian author, **1837**; Wilhelm Konrad von Röntgen, German physicist, **1923**; Edgar Wallace, English thriller writer, **1932**; Billy Rose, US producer and lyricist, **1966**; Sophie Tucker, US singer, **1966**.

NOTES

February 11

"I have cherished the idea of a democratic and free society in which all persons live together in harmony and with equal opportunity ... if needs be, it is an idea for which I am prepared to die."
—NELSON MANDELA, *on release after 26 years in jail*

EVENTS

1858 Bernadette Soubirous, a peasant girl, allegedly had a vision of the Virgin Mary in a grotto in Lourdes. **1945** The Yalta Conference ended, at which the Allied leaders planned the final defeat of Germany and agreed on the establishment of the United Nations. **1975** Margaret Thatcher became the first woman leader of a British political party, the Conservative party. **1990** After more than 27 years in prison, ANC President Nelson Mandela walked to freedom from a prison near Cape Town, South Africa. **1990** James "Buster" Douglas knocked out Mike Tyson to win the world heavyweight boxing title.

BIRTHS

Thomas Edison, US inventor, **1847**; Joseph Mankiewicz, US film writer and director, **1909**; Mary Quant, English fashion designer, **1934**; Burt Reynolds, US film actor, **1936**.

DEATHS

Lazaro Spallanzani, Italian physiologist and chemist, **1799**; Honoré Daumier, French caricaturist, **1879**; John Buchan, Canadian statesman and novelist, **1940**; Sergei Mikhailovich Eisenstein, Russian film director, **1948**; Silvia Plath, US poet, **1963**; Lee J. Cobb, US actor, **1976**; William Conrad, US actor, **1994**.

NOTES

February 12

*"In giving freedom to the slave we assure freedom to the free—
honorable alike in what we give and what we preserve. We shall
nobly save, or meanly lose, the last best hope of earth."*
—ABRAHAM LINCOLN, *annual message to Congress, Dec. 1, 1862*

EVENTS

1554 Lady Jane Grey, queen of England for nine days, was executed on Tower Green for high treason. **1818** Independence was proclaimed by Chile. **1851** Prospector Edward Hargreaves made a discovery at Summerhill Creek, New South Wales, which set off a gold rush in Australia. **1912** China became a republic following the overthrow of the Manchu dynasty. **1955** The US began sending military advisers to train South Vietnamese troops. **1973** The first US prisoners of war were released from North Vietnam. **1993** The South African government and the ANC reached an agreement on a transitional "government of national unity."

BIRTHS

Abraham Lincoln, 16th US president, **1809**; Charles Darwin, English scientist, **1809**; George Meredith, English novelist, **1828**; Omar Bradley, US general in World War II, **1893**; Franco Zeffirelli, Italian opera and film director, **1923**.

DEATHS

Immanuel Kant, German philosopher, **1804**; Hans Guido von Bülow, German pianist and conductor, **1894**; Lillie Langtry, English actress, **1929**; Auguste Escoffier, French chef and cookery-writer, **1935**; Henry Hathaway, US filmmaker, **1985**; Lorne Greene, Canadian-born US film and TV actor, **1987**.

NOTES

February 13

"Writing is not a profession but a vocation of unhappiness."
—GEORGES SIMENON

EVENTS

1689 William of Orange and Mary ascended the British throne as joint sovereigns. **1692** The massacre of the Macdonalds at Glencoe in Scotland was carried out by their traditional enemies, the Campbells. **1793** Britain, Prussia, Austria, Holland, Spain, and Sardinia formed an alliance against France. **1867** Strauss's waltz *The Blue Danube* was first played publicly, in Vienna. **1886** The James Younger gang made its first "hit," robbing $60,000 from a Missouri bank. **1917** Dutch spy Mata Hari was arrested by the French. **1960** The French tested their first atomic bomb in the Sahara. **1974** Russian novelist Alexander Solzhenitsyn was expelled from the USSR.

BIRTHS

Fyodor Chaliapin, Russian operatic bass, **1873**; Georges Simenon, Belgian novelist, **1901**; Kim Novak, US film actress, **1933**; George Segal, US film actor, **1934**; Oliver Reed, British film actor, **1938**; Stockard Channing, US film actress, **1944**.

DEATHS

Catherine Howard, fifth wife of Henry VIII of England, executed, **1542**; Benvenuto Cellini, Italian sculptor and goldsmith, **1571**; Cotton Mather, US colonist and writer, **1728**; Richard Wagner, German composer, **1883**; Georges Rouault, French painter, **1958**; Jean Renoir, French-born US film director, **1979**.

NOTES

February 14

---

*"Like so many substantial Americans, he had married young
and kept on marrying, springing from blonde to blonde
like the chamois of the Alps leaping from crag to crag."*
—P.G. WODEHOUSE

St. Valentine's Day.

EVENTS

1859 Oregon became the 33rd state. **1912** Arizona became the 48th state. **1929** The St. Valentine's Day Massacre took place in Chicago, when seven members of Bugsy Moran's gang were gunned down in a warehouse. **1945** The first American bombing of Dresden, Germany, took place by the US 8th Air Force. **1956** At the 20th Soviet Communist Party Conference, Nikita Khrushchev denounced the policies of Stalin. **1962** US military advisers in Vietnam were given authority to defend themselves if fired upon. **1975** The Northern Mariana Islands became a US commonwealth territory.

BIRTHS

Francesco Cavalli, Italian composer, **1602**; Thomas Malthus, English economist, **1766**; Christopher Sholes, US inventor of the typewriter, **1819**; Jack Benny, US comedian and actor, **1894**.

DEATHS

Richard II, king of England, **1400**; Fiorenzo di Lorenzo, Italian painter, **1525**; William Tecumseh Sherman, US general, **1891**; P.G. Wodehouse, English novelist, **1975**; Frederick Loewe, US composer, **1988**.

NOTES

February 15

"Float like a butterfly, sting like a bee."
—MOHAMMED ALI *(Cassius Clay)*

EVENTS

1898 The USS *Maine*, sent to Cuba on a goodwill tour, was struck by a mine and sank in Havana harbor, with the loss of 260 lives. **1922** The first session of the Permanent Court of International Justice in The Hague was held. **1942** Singapore surrendered to Japanese forces. **1945** US infantry landed successfully on Bataan peninsula in the Philippines. **1974** The battle for the strategic Golan Heights between Israeli and Syrian forces began. **1978** Mohammed Ali lost his world heavyweight boxing title to Leon Spinks in Las Vegas.

BIRTHS

Pedro Menendez de Avilés, Spanish navigator, **1519**; Galileo Galilei, Italian astronomer, **1564**; Jeremy Bentham, English philosopher and writer, **1748**; Claire Bloom, English actress, **1931**; Jane Seymour, English actress, **1951**.

DEATHS

Gotthold Ephraim Lessing, German author, **1781**; Mikhail Ivanovich Glinka, Russian composer, **1857**; Herbert Henry Asquith, British prime minister, **1928**; Nat "King" Cole, US singer, **1965**; Ethel Merman, US singer and actress, **1984**; Richard Feynman, US scientist, **1988**.

NOTES

February 16

"I've a woman's ability to stick to a job and get on with it when everyone else walks off and leaves it."
—MARGARET THATCHER, *reported on Feb. 16, 1975*

EVENTS

1932 The Irish general election was won by the Fianna Fáil party, led by Éamon de Valera. **1937** US scientist W.H. Carothers obtained a patent for nylon. **1959** Fidel Castro became president of Cuba. **1960** The US nuclear submarine *Triton* set off to circumnavigate the world underwater.

BIRTHS

Giambattista Bodoni, Italian typographer, **1740**; Francis Galton, English scientist and founder of eugenics, **1822**; Ernst Haeckel, German naturalist and philosopher, **1834**; Charles Taze Russell, US founder of the Jehovah's Witness sect, **1852**; John Schlesinger, US film director, **1926**; Sonny Bono, US singer and congressman, **1935**; John McEnroe, US tennis player, **1959**.

DEATHS

Alfonso III, king of Portugal, **1279**; Pierre-Paul Prud'hon, French painter, **1823**; Henry Walter Bates, English naturalist and explorer, **1892**.

NOTES

February 17

*"Sleep is good, death is better; but of course, the best
thing would be never to have been born at all."*
—HEINRICH HEINE, *"Morphine"*

EVENTS

1859 The first production of Verdi's opera *Un Ballo in Maschera*
took place in Rome. **1864** The first successful submarine torpedo
attack took place when the USS *Housatonic* was sunk by the
Confederate submarine *H.L. Hunley* in Charleston's harbor; however, the force of the explosion was so great that the submarine
itself was also blown up, killing all on board. **1880** An attempt was
made to assassinate the Russian czar Alexander II with a bomb at
the Winter Palace, St. Petersburg. **1904** First production of
Puccini's opera *Madama Butterfly*, in Milan. **1968** French skier Jean-
Claude Killy won three gold medals at the Winter Olympics in
Grenoble. **1972** The House of Commons voted in favor of Britain
joining the European Community (now the European Union).

BIRTHS

Arcangelo Corelli, Italian composer, **1653**; Thomas Malthus,
English economist, **1766**; Marian Anderson, US operatic con-
tralto, **1902**; Hal Holbrook, US actor, **1925**; Yassir Arafat,
Palestinian leader, **1929**; Alan Bates, English actor, **1934**.

DEATHS

Tamerlane (the Great), Mongol leader, **1405**; Molière, French
dramatist, **1673**; Heinrich Heine, German poet, **1856**; Geronimo,
Apache warrior chief, **1909**; Graham Sutherland, English painter,
1980; Lee Strasburg, US actor, **1982**; Thelonious Monk, US jazz
pianist, **1982**.

NOTES

February 18

"He that is down needs fear no fall
He that is low no pride."
—JOHN BUNYAN, Pilgrim's Progress

The national days of Gambia and Nepal.

EVENTS

1678 Publication of John Bunyan's *Pilgrim's Progress*. **1930** US astronomer Clyde Tombaugh discovered the planet Pluto. **1948** After 16 years in power, the Fianna Fáil party was defeated in the Irish general elections. **1965** The Gambia became an independent state within the British Commonwealth. **1970** The "Chicago 7" were found not guilty of inciting riots at the 1968 Democratic National Convention, but five were convicted of intent to incite riots.

BIRTHS

Alessandro Volta, Italian scientist and inventor of the electric battery, **1745**; Niccolò Paganini, Italian violinist, **1784**; Andrés Segovia, Spanish classical guitarist, **1894**; Jack Palance, US film actor, **1920**; Helen Gurley Brown, US magazine editor, **1922**; Len Deighton, English novelist, **1929**; John Travolta, US film actor, **1954**; Matt Dillon, US film actor, **1964**.

DEATHS

Fra Angelico, Florentine painter, **1455**; Martin Luther, German leader of the Reformation, **1546**; Michelangelo Buonarroti, Italian painter and sculptor, **1564**; Richard Wagner, German composer, **1833**; Robert Oppenheimer, US physicist, developer of the atomic bomb, **1967**.

NOTES

February 19

EVENTS

1800 Napoleon Bonaparte proclaimed himself First Consul of France. **1878** US inventor Thomas Edison patented the phonograph. **1906** William Kellogg established the Battle Creek Toasted Cornflake Company, selling breakfast cereals originally developed as a health food for psychiatric patients. **1945** US Marines landed on Iwo Jima. **1959** Britain, Greece, and Turkey signed an agreement guaranteeing the independence of Cyprus. **1976** Iceland broke off diplomatic relations with Britain over fishing limits in the "cod war."

BIRTHS

Nicolaus Copernicus, Polish astronomer, **1473**; David Garrick, English actor and theater manager, **1717**; Luigi Boccherini, Italian cellist and composer, **1743**; Adelina Patti, Italian operatic soprano, **1843**; Merle Oberon, Tasmanian-born US film actress, **1911**; Stan Kenton, US composer and bandleader, **1912**; Lee Marvin, US film actor, **1924**; John Frankenheimer, US film director, **1930**; Margaux Hemingway, US actress, **1955**.

DEATHS

Georg Büchner, German poet and dramatist, **1837**; Charles Blondin, French tightrope walker, **1897**; Ernst Mach, Austrian physicist, **1916**; André Gide, French novelist, **1951**; Luigi Dallapiccola, Italian composer, **1975**; Michael Powell, English film director and producer, **1990**.

NOTES

February 20

EVENTS

1811 Austria declared itself bankrupt. **1917** The US bought the Dutch West Indies for defense reasons. **1938** Anthony Eden resigned as British foreign secretary in protest against Prime Minister Neville Chamberlain's appeasement policy. **1947** Lord Louis Mountbatten was appointed viceroy of India, the last person to hold this office. **1962** US astronaut John Glenn orbited the Earth three times in the space capsule *Friendship 7*. **1985** Contraceptives went on sale in the Irish Republic for the first time.

BIRTHS

Voltaire, French writer and philosopher, **1694**; Honoré Daumier, French painter, **1808**; Marie Rambert, British dancer and founder of the Ballet Rambert, **1888**; Enzo Ferrari, Italian automobile manufacturer, **1898**; Robert Altman, US film director, **1925**; Sidney Poitier, US film actor, **1927**; Sandy Duncan, US film actress, **1946**.

DEATHS

James I, king of Scotland, assassinated **1437**; Benedict Spinoza, Dutch philosopher, **1677**; Aurangzeb, last of the Mogul rulers of India, **1707**; Percy Grainger, Australian-born US composer, **1961**; Walter Winchell, US journalist, **1972**; Mikhail Sholokhov, Russian author, **1984**.

NOTES

February 21

EVENTS

1804 British engineer Richard Trevithick demonstrated the first steam engine to run on rails. **1916** In World War I, the Battle of Verdun began (it continued until December 16). **1960** All private businesses in Cuba were nationalized by Fidel Castro. **1972** President Richard Nixon arrived in Beijing on a visit intended to improve US-Chinese relations. **1975** Watergate defendants John Mitchell, John Ehrlichman, and H.R. Haldeman were sentenced to prison terms. **1989** Czech writer Václav Havel was jailed for antigovernment demonstrations. **1994** Aldrich Ames, a CIA counterintelligence officer, and his wife were arrested on charges of spying for the Soviet Union and Russia.

BIRTHS

Antonio López de Santa Anna, Mexican revolutionary and dictator, **1794**; W.H. Auden, English poet, **1907**; Robert Mugabe, first prime minister of Zimbabwe, **1924**; Erma Bombeck, US columnist, **1927**; Nina Simone, US singer, **1934**.

DEATHS

Jethro Tull, English agriculturalist, **1741**; Nikolai Gogol, Russian novelist and dramatist, **1852**; George Ellery Hale, US astronomer, **1938**; Malcolm X, US Black Muslim leader, shot dead at a meeting, **1965**; Howard Walter Florey, Australian pathologist who developed penicillin, **1968**; Margot Fonteyn, English ballet dancer, **1991**.

NOTES

February 22

"The basis of our political system is the right of the people to make and to alter their constitutions of government."
—GEORGE WASHINGTON, *Farewell Address*

EVENTS

1819 Spain ceded Florida to the US. **1860** Some 20,000 shoe workers in New England won raises after a successful strike. **1868** President Andrew Johnson was impeached by the House of Representatives (but later acquitted by the Senate). **1879** US storekeeper F.W. Woolworth opened his first "five-and-ten-cent" store in Utica, New York. **1940** Five-year-old Tenzin Gyatso was enthroned as the 14th Dalai Lama in Lhasa, Tibet. **1946** Dr. Selman Abraham Waksman, US biochemist, announced that he had discovered streptomycin, an antibiotic. **1995** The District of Columbia was declared insolvent by Congress.

BIRTHS

George Washington, 1st US president, **1732**; Arthur Schopenhauer, German philosopher, **1788**; Robert Baden-Powell, English soldier and founder of the Boy Scout movement, **1857**; Luis Buñuel, Spanish film director, **1900**; Robert Young, US actor, **1907**; John Mills, English actor, **1908**; Drew Barrymore, US film actress, **1975**.

DEATHS

Amerigo Vespucci, Italian navigator after whom America is named, **1512**; Jean-Baptiste-Camille Corot, French painter, **1875**; Stefan Zweig, Austrian writer, **1942**; Elizabeth Bowen, Irish novelist, **1973**; Oskar Kokoschka, Austrian painter, **1980**.

NOTES

February 23

"In the future everyone will be famous for 15 minutes."
—ANDY WARHOL

EVENTS

1732 First performance of Handel's oratorio *Esther*, in London. **1836** The siege of the Alamo began, under the Mexican general Santa Anna. **1898** Emile Zola was imprisoned for writing his open letter *J'accuse*, accusing the French government of anti-Semitism and of wrongly imprisoning the army officer Captain Alfred Dreyfus. **1901** The US Steel Corporation was founded. **1919** Benito Mussolini founded the Italian Fascist party. **1981** Spanish fascist army officers led by Lt. Colonel Antonio Tejero attempted a coup in the Cortes (parliament).

BIRTHS

Samuel Pepys, English civil servant and diarist, **1633**; George Frederick Handel, German-born British composer, **1685**; Victor Fleming, US film director who made *The Wizard of Oz*, **1883**; Erich Kästner, German children's author, **1899**; Peter Fonda, US film actor, **1939**.

DEATHS

Joshua Reynolds, English painter, **1792**; John Keats, English poet, **1821**; John Quincy Adams, 6th US president, **1848**; Karl Gauss, German mathematician and astronomer, **1855**; Nellie Melba, Australian operatic soprano, **1931**; Edward Elgar, English composer, **1934**; Stan Laurel, English-born US film comedian, **1965**; Adrian Boult, English conductor, **1983**; Andy Warhol, US pop artist, **1987**.

NOTES

February 24

"I married beneath me, all women do."
—LADY ASTOR

EVENTS

303 Galerius Valerius Maximianus issued an edict demanding the persecution of Christians. **1582** The Gregorian calendar was introduced by Pope Gregory XIII; it replaced the Julian calendar. **1905** The Simplon Tunnel through the Alps was completed. **1920** American-born Nancy Astor became the first woman to address the British Parliament. **1932** Britain's Malcolm Campbell beat his own land speed record in *Bluebird* at Daytona Beach, Florida; he reached a speed of 253.96 mph/408.88 kph. **1946** Juan Perón was elected president of Argentina. **1984** The US completed the withdrawal of its Marines from Lebanon (after more than 200 had been killed by a terrorist bomb on October 23, 1983.)

BIRTHS

Charles V, Holy Roman Emperor, **1500**; Wilhelm Grimm, German philologist and, with his brother Jakob, compiler of fairy tales, **1786**; Arnold Dolmetsch, Swiss maker and restorer of musical instruments, **1858**; Michel Legrand, French composer of film music, **1932**; James Florentino, US film actor, **1938**.

DEATHS

Thomas Bowdler, English editor who produced "bowdlerized," or expurgated, versions of great literary works such as Shakespeare and the Old Testament, **1825**; Nikolai Bulganin, Soviet prime minister, **1975**; "Memphis Slim," US blues singer, **1987**; Dinah Shore, US singer, **1994**.

NOTES

February 25

*"Of course we were brought to the verge of war.
If you are scared to go to the brink, you are lost."*
—JOHN FOSTER DULLES, *reported on Jan. 16, 1956*

The national day of Kuwait.

EVENTS

1793 President George Washington met with heads of government departments, the first "Cabinet" meeting. **1913** US federal income tax was introduced by law. **1913** English suffragist Emmeline Pankhurst went on trial for a bomb attack on the home of David Lloyd George, chancellor of the Exchequer. **1948** The Communists seized complete control of Czechoslovakia.

BIRTHS

Carlo Goldoni, Italian playwright, **1707**; Pierre-Auguste Renoir, French Impressionist painter, **1841**; Enrico Caruso, Italian operatic tenor, **1873**; John Foster Dulles, US secretary of state known for "brinkmanship," **1888**; Anthony Burgess, English novelist, **1917**; George Harrison, English pop musician and former member of the Beatles, **1943**.

DEATHS

Christopher Wren, English architect, **1723**; Paul Julius von Reuter, founder of Reuters international news agency, **1899**; John Tenniel, English artist and illustrator, **1914**; Mark Rothko, US painter, **1970**; Tennessee Williams, US dramatist, **1983**.

NOTES

February 26

EVENTS

1531 An earthquake in Lisbon, Portugal, killed 20,000 people. **1815** Napoleon escaped from exile on the island of Elba. **1935** Robert Watson-Watt gave the first demonstration of Radar at Daventry, England. **1936** Adolf Hitler launched the Volkswagen ("people's automobile"), intended to compete with Ford's Model T and boost the German economy. **1986** Robert Penn Warren was named the first official US poet laureate. **1993** Six people were killed by a bomb in the underground parking area of New York's World Trade Center. **1994** A jury found 11 members of the Branch Davidian religious cult not guilty of murder and conspiracy in the February 1993 deaths of 4 federal agents besieging their armed compound at Waco, Texas.

BIRTHS

Victor Hugo, French novelist and playwright, **1802**; William Cody ("Buffalo Bill"), US showman, **1846**; Tony Randall, US comic actor, **1920**; Betty Hutton, US film actress and singer, **1921**; Fats Domino, US singer, **1928**; Johnny Cash, US country singer, **1932**.

DEATHS

Roger II, king of Sicily, **1154**; John Philip Kemble, English actor, **1823**; Richard Gatling, US inventor of the Gatling gun, **1903**; Slim Gaillard, US jazz musician, **1991**.

NOTES

February 27

"Some of my best leading men have been dogs and horses."
—ELIZABETH TAYLOR, The Times, *Feb. 18, 1981*

EVENTS

1782 The British Parliament voted to abandon the American war. **1879** US chemists Ira Remsen and Constantine Fahlberg announced their discovery of the artificial sweetner, saccharin. **1933** The German Reichstag (parliament building) in Berlin was destroyed by fire; it is believed that the Nazis were responsible, though they blamed the Communists. **1991** The Gulf War came to an end with the liberation of Kuwait and the retreat of Iraqi forces.

BIRTHS

Constantine I (the Great), Roman emperor, **288**; Henry Wadsworth Longfellow, US poet, **1807**; Rudolf Steiner, Austrian philosopher, **1861**; John Steinbeck, US novelist, **1902**; Lawrence Durrell, English poet and novelist, **1912**; Joanne Woodward, US film actress, **1930**; Elizabeth Taylor, English-born US film actress, **1932**; Chelsea Clinton, daughter of President and Mrs. Clinton, **1980**.

DEATHS

General Francis Marion, US Revolutionary hero known as the "Swamp Fox," **1795**; Alexander Borodin, Russian composer and chemist, **1887**; Ivan Pavlov, Russian psychologist, **1936**; Peter Behrens, German architect, **1940**; Henry Cabot Lodge, US politician and diplomat, **1985**; Lilian Gish, US film actress, **1993**.

NOTES

February 28

*"What is character but the determination of incident?
What is incident but the illustration of character?"*
—HENRY JAMES, Partial Portraits

EVENTS

1784 John Wesley, English founder of Methodism, signed its deed of declaration. **1854** The Republican party was founded at Ripon, Wisconsin, to oppose the extension of slavery. **1912** The first parachute jump was made, over Missouri. **1948** The last British troops left India. **1986** Swedish Prime Minister Olof Palme was shot dead as he walked home from a movie theater in Stockholm. **1993** Four US agents were killed while storming the headquarters of the Branch Davidian cult in Waco, Texas. **1994** NATO aircraft shot down four Serb warplanes, recording the first offensive action in the organization's history.

BIRTHS

René Antoine de Réaumur, French scientist and inventor of a thermometer scale, **1683**; Linus Pauling, US physicist and chemist, **1909**; Stephen Spender, English poet and critic, **1909**; Vincente Minnelli, US film director, **1913**; Peter Medawar, English immunologist, **1915**.

DEATHS

Alphonse de Lamartine, French poet, **1869**; Henry James, US-born British novelist, **1916**; Alfonso XIII, king of Spain, **1941**; Rajendra Prasad, first president of India, **1963**; Henry Luce, US magazine publisher, **1967**.

NOTES

February 29

Leap Year Day.

EVENTS

1880 The St. Gotthard railroad tunnel through the Alps was completed, linking Italy with Switzerland. **1956** Pakistan became an Islamic republic. **1960** An earthquake killed about 12,000 people in Agadir, Morocco. **1964** President Lyndon Johnson denied reports that the US was considering an intensification of the war in Vietnam. **1968** English astronomer Jocelyn Burnell announced the discovery of the first pulsar.

BIRTHS

Ann Lee, English founder of the American Society of Shakers, **1736**; Gioacchino Rossini, Italian composer, **1792**; John Holland, US submarine inventor, **1840**; Shri Morarji Desai, Indian politician, **1896**; Jimmy Dorsey, US bandleader, **1904**; Mario Andretti, Italian-born US racing driver, **1940**.

DEATHS

St. Hilarius, 46th pope, **468**; Patrick Hamilton, Scottish Protestant martyr, **1528**; John Landseer, English painter, **1852**.

NOTES

_____

_____

_____

_____

March 1

---

*"Perhaps of all the creations of man language
is the most astonishing."*
—LYTTON STRACHEY, Words and Poetry

The national day of Wales.

EVENTS

1780 Pennsylvania became the first state to abolish slavery. **1790** Congress passed the act requiring a regular census. **1803** Ohio became the 17th state. **1845** The US annexed Texas. **1867** Nebraska became the 37th state. **1932** Charles Lindbergh's baby son was kidnapped (and found dead May 12). **1949** Heavyweight boxing champion Joe Louis retired after successfully defending his title 25 times. **1954** The US conducted its first hydrogen-bomb test at Bikini Atoll, in the Marshall Islands. **1954** Five congressmen were wounded by Puerto Rican separatists in the House of Representatives. **1966** The unmanned Soviet spacecraft *Venus 3* landed on Venus. **1993** US forces began to drop relief supplies to civilians in war-torn Bosnia-Herzegovina.

BIRTHS

Frédéric Chopin, Polish pianist and composer, **1810**; Lytton Strachey, English biographer, **1880**; Glenn Miller, US bandleader, **1904**; David Niven, Scottish-born US film actor, **1910**; Dinah Shore, US singer, **1918**; Harry Belafonte, US singer, **1927**; Ron Howard, US actor and director, **1958**.

DEATHS

George Herbert, English poet, **1633**; Girolamo Frescobaldi, Italian composer, **1643**; Jackie Coogan, US film actor who in 1921 played the child in Charlie Chaplin's *The Kid*, **1984**.

NOTES

March 2

"No party has a monopoly over what is right."
—MIKHAIL GORBACHEV, *reported on March 2, 1986*

EVENTS

1836 Texas proclaimed independence from Mexico and became a republic. **1877** Rutherford B. Hayes was declared president by one vote by an electoral commission after the electoral votes were disputed. **1949** US Air Force Captain James Gallagher returned to Fort Worth, Texas, after flying non-stop around the world in 94 hours with a crew of 13 men; tanker aircraft refueled their plane four times during the flight. **1955** Severe flooding in north and west Australia killed 200 people. **1969** The French-built supersonic aircraft *Concorde* made its first test flight from Toulouse. **1970** Rhodesia proclaimed itself a republic.

BIRTHS

Bedřich Smetana, Czech composer, **1824**; Kurt Weill, German composer who worked with Bertolt Brecht, **1900**; Jennifer Jones, US film actress, **1919**; Mikhail Gorbachev, Soviet leader, **1931**; John Irving, US novelist, **1942**; Ian Woosnam, Welsh golfer, **1958**; Jon Bon Jovi, US rock singer, **1962**.

DEATHS

John Wesley, English founder of Methodism, **1791**; Horace Walpole, English novelist and historian, **1797**; D.H. Lawrence, English novelist, **1930**; Howard Carter, English Egyptologist who discovered Tutankhamen's tomb, **1939**; Randolph Scott, US film actor, **1987**.

NOTES

March 3

*"Morocco is like a tree nourished by roots
deep in the soil of Africa which breathes through
foliage rustling to the winds of Europe."*
—KING HASSAN II OF MOROCCO, The Challenge

The national day of Morocco.

EVENTS

1802 Beethoven's "Moonlight Sonata" published. **1820** The Missouri Compromise bill passed Congress, allowing slavery in that state but restricting it in the northwest. **1845** Florida became the 27th state. **1875** The first performance of Bizet's opera *Carmen* was staged, at the Opéra Comique, Paris. **1931** "The Star-Spangled Banner" was adopted as the US national anthem. **1969** US spacecraft *Apollo 9* was launched. **1991** Latvia and Estonia voted to secede from the Soviet Union.

BIRTHS

George Pullman, US designer of luxury railroad cars, **1831**; Alexander Graham Bell, Scottish-born US inventor of the telephone, **1847**; Jean Harlow, US film actress, **1911**; Richard Chamberlain, US film actor, **1935**; Miranda Richardson, English actress, **1958**.

DEATHS

Robert Hooke, English physicist, **1703**; Robert Adam, Scottish architect, **1792**; Giandomenico Tiepolo, Italian artist, **1804**; Lou Costello, US comedian, **1959**; Arthur Koestler, Hungarian-born writer, **1983**; Danny Kaye, US comedian, **1987**.

NOTES

March 4

*"No pain, no palm; no thorns, no throne; no gall,
no glory; no cross, no crown."*
—WILLIAM PENN, No Cross, No Crown

EVENTS

1681 Quaker William Penn received a charter to establish the colony of Pennsylvania. **1791** Vermont became the 14th state. **1861** Abraham Lincoln was sworn in as the 16th president of the US. **1877** The Russian Imperial Ballet staged the first performance of the ballet *Swan Lake,* in Moscow. **1968** Tennis authorities voted to admit professional players to Wimbledon, previously open only to amateur players. **1994** After a five-month trial, four Muslim fundamentalists were convicted of bombing New York's World Trade Center on February 26, 1993.

BIRTHS

Prince Henry the Navigator, Portuguese patron of explorers, **1394**; Antonio Vivaldi, Italian composer, **1678**; Bernard Haitink, Dutch conductor, **1929**; Miriam Makeba, South African singer, **1931**.

DEATHS

Saladin, Kurdish-born Muslim leader who defeated the Crusaders, **1193**; Thomas Malory, English author of the *Morte d'Arthur*, **1470**; Jean-François Champollion, French Egyptologist, **1832**; Nikolai Gogol, Russian novelist and playwright, **1852**; William Carlos Williams, US poet, **1963**; John Candy, Canadian-born US comic actor, **1994**.

NOTES

March 5

EVENTS

1770 British troops killed five civilians when they fired into a crowd of demonstrators in Boston; the incident became known as the "Boston Massacre." **1927** US Marines landed in China to protect American property during civil war. **1933** The Nazi party won almost half the seats in the German general election. **1936** The *Spitfire* British fighter plane made its first test flight from Eastleigh, Southampton. **1946** The term "iron curtain" was first used, by Winston Churchill in a speech in Missouri. **1994** White House legal counsel Bernard Nessbaum resigned after being accused of prying into the Whitewater scandal investigation.

BIRTHS

Henry II, king of England, **1133**; Gerardus Mercator, Flemish cartographer, **1512**; Augusta Gregory, Irish playwright, **1852**; Heitor Villa-Lobos, Brazilian composer, **1887**; Rex Harrison, English actor, **1908**.

DEATHS

Antonio Correggio, Italian painter, **1534**; Friedrich Mesmer, Austrian physician and founder of mesmerism, or "animal magnetism," **1815**; Alessandro Volta, Italian physicist, **1827**; Joseph Stalin, Soviet dictator, **1953**; Sergei Prokofiev, Russian composer, **1953**; Tito Gobbi, Italian operatic baritone, **1984**; John Belushi, US comic actor, **1982**; William Powell, US film actor, **1984**.

NOTES

March 6

*"It is better to be first with an ugly woman
than the hundredth with a beauty."*
—PEARL BUCK, The Good Earth

The national day of Ghana.

EVENTS

1836 The 12-day siege of the Alamo ended, with the entire garrison of over 180 killed. **1857** The Supreme Court ruled in the *Dred Scott* case that slaves could not become citizens. **1899** Aspirin was patented by chemist Felix Hoffman. **1930** Clarence Birdseye's first frozen foods went on sale in Springfield, Massachusetts. **1957** Ghana became independent, the first British colony to do so. **1987** A cross-channel ferry left Zeebrugge, Belgium, with its bow doors open; it capsized suddenly outside the harbor, killing over 180 passengers.

BIRTHS

Cyrano de Bergerac, French novelist and playwright, **1619**; Elizabeth Barrett Browning, English poet, **1806**; Philip Henry Sheridan, Union general in the Civil War, **1831**; Andrzej Wajda, Polish film director, **1926**; Valentina Tereshkova, Soviet astronaut, **1937**; Kiri Te Kanawa, New Zealand operatic soprano, **1944**.

DEATHS

Louisa May Alcott, US novelist, **1888**; Gottlieb Daimler, German motor engineer who invented the motorcycle, **1900**; Oliver Wendell Holmes, US Supreme Court justice, **1935**; Pearl Buck, US novelist, **1971**; Donald Maclean, English-born Soviet spy, **1984**.

NOTES

March 7

EVENTS

1838 Swedish soprano Jenny Lind gave her debut performance in Weber's *Der Freischütz*. **1876** Alexander Graham Bell patented the telephone. **1912** French aviator Henri Seimet made the first non-stop flight from Paris to London. **1926** A radio-telephone link was established between New York and London. **1971** Women in Switzerland achieved the right to vote and hold federal office. **1994** California passed a new "three strikes and you are out" crime law doubling the penalty if a person convicted of a felony had previously been convicted of a serious crime. **1995** New York State brought back the death penalty, becoming the 38th state to do so; the last New York execution had been in 1963.

BIRTHS

Luther Burbank, US botanist and plant breeder, **1849**; Tomáš Masaryk, Czech leader, **1850**; Piet Mondrian, Dutch painter, **1872**; Maurice Ravel, French composer, **1875**; Ivan Lendl, Czech tennis player, **1960**.

DEATHS

Antoninus Pius, Roman emperor, **161**; St. Thomas Aquinas, Italian theologian, **1274**; Herman Mankiewicz, US screenwriter, **1953**; Percy Wyndham Lewis, English writer and artist, **1957**; Stevie Smith, English poet and novelist, **1971**.

NOTES

March 8

---

*"There is nothing—absolutely nothing—half so much worth doing
as simply messing about in boats."*
—KENNETH GRAHAME, The Wind in the Willows

EVENTS

1702 Anne became queen of Britain after William III died in a riding accident. **1910** The first pilot's licenses were issued, to an Englishman, J.T.C. Moore Brabazon, and a Frenchwoman, Elise Deroche. **1917** The February Revolution began in Petrograd (St. Petersburg), Russia. **1930** In India, a campaign of civil disobedience began, led by Mahatma Gandhi. **1965** Some 3,500 US Marines landed in South Vietnam. **1971** US boxer Mohammed Ali was defeated by Joe Frazier.

BIRTHS

Oliver Wendell Holmes, US jurist, **1841**; Kenneth Grahame, Scottish author of *The Wind in the Willows*, **1859**; Otto Hahn, German physicist and chemist, **1879**; Cyd Charisse, US film actress and dancer, **1921**.

DEATHS

Abraham Darby, English ironmaster, the first to use coke for smelting iron, **1717**; Hector Berlioz, French composer, **1869**; Millard Fillmore, 13th US president, **1874**; John Ericsson, Swedish-born US inventor of the screw propeller, **1889**; William Howard Taft, 27th US president, **1930**; Thomas Beecham, English conductor, **1961**; Harold Lloyd, US silent-film comedian, **1971**.

NOTES

March 9

*"You begin saving the world by saving one man at a time;
all else is grandiose romanticism or politics."*
—CHARLES BUKOWSKI, Tales of Ordinary
Madness, *"Too Sensitive"*

EVENTS

1074 Pope Gregory VII excommunicated all married priests. **1796** French army commander Napoleon Bonaparte married Josephine de Beauharnais. **1831** The French Foreign Legion was founded in Algeria; its headquarters moved to France in 1962. **1862** The first naval battle between ironclads was a standoff in the Civil War between the Union's *Monitor* and the Confederacy's *Virginia* (the *Merrimack* renamed the previous day) at Hampton Roads, Virginia. **1918** The Russian capital was transferred from Petrograd (St. Petersburg) to Moscow. **1956** Archbishop Makarios of Cyprus was deported to the Seychelles to prevent his involvement in terrorist activities. **1961** The Russian dog Laika was launched into space aboard *Sputnik 9*.

BIRTHS

William Cobbett, English author and politician, **1763**; Vyacheslav Molotov, Soviet politician, **1890**; Yuri Gagarin, Soviet astronaut, the first man in space, **1934**; Bobby Fischer, US world chess champion, **1943**.

DEATHS

Jules Mazarin, French cardinal and politician, **1661**; Wilhelm I, king of Prussia, **1888**; Menachem Begin, Israeli prime minister, **1992**; Bob Crosby, US bandleader, **1993**; Fernando Rey, Spanish actor, **1994**; Charles Bukowski, US novelist and poet, **1994**.

NOTES

March 10

*"If you pick up a starving dog and make him
prosperous he will not bite you. This is the principal
difference between a dog and a man."*
—MARK TWAIN, *What Is Man?*

EVENTS

1914 English suffragist Mary Richardson slashed Velázquez'
Rokeby Venus with a meat cleaver. **1969** James Earl Ray was sentenced to 99 years' imprisonment after pleading guilty to the
murder of civil-rights leader Martin Luther King. **1974** A
Japanese soldier was discovered hiding on Lubang Island in the
Philippines. He was unaware that World War II had ended and
was waiting to be picked up by his own forces. **1994** The US
Centers for Disease Control and Prevention announced that new
AIDS cases in the US had more than doubled in 1993 to 103,500
from 49,016 the previous year.

BIRTHS

Marcello Malpighi, Italian physiologist, **1628**; Tamara Karsavina,
Russian ballet dancer, **1885**; Arthur Honegger, French composer,
1892; Bix Beiderbecke, US jazz musician and composer, **1903**;
Prince Edward, youngest son of Queen Elizabeth II, **1964**.

DEATHS

Giuseppe Mazzini, Italian nationalist, **1832**; Mikhail Bulgakov,
Russian novelist and playwright, **1940**; Jan Masaryk, Czech
politician, allegedly committed suicide after Communist
takeover, **1948**; Konstantin Chernenko, Soviet leader, **1985**; Ray
Milland, US film actor, **1986**.

NOTES

March 11

EVENTS

1702 The first successful English daily newspaper, the *Daily Courant*, was published in London. **1941** Congress passed the Lend-Lease Bill, authorizing billions in loans to its allies in World War II. **1961** The Port of Authority of New York and New Jersey recommended the building of a $355 million World Trade Center in lower Manhattan. **1985** Mikhail Gorbachev became leader of the USSR. **1990** US tennis player Jennifer Capriati, aged 13, became the youngest-ever finalist in a professional tennis contest.

BIRTHS

Urbain Leverrier, French astronomer, **1811**; Harold Wilson, British prime minister, **1916**; Rupert Murdoch, Australian-born US news media proprietor, **1931**; Sam Donaldson, US TV newsman, **1934**; Douglas Adams, English author of *The Hitch-Hiker's Guide to the Galaxy*, **1952**.

DEATHS

Johnny Appleseed (John Chapman), American pioneer who planted apple trees throughout the Midwest, **1845**; Rolf Boldrewood, Australian author, **1915**; Alexander Fleming, Scottish bacteriologist who discovered penicillin, **1955**; Richard Evelyn Bird, US aviator and explorer, **1957**; Erle Stanley Gardner, US crime writer and lawyer, **1970**.

NOTES

_____

_____

_____

_____

March 12

*"I don't act for public opinion. I act for the nation
and for my own satisfaction."*
—KEMAL ATATÜRK

EVENTS

1789 The US Post Office was established. **1881** France made Tunisia a protectorate. **1912** The American Girl Guides were established (renamed the Girl Scouts in 1913). **1930** Indian leader Mahatma Gandhi began his walk to the sea, known as the Salt March, in defiance of the British government's tax on salt and monopoly of the salt trade in India. **1938** Germany annexed Austria. **1940** The Russo-Finnish War ended with Finland signing over territory to the USSR. **1993** Janet Reno became the first woman to serve as US attorney general. **1994** The Church of England ordained its first women priests; 32 women became priests at the service in Bristol Cathedral.

BIRTHS

Kemal Atatürk, Turkish leader, **1881**; Vaslav Nijinsky, Russian ballet dancer, **1890**; Max Wall, English actor and comedian, **1908**; Liza Minnelli, US film actress and singer, **1946**; James Taylor, US singer and songwriter, **1948**.

DEATHS

St. Gregory, pope, **604**; Cesare Borgia, Italian cardinal and politician, **1507**; Sun Yat-sen, Chinese revolutionary leader, **1925**; Anne Frank, Dutch Jewish diarist, died in a Nazi concentration camp, **1945**; Charlie "Bird" Parker, US jazz saxophonist, **1955**; Eugene Ormandy, US conductor, **1985**.

NOTES

March 13

EVENTS

1781 German-born British astronomer William Herschel discovered the planet Uranus. **1881** Czar Alexander II of Russia died after a bomb was thrown at him in St. Petersburg. **1884** US Standard Time came into being. **1894** The first public striptease act was performed in Paris. **1928** A dam burst near Los Angeles and 450 people drowned. **1930** US astronomer Clyde Tombaugh discovered the planet Pluto; its existence had been predicted 14 years earlier by US astronomer Percy Lowell. **1979** A Marxist coup led by Maurice Bishop took place in Grenada.

BIRTHS

Joseph Priestley, English scientist, **1733**; Percy Lowell, US astronomer, **1855**; Hugh Walpole, English novelist, **1884**; Henry Hathaway, US film director, **1898**; Neil Sedaka, US singer and songwriter, **1939**.

DEATHS

Richard Burbage, English actor who built the Globe Theatre, **1619**; Benjamin Harrison, 23rd US president, **1901**; Susan Anthony, US feminist, **1906**; Stephen Vincent Benét, US poet who wrote "John Brown's Body," **1943**; John Middleton Murry, English writer and critic, **1957**.

NOTES

March 14

"Equations are more important to me because politics is for the present, but an equation is something for eternity."
—ALBERT EINSTEIN

EVENTS

1492 Queen Isabella of Castile ordered the expulsion of 150,000 Jews from Spain, unless they accepted Christian baptism. **1743** The first town meeting was held, in Faneuil Hall in Boston. **1885** Gilbert and Sullivan's *The Mikado* was first performed, at the Savoy Theatre, London. **1888** A four-day blizzard ended in the US East with some 400 dead. **1891** The submarine *Monarch* laid the first underwater telephone cable. **1986** Halley's Comet returned and was photographed by five space probes, including *Giotto*, which flew into the comet's tail.

BIRTHS

Georg Philipp Telemann, German composer, **1681**; Mrs. Isabella Beeton, English cookbook writer, **1836**; Maxim Gorky, Russian playwright and novelist, **1868**; Albert Einstein, German-born US physicist, **1879**; Michael Caine, English film actor, **1933**; Billy Crystal, US film actor, **1947**.

DEATHS

Karl Marx, German philosopher, **1883**; George Eastman, US inventor of the Kodak camera, **1932**; Nikolai Bukharin, Russian politician, **1938**; Susan Hayward, US film actress, **1975**; Busby Berkeley, US film choreographer, **1976**.

NOTES

March 15

EVENTS

1820 Maine became the 23rd state. **1892** US inventor Jesse Reno patented the first escalator. **1909** US entrepreneur G.S. Selfridge opened Selfridges, Britain's first department store, in London. **1917** Czar Nicholas II of Russia abdicated. **1919** The American Legion was founded. **1933** Nazi leader Adolf Hitler proclaimed the Third Reich in Germany; he also banned left-wing newspapers and kosher food.

BIRTHS

Andrew Jackson, 7th US president, **1767**; John Snow, English physician who pioneered the use of ether as an anesthetic, **1813**; Emil von Behring, German bacteriologist, **1854**; Joseph Cotton, US film actor, **1905**; Mai Zetterling, Swedish-born actress and director, **1925**; Mike Love, US pop singer, member of the Beach Boys, **1941**; Ry Cooder, US guitarist, **1947**.

DEATHS

Julius Caesar, Roman general and dictator, assassinated, **44 BC**; Henry Bessemer, English metallurgist who invented the Bessemer converter, **1898**; Aristotle Onassis, Greek shipping tycoon, **1975**; Rebecca West, English novelist, **1983**.

NOTES

March 16

EVENTS

1660 The Long Parliament of England was dissolved, after sitting for 20 years. **1802** The US Military Academy was established at West Point, New York. **1926** The first rocket fueled by gasoline and liquid oxygen was successfully launched at Auburn, Massachusetts, by US physicist Robert Goddard. **1973** The new London Bridge was opened. **1994** Figure skater Tonya Harding pleaded guilty in Portland, Oregon, to covering up a plot to assault her Olympic rival Nancy Kerrigan. **1995** Mississippi finally ratified the US Constitution's 13th Amendment, which abolishes slavery; it was nationally adopted 130 years earlier.

BIRTHS

James Madison, 4th US president, **1751**; Matthew Flinders, English navigator who explored the coast of Australia, **1774**; Georg Ohm, German physicist, **1787**; Leo McKern, Australian actor, **1920**; Jerry Lewis, US comedy film actor, **1926**; Bernardo Bertolucci, Italian film director, **1941**.

DEATHS

Tiberius Claudius Nero, Roman emperor, **37**; Aubrey Beardsley, English illustrator, **1898**; Miguel Primo de Rivera, Spanish politician and dictator, **1930**; William Henry Beveridge, English economist who wrote the report on which the British welfare state was founded, **1963**.

NOTES

_____

_____

_____

_____

March 17

"I am just going outside and may be some time."
—CAPTAIN LAWRENCE OATES, *a member of Scott's Antarctic expedition, his last words as he walked out into a blizzard*

The national day of Ireland.

EVENTS

1766 Britain's Parliament repealed the Stamp Act that had provoked the American slogan "No taxation without representation." **1897** English-born New Zealand boxer Bob Fitzsimmons won the world heavyweight title from US champion Jim Corbett. **1969** Golda Meir, aged 70, took office as prime minister of Israel, the first woman to do so. **1978** The oil tanker *Amoco Cadiz* ran aground on the coast of Brittany, spilling over 220,000 tons of crude oil and causing extensive pollution. **1990** The Bastille opera house, Paris, was opened.

BIRTHS

Bobby Jones, US golfer, **1902**; Nat "King" Cole, US singer, **1919**; Penelope Lively, English novelist, **1933**; Rudolf Nureyev, Russian ballet dancer, **1938**; Robin Knox-Johnston, British yachtsman, the first to sail single-handed, non-stop around the world, **1939**.

DEATHS

Marcus Aurelius, Roman emperor, **180**; Daniel Bernoulli, Swiss mathematician and physicist, **1782**; Christian Doppler, Austrian physicist, **1853**; Lawrence Oates, English Antarctic explorer, **1912**; George Wilkins, Australian polar explorer, **1958**.

NOTES

March 18

"I believe it is peace in our time ... peace with honor."
—NEVILLE CHAMBERLAIN

EVENTS

1662 The first public bus service began operating, in Paris. **1891** The London-Paris telephone link came into operation. **1922** Indian leader Mahatma Gandhi was jailed for six years for sedition. **1931** The first electric razors were manufactured in the US. **1965** Soviet astronaut Alexei Leonov made the first "walk" in space. **1987** The US speed limit was raised from 55 mph to 65 mph on rural highways.

BIRTHS

Grover Cleveland, 22nd and 24th US president, **1837**; Nikolai Rimsky-Korsakov, Russian composer, **1844**; Rudolf Diesel, German engineer who invented the engine named after him, **1858**; Neville Chamberlain, British prime minister who tried unsuccessfully to make peace with Hitler, **1869**; Lavrenti Beria, Soviet chief of secret police, **1889**; Peter Graves, US film actor, **1926**; Matt Dillon, US film actor, **1964**.

DEATHS

Fra Angelico, Italian monk and painter, **1455**; Ivan IV (the Terrible), **1584**; Robert Walpole, first prime minister of Britain, **1745**; Laurence Sterne, Irish novelist, **1768**.

NOTES

March 19

EVENTS

721 BC The first-ever recorded solar eclipse was seen from Babylon. **1628** The New England Company was formed in Massachusetts Bay. **1913** Russian composer Modest Mussorgsky's opera *Boris Godunov* was first performed in full at the Metropolitan Opera, New York. **1920** The US Senate failed to ratify the Versailles Treaty ending World War I and establishing the League of Nations. **1932** The Sydney Harbour Bridge, New South Wales, Australia, was opened; it was the world's longest single-span arch bridge, at 1,650 ft/503 m.

BIRTHS

Georges de la Tour, French painter, **1593**; Tobias Smollett, Scottish physician and author, **1721**; David Livingstone, Scottish missionary and explorer, **1813**; Richard Burton, English explorer and scholar, **1821**; Wyatt Earp, US law officer, **1848**; Sergei Diaghilev, Russian ballet impresario, **1872**; Philip Roth, US novelist, **1933**; Glenn Close, US actress, **1947**.

DEATHS

Mary Anning, English paleontologist who discovered the first ichthyosaurus, **1847**; Arthur James Balfour, British prime minister, **1930**; Edgar Rice Burroughs, US novelist who wrote the Tarzan stories, **1950**; Bruce Willis, US film actor, **1955**.

NOTES

March 20

"I shall return."
—DOUGLAS MACARTHUR, *promise to the Filipinos on March 20, 1942*

EVENTS

1602 The Dutch government founded the Dutch East India Company. **1815** Napoleon returned to Paris from banishment on the island of Elba to begin his last 100 days of power that ended with defeat and exile. **1852** US author Harriet Beecher Stowe's novel *Uncle Tom's Cabin* was published. **1934** Radar was first demonstrated at Kiel Harbor, Germany. **1956** Tunisia achieved independence from France. **1990** Namibia achieved independence from South Africa.

BIRTHS

Ovid, Roman poet, **43 BC**; Henrik Ibsen, Norwegian playwright, **1828**; Beniamino Gigli, Italian operatic tenor, **1890**; Michael Redgrave, English actor, **1908**; Vera Lynn, English singer, **1917**; William Hurt, US film actor, **1950**; Spike Lee, US actor, director, and producer, **1957**; Holly Hunter, US film actress, **1958**.

DEATHS

Henry IV, king of England, **1413**; Isaac Newton, English scientist, **1727**; Lajos Kossuth, Hungarian revolutionary leader, **1894**; Ferdinand Foch, French Army marshal, **1929**.

NOTES

_____

_____

_____

_____

March 21

*"I was obliged to work hard. Whoever is
equally industrious will succeed just as well."*
—J.S. BACH

EVENTS

1933 Germany's first Nazi parliament was officially opened in a ceremony at the garrison church in Potsdam. **1946** British minister Aneurin Bevan announced the Labour government's plans for the National Health Service. **1952** Kwame Nkrumah was elected prime minister of the Gold Coast (later Ghana.) **1960** The Sharpeville Massacre took place in South Africa: a peaceful demonstration against the pass laws ended with about 70 deaths when police fired on demonstrators. **1963** Alcatraz, the maximum-security prison in San Francisco Bay, was closed. **1990** A demonstration in London against the poll tax became a riot, in which over 400 people were arrested.

BIRTHS

Johann Sebastian Bach, German composer, **1685**; Paul Tortelier, French cellist, **1914**; Peter Brook, English stage and film director, **1925**; Ayrton Senna, Brazilian racing driver, **1960**.

DEATHS

Thomas Cranmer, archbishop of Canterbury, burned at the stake, **1556**; James Ussher, Irish theologian and archbishop of Armagh, who fixed the date of the creation at 4004 BC, **1656**; Robert Southey, English poet, **1843**; Alexander Glazunov, Russian composer, **1936**; Robert Preston, US film actor, **1986**.

NOTES

March 22

"The concerts you enjoy together
Neighbors you annoy together
Children you destroy together
That make marriage a joy."
—STEPHEN SONDHEIM, *"The Little Things You Do Together"*

The earliest possible date for Easter.

EVENTS

1895 French cinema pioneers Auguste and Louis Lumière gave the first demonstration of celluloid film, in Paris. **1942** The BBC began broadcasting in Morse code to the French Resistance. **1945** The Arab League was founded in Cairo. **1946** Jordan achieved independence from British rule.

BIRTHS

Maximilian I, Holy Roman Emperor, **1459**; Karl Malden, US film actor, **1913**; Marcel Marceau, French mime artist, **1923**; Stephen Sondheim, US composer and lyricist, **1930**; William Shatner, Canadian-born US actor who played Captain Kirk in the *Star Trek* TV series and films, **1931**; Andrew Lloyd Webber, English composer of musicals, **1948**.

DEATHS

Johann Wolfgang von Goethe, German poet, novelist, and playwright, **1832**; Thomas Hughes, English author of *Tom Brown's Schooldays*, **1896**; Mike Todd, US film producer, **1958**; Walter Lantz, US animator who created Woody Woodpecker, **1994**.

NOTES

March 23

The national day of Pakistan.

EVENTS

1743 Handel's *Messiah* was performed for the first time, in London. **1765** The British Parliament passed the Stamp Act, imposing a tax on all publications and official documents in America. **1775** Patrick Henry said "Give me liberty or give me death." **1919** The Italian Fascist party was formed by Benito Mussolini. **1925** Authorities in Tennessee forbade the teaching of Darwinian theory in schools. **1956** Pakistan was declared an Islamic republic within the British Commonwealth.

BIRTHS

Juan Gris, Spanish painter, **1887**; Joan Crawford, US film actress, **1904**; Akira Kurosawa, Japanese film director, **1910**; Wernher von Braun, German-born US rocket engineer, **1912**; Roger Bannister, English neurologist who, as a student, was the first person to run a mile in under four minutes (3 min, 59.4 sec), **1929**.

DEATHS

Stendhal, French novelist, **1945**; Raoul Dufy, French painter, **1953**; Peter Lorre, Hungarian-born US film actor, **1964**.

NOTES

March 24

---

*"Lives of great men remind us
We can make our lives sublime,
And departing, leave behind us,
Footprints on the sand of time."*
—HENRY WADSWORTH LONGFELLOW, *"A Psalm of Life"*

EVENTS

1401 Tamerlane the Great captured Damascus. **1603** The crowns of England and Scotland were united when King James VI of Scotland succeeded to the English throne as James I. **1976** Isabel Perón, president of Argentina, was deposed. **1989** America's largest oil spill (some 240,000 barrels) occurred in Prince William Sound, Alaska, when the tanker *Exxon Valdez* struck a reef. **1994** Luis Donaldo Colosio, presidential candidate for Mexico's ruling Institutional Revolutionary party, was assassinated in Tijuana.

BIRTHS

Fanny Crosby, US blind composer of more than 6,000 pieces, mostly hymns, **1820**; William Morris, English socialist and craftsman, **1834**; Roscoe "Fatty" Arbuckle, US silent film actor, **1887**; Ub Iwerks, US animator who worked with Walt Disney on the creation of Mickey Mouse, **1901**; Steve McQueen, US film actor, **1930**.

DEATHS

Elizabeth I, queen of England, **1603**; Henry Wadsworth Longfellow, US poet, **1882**; Jules Verne, French novelist, **1905**; J.M. Synge, Irish playwright, **1909**; Bernard, Viscount Montgomery of Alamein, British field-marshal, **1976**.

NOTES

March 25

The national day of Greece.

EVENTS

1306 Robert I (the Bruce) was crowned king of Scots. **1609** English explorer Henry Hudson set off from Amsterdam, on behalf of the Dutch East India Company, in search of the Northwest Passage. **1807** The British parliament abolished the slave trade in British territory. **1957** Six European countries (France, Belgium, Luxembourg, West Germany, Italy, and the Netherlands) signed the Treaty of Rome, establishing the European Community (now the European Union). **1994** The final US peacekeeping forces left Somalia, being replaced by UN troops.

BIRTHS

Henry II, king of England, 1133; Arturo Toscanini, Italian conductor, 1867; Béla Bartók, Hungarian composer, 1881; David Lean, English film director, 1908; Gloria Steinem, US feminist and writer, 1934; Aretha Franklin, US singer, 1942; Elton John, English pop singer and songwriter, 1947.

DEATHS

Anna Seward, English novelist who wrote *Black Beauty*, 1809; Frédéric Mistral, French poet, 1914; Claude Debussy, French composer, 1918; King Faisal of Saudi Arabia, assassinated by his nephew, 1975.

NOTES

March 26

*"It was a blonde to make a bishop kick a
hole in a stained glass window."*
—RAYMOND CHANDLER, Farewell My Lovely

EVENTS

1920 British special constables known as the Black and Tans arrived in Ireland. **1964** *Funny Girl* opened on Broadway, establishing Barbra Streisand as a star. **1971** The Awami League declared the independence of East Pakistan as Bangladesh. **1973** The first women were allowed on the floor of the London Stock Exchange. **1979** Israeli Prime Minister Menachem Begin and Egyptian President Anwar Sadat signed a historic peace treaty after two years of negotiations.

BIRTHS

A.E. Housman, English poet, 1859; Robert Frost, US poet, 1874; Pierre Boulez, French conductor and composer, 1925; Alan Arkin, US actor, 1934; Leonard Nimoy, US actor who played Mr. Spock in the TV series *Star Trek*, 1931; James Caan, US film actor, 1939; Erica Jong, US novelist, 1942; Diana Ross, US singer, 1944.

DEATHS

Ludwig von Beethoven, German composer, 1827; Walt Whitman, US poet, 1892; Cecil Rhodes, English-born South African politician, 1902; Sarah Bernhardt, French actress, 1923; Raymond Chandler, US novelist who created private eye Philip Marlowe, 1959; Noël Coward, English playwright, songwriter, and entertainer, 1973.

NOTES

March 27

"When a woman behaves like a man, why doesn't she behave like a nice man?"
—EDITH EVANS

EVENTS

1794 The United States Navy was formed. **1914** The first successful blood transfusion was performed, in a Brussels hospital. **1958** Nikita Khrushchev became leader of the Soviet Union. **1964** Britain's ten "Great Train Robbers" were sentenced to a total of 307 years in prison. **1977** PanAm and KLM jumbo jets collided on the runway at Tenerife airport, in the Canary Islands, killing 574 people.

BIRTHS

Henry Royce, English automobile designer and manufacturer, **1863**; Ludwig Mies van der Rohe, German architect, **1886**; Dashiell Hammett, US writer, **1894**; Gloria Swanson, US film actress, **1899**; Cyrus Vance, US secretary of state, **1917**; Sarah Vaughan, US jazz singer, **1924**; Mstislav Rostropovich, Russian-born US cellist and conductor, **1927**.

DEATHS

James I, king of England (and of Scotland as James VI), **1625**; Giovanni Battista Tiepolo, Italian painter, **1770**; James Dewar, Scottish physicist and chemist who invented the thermos flask, **1923**; Yuri Gagarian, Soviet cosmonaut, **1968**; Anthony Blunt, English art historian and Soviet spy, **1983**.

NOTES

March 28

"Every gun that is made, every warship launched, every rocket fired signifies, in the final sense, a theft from those who hunger and are not fed, those who are cold and are not clothed."
—DWIGHT D. EISENHOWER, *speech, April 16, 1953*

EVENTS

1910 The first seaplane took off near Marseille, in south France. **1930** The cities of Angora and Constantinople, in Turkey, changed their names to Ankara and Istanbul, respectively. **1939** The Spanish Civil War came to an end as Madrid surrendered to General Franco. **1979** The nuclear power station at Three Mile Island in Pennsylvania suffered a meltdown in the core of one of its reactors.

BIRTHS

Raphael, Italian painter, **1483**; St. Teresa of Avila, Carmelite nun, **1515**; George I, king of Britain and Ireland, **1660**; Paul Whiteman, US musician and bandleader, **1891**; Dirk Bogarde, English actor and author, **1921**.

DEATHS

James Thomas Brudenell, 7th earl of Cardigan, leader of the disastrous Charge of the Light Brigade at Balaclava, **1868**; Virginia Woolf, English novelist, **1941**; Sergei Rachmaninov, Russian pianist and composer, **1943**; W.C. Handy, US blues composer, **1958**; Dwight D. Eisenhower, 34th US president, **1969**; Marc Chagall, Russian-born French painter, **1985**; Eugène Ionesco, Romanian-born French playwright of the Theater of the Absurd, **1994**.

NOTES

March 29

"Great God! This is an awful place."
—ROBERT FALCON SCOTT, *diary entry on the South Pole*

EVENTS

1867 Quebec, Ontario, Nova Scotia, and New Brunswick gained self-governing status as the Dominion of Canada. **1886** Coca-Cola went on sale in the US; it was marketed as a "brain tonic" and was claimed to relieve exhaustion. **1951** Julius and Ethel Rosenberg were found guilty of wartime espionage. **1973** The last US troops left Vietnam. **1974** US spacecraft *Mariner 10* took close-up photographs of the planet Mercury.

BIRTHS

John Tyler, 10th US president, 1790; Elihu Thomson, US inventor, 1853; Pearl Bailey, US singer, 1918; John Major, British prime minister, 1943.

DEATHS

Charles Wesley, English evangelist and hymn-writer whose brother John founded Methodism, 1788; Georges-Pierre Seurat, French painter, 1891; Robert Falcon Scott, English Antarctic explorer, 1912; Joyce Cary, Irish novelist, 1957.

NOTES

March 30

*"Oh, the beautiful sun of midsummer! It beats upon my head,
and I do not doubt it makes one a little queer."*
—VINCENT VAN GOGH, *letter to his brother Theo*

EVENTS

1775 The British parliament passed an act forbidding its North American colonies to trade with anyone other than Britain. **1842** Ether was first used as an anesthetic during surgery, by US doctor Crawford Long. **1856** The Crimean War was brought to an end by the signing of the Treaty of Paris. **1867** The US bought Alaska from Russia for $7.2 million (oil had not yet been discovered). **1981** In Washington, DC, would-be assassin John Hinckley shot President Reagan in the chest.

BIRTHS

Francisco de Goya, Spanish painter, **1746**; Paul Verlaine, French poet, **1844**; Vincent Van Gogh, Dutch painter, **1853**; Sean O'Casey, Irish playwright, **1880**; Melanie Klein, Austrian-born British psychologist, **1882**; Frankie Laine, US singer, **1913**; Warren Beatty, US film actor, **1937**; Eric Clapton, English guitarist, **1945**.

DEATHS

William Hunter, Scottish anatomist and obstetrician, **1783**; "Beau" Brummel, English dandy, **1840**; Rudolf Steiner, Austrian philosopher, **1925**; Friedrich Bergius, German scientist, **1949**; Léon Blum, French politician, **1950**; James Cagney, US film actor, **1986**.

NOTES

_____

_____

_____

_____

March 31

"Common sense is the best-distributed commodity in the world, for every man is convinced that he is well supplied with it."
—RENÉ DESCARTES

EVENTS

1282 The Sicilian Vespers, a massacre of the French in Sicily, begun the previous evening, ended. **1889** In Paris, the Eiffel Tower, built for the Universal Exhibition, was inaugurated. **1896** The first zipper was patented in the US by its inventor, Whitcomb Judson. **1959** Tibetan Buddhist leader, the Dalai Lama, fled from Chinese-occupied Tibet. **1971** Lt. William Calley was sentenced to life imprisonment after being found guilty of murdering civilians in the South Vietnamese village of My Lai in 1969.

BIRTHS

René Descartes, French philosopher and mathematician, **1596**; Andrew Marvell, English poet, **1621**; Franz Joseph Haydn, Austrian composer, **1732**; Nikolai Gogol, Russian novelist, **1809**; Robert Bunsen, German chemist, **1811**; Jack Johnson, US boxer who was the first black world heavyweight champion, **1878**; John Fowles, English novelist, **1927**; Shirley Jones, US film actress and singer, **1934**; Herb Alpert, US musician, **1935**; Albert Gore, US vice president, **1948**.

DEATHS

Francis I, king of France, **1547**; Philip III, king of Spain, **1621**; John Donne, English poet, **1631**; John Constable, English painter, **1837**; Charlotte Brontë, English novelist, **1855**; Jesse Owens, US athlete, **1980**.

NOTES

_____

_____

_____

_____

April 1

All Fools' Day.

EVENTS

1918 The British Royal Air Force was formed. **1945** US Marines invaded Okinawa. **1948** The USSR began its blockade of Berlin. **1954** The US Air Force Academy was established. **1960** The US launched the world's first weather satellite, *Tiros I*. **1973** North Vietnam released 590 US prisoners of war.

BIRTHS

William Harvey, English physician who explained the circulation of the blood, **1578**; Otto von Bismarck, first chancellor of the German Empire, **1815**; Edmond Rostand, French playwright, author of *Cyrano de Bergerac*, **1868**; Lon Chaney, US silent-film actor, **1883**; Jane Powell, US film actress and singer, **1928**; Debbie Reynolds, US film actress, **1932**; Ali MacGraw, US film actress, **1938**.

DEATHS

Eleanor of Aquitaine, queen of England and France, **1204**; Robert III, king of Scotland, **1406**; Scott Joplin, US ragtime composer, **1917**; Karl Franz Josef, emperor of Austria, **1922**; Max Ernst, German surrealist painter, **1976**; Marvin Gaye, US singer, **1984**.

NOTES

April 2

"A statesman is a politician who places himself at the service of the nation. A politician is a statesman who places the nation at his service."
—GEORGES POMPIDOU

EVENTS

1792 The first US mint was established at Philadelphia. **1801** At the Battle of Copenhagen, British naval hero Horatio Nelson ignored Admiral Parker's signal to stop fighting and won the battle. **1849** Britain annexed the Punjab. **1860** The first parliament of the united Italy met at Turin. **1979** Israeli Prime Minister Menachem Begin became the first Israeli leader to visit Cairo when he met Egyptian President Anwar Sadat. **1982** Argentina invaded the Falkland Islands.

BIRTHS

Charlemagne, king of the Franks, **742**; Hans Christian Andersen, Danish author, **1805**; Emile Zola, French novelist, **1840**; Buddy Ebsen, US TV and film actor, **1908**; Alec Guinness, English actor, **1914**; Jack Brabham, Australian racing driver, **1926**; Emmylou Harris, US country and pop singer, **1948**.

DEATHS

Honoré Mirabeau, French politician and writer, **1791**; Samuel Morse, US inventor of the telegraph, **1872**; C.S. Forester, English novelist, **1966**; Georges Pompidou, president of France, **1974**.

NOTES

April 3

"An actor's a guy who, if you ain't talking about him, ain't listening."
—MARLON BRANDO

EVENTS

1721 Robert Walpole became the first prime minister of Britain. **1860** The Pony Express began operations with dispatch riders regularly making the 2,000-mi/3,000-km trip from St. Joseph Missouri, to San Francisco. **1882** The train robber Jesse James was shot in the back and killed by his gang member, Robert Ford. **1922** In the USSR, Stalin was appointed as general secretary of the Communist party. **1930** Haile Selassie became emperor of Ethiopia.

BIRTHS

Henry IV, first Lancastrian king of England, **1367**; Washington Irving, US historian and short-story writer, **1783**; Doris Day, US film actress and singer, **1924**; Marlon Brando, US actor, **1924**; Helmut Kohl, German politician, **1930**; Eddie Murphy, US film actor, **1961**.

DEATHS

Bartolomé Murillo, Spanish painter, **1682**; James Clark Ross, English explorer, **1862**; Jesse James, US outlaw, **1882**; Johannes Brahms, German composer, **1897**; Graham Greene, English novelist, **1991**; Martha Graham, US dancer and choreographer, **1991**; Dieter Plage, German wildlife photographer, **1993**.

NOTES

_____

_____

_____

_____

April 4

*"We must learn to live together as brothers
or perish together as fools."*
—MARTIN LUTHER KING

The national day of Hungary.

EVENTS

1541 Spanish Jesuit Ignatius de Loyola, the order's founder, became its first superior-general. **1581** English navigator Francis Drake returned home after sailing around the world and was knighted by Queen Elizabeth I. **1949** The North Atlantic Treaty Organization (NATO) was formed in Washington, DC; 11 countries signed the treaty. **1979** Zulfikar Ali Bhutto, ousted prime minister of Pakistan and father of Benazir Bhutto, was executed by Pakistan's military government for conspiracy to murder.

BIRTHS

Grinling Gibbons, Dutch-born woodcarver and sculptor, **1648**; Linus Yale, US inventor of the Yale lock, **1821**; William Siemens, German-born British metallurgist and inventor, **1823**; Muddy Waters, US blues singer, **1915**; Cloris Leachman, US film actress, **1926**; Maya Angelou, US author, **1928**; Anthony Perkins, US actor, **1932**.

DEATHS

Oliver Goldsmith, Irish playwright, **1774**; William Henry Harrison, 9th US president, **1841**; Karl Benz, German automobile engineer, **1929**; André Michelin, French tire manufacturer, **1931**; Martin Luther King, US civil-rights leader, assassinated, **1968**; Gloria Swanson, US film actress, **1983**.

NOTES

April 5

"I have eyes like a bullfrog, a neck like an ostrich, and limp hair. You have to be good to survive with that equipment."
—BETTE DAVIS

EVENTS

1874 Johann Strauss's operetta *Die Fledermaus* was first performed, in Vienna. **1915** Jess Willard, the "great white hope," won the world heavyweight boxing title from Jack Johnson. **1986** A bomb attack on "La Belle" discotheque in West Berlin, frequented by US servicemen, killed 2 and injured 200.

BIRTHS

Thomas Hobbes, English philosopher, **1588**; Elihu Yale, American merchant and founder of the college named for him, **1649**; Spencer Tracey, US film actor, **1900**; Bette Davis, US film actress, **1908**; Herbert von Karajan, Austrian conductor, **1908**; Gregory Peck, US film actor, **1916**; Colin Powell, US general and chairman of the Joint Chiefs of Staff, the highest-ranking black military officer in US history, **1937**.

DEATHS

Georges Danton, French revolutionary leader, guillotined, **1794**; George Herbert, earl of Carnarvon, British Egyptologist, **1923**; Douglas MacArthur, US general, **1964**; Chiang Kai-shek, Chinese soldier and politician, **1975**; Howard Hughes, US multi-millionaire industrialist and moviemaker, **1976**.

NOTES

_____

_____

_____

_____

April 6

*"If my doctor told me I only had six months to live,
I wouldn't brood. I'd type a little faster."*
—ISAAC ASIMOV, Life

EVENTS

1830 Joseph Smith founded the Mormon Church in New York State. **1862** The Civil War battle at Shiloh, Tennessee, began. **1896** The first modern Olympic Games began in Athens. **1909** US explorer Robert Peary became the first person to reach the North Pole. **1917** The US declared war on Germany. **1965** *Early Bird,* the first commercial communications satellite, was launched by the US. **1978** The US raised the mandatory retirement age from 65 to 70.

BIRTHS

Gustave Moreau, French painter, **1826**; Harry Houdini, US escapologist, **1874**; John Betjeman, English poet, **1906**; James Watson, US biologist, **1928**; André Previn, German-born US conductor, **1929**; Merle Haggard, US country singer, **1937**.

DEATHS

Richard I (the Lion-Hearted), king of England, **1199**; Albrecht Dürer, German painter, **1528**; Jules Bordet, Belgian bacteriologist, **1961**; Igor Stravinsky, Russian composer, **1971**; Isaac Asimov, Russian-born US science and science-fiction writer, **1992**.

NOTES

April 7

*"Mom and pop were just a couple of kids when they got married. He
was 18, she was 16 and I was 3."*
—BILLIE HOLIDAY, Lady Sings the Blues

EVENTS

1827 The first matches were sold in Stockton, England, by their
inventor, chemist John Walker. **1862** Union forces won the Civil
War's Battle of Shiloh. **1906** A major eruption of the Italian volcano, Vesuvius, took place. **1939** Italy invaded Albania. **1948** The
World Health Organization (WHO) was established. **1980** The
Federal Trade Commission voted to restructure and deregulate
the telephone industry.

BIRTHS

St. Francis Xavier, Spanish Jesuit missionary, **1506**; William
Wordsworth, English poet, **1770**; Billie Holiday, US jazz singer,
1915; Ravi Shankar, Indian sitar player, **1920**; James Garner, US
film actor, **1928**; David Frost, English TV host and interviewer,
1939; Francis Ford Coppola, US film director, **1939**.

DEATHS

El Greco, Greek-born Spanish painter, **1614**; Dick Turpin, English
highwayman, **1739**; Phineas T. Barnum, US showman, **1891**;
Henry Ford, US automobile manufacturer, **1947**; Theda Bara, US
silent-film actress, **1955**.

NOTES

April 8

EVENTS

1513 Spanish explorer Juan Ponce de León arrived in Florida and claimed it for Spain. **1838** Isambard Brunel's *Great Western*, the first transatlantic steamship, set off on its first voyage, from Bristol, England, to New York; the journey took 15 days. **1908** Herbert Asquith became prime minister of Britain. **1939** In Albania, King Zog abdicated after Italy occupied the country. **1946** The League of Nations met for the last time. **1953** British colonial authorities in Kenya sentenced Jomo Kenyatta to seven years' imprisonment for allegedly organizing the Mau Mau guerrillas.

BIRTHS

Adrian Boult, English conductor, **1889**; Mary Pickford, US film actress, **1893**; Ian Smith, Rhodesian prime minister, **1919**; Dorothy Tutin, English actress, **1931**.

DEATHS

Caracalla, Roman emperor, assassinated, **217**; Gaetano Donizetti, Italian composer, **1848**; Elisha Graves Otis, US inventor of the safety elevator, **1861**; Pablo Picasso, Spanish painter, **1973**; Marian Anderson, US operatic contralto, **1993**; Kurt Cobain, lead singer with Nirvana, **1994**.

NOTES

April 9

EVENTS

1682 Louisiana was claimed for France and named by Robert Cavelier, Sieur de La Salle. **1770** English navigator James Cook arrived in Botany Bay, Australia, the first European to do so. **1865** The Civil War ended when Confederate General Robert E. Lee surrendered to Union General Ulysses S. Grant, at Appomattox Courthouse, Virginia. **1869** The Hudson Bay Company agreed to transfer its territory to Canada. **1969** The British supersonic aircraft *Concorde* made its first test flight. **1992** Manuel Noriega, former ruler of Panama, was convicted in Miami of drug trafficking.

BIRTHS

Charles Baudelaire, French poet, **1821**; Efrem Zimbalist, Russian-born US violinist and composer, **1889**; Paul Robeson, US actor and singer, **1898**; Dennis Quaid, US film actor, **1954**; Severiano Ballesteros, Spanish golfer, **1957**.

DEATHS

Lorenzo de' Medici, Florentine ruler, **1492**; Francis Bacon, English philosopher and politician, **1626**; Dante Gabriel Rossetti, English painter and poet, **1882**; Dietrich Bonhoeffer, German theologian, **1945**; Frank Lloyd Wright, US architect, **1959**.

NOTES

April 10

*"Anyone who has been to an English public school
will always feel comparatively at home in prison."*
—EVELYN WAUGH, Decline and Fall

EVENTS

1790 The US patent system began. **1841** The *New York Tribune* was first published. **1849** The safety pin was patented in the US. **1864** Austrian Archduke Maximilian was made emperor of Mexico. **1945** Soldiers of the US 80th Division liberated the concentration camp at Buchenwald, Germany. **1946** Japanese women voted for the first time. **1972** Earthquakes in Iran killed over 3,000 people.

BIRTHS

James V, king of Scotland, **1512**; William Hazlitt, English essayist and critic, **1778**; William Booth, English founder of the Salvation Army, **1827**; Lew Wallace, US general and novelist who wrote *Ben-Hur*, **1829**; Joseph Pulitzer, US newspaper proprietor who founded the Pulitzer Prize for literature and journalism, **1847**; Max von Sydow, Swedish actor, **1929**; Omar Sharif, Egyptian film actor, **1932**; Paul Theroux, US writer, **1941**.

DEATHS

Joseph-Louis Lagrange, French mathematician, **1813**; Algernon Charles Swinburne, English poet, **1909**; Emiliano Zapata, Mexican revolutionary leader, shot by government troops, **1919**; Auguste Lumière, French cinema pioneer, **1954**; Evelyn Waugh, English novelist, **1966**; Chris Hani, South African ANC leader, assassinated, **1993**.

NOTES

April 11

"Never despise what it says in the women's magazines:
It may not be subtle but neither are men."
—ZSA ZSA GABOR, *reported on April 11, 1976*

EVENTS

1713 The War of the Spanish Succession was ended by the signing of the Treaty of Utrecht; France ceded Newfoundland and Gibraltar to Britain. **1814** Napoleon abdicated and was exiled to the island of Elba; Louis XVIII became king of France. **1945** Allied troops liberated the Nazi concentration camp at Buchenwald. **1947** Jackie Robinson of the Brooklyn Dodgers became the first black major league baseball player. **1951** US General Douglas MacArthur was relieved of his command in Korea, after a disagreement with President Truman. **1961** Nazi war criminal Adolf Eichmann went on trial in Jerusalem after being captured in Argentina, where he had fled after World War II.

BIRTHS

James Parkinson, English physician who discovered Parkinson's disease, **1755**; Nick La Rocca, US founder of the Original Dixieland Jazz Band, **1889**; Dean Acheson, US secretary of state, **1893**; Joel Grey, US actor and singer, **1932**.

DEATHS

Donato Bramante, Italian architect who began St. Peter's, Rome, **1514**; Luther Burbank, US botanist, **1926**; Archibald McIndoe, New Zealand-born plastic surgeon, **1960**; John O'Hara, US novelist, **1970**; Erskine Caldwell, US novelist, **1987**.

NOTES

April 12

"Let me assert my firm belief that the only thing we have to fear is fear itself—nameless, unreasoning, unjustified terror which paralyzes needed efforts to convert retreat into advance."
—FRANKLIN D. ROOSEVELT, *inaugural address, March 4, 1933*

EVENTS

1606 The Union Jack was adopted as the official flag of Great Britain. **1861** The Civil War began when Confederate troops fired on the federal garrison at Fort Sumter off Charleston, South Carolina; it was captured two days later. **1961** Soviet cosmonaut Yuri Gagarin became the first person to orbit the Earth. **1980** The US Olympic Committee, at President Carter's urging, voted to boycott the Moscow Olympics because of the Soviet occupation of Afghanistan. **1981** The US space shuttle *Columbia* was launched from Cape Canaveral.

BIRTHS

Henry Clay, American politician, **1777**; Lionel Hampton, US bandleader, **1913**; Raymond Barre, French politician, **1924**; David Letterman, US TV talkshow host, **1947**; Scott Turow, US novelist and lawyer, **1949**; David Cassidy, US singer and actor, **1950**.

DEATHS

Franklin D. Roosevelt, 32nd US president, **1945**; Josephine Baker, US-born French singer and dancer, **1975**; Joe Louis, US heavyweight boxing champion, **1981**; Alan Paton, South African novelist and politician, **1988**; Sugar Ray Robinson, US welterweight boxing champion, **1989**.

NOTES

April 13

EVENTS

1598 Henry IV of France issued the Edict of Nantes, giving religious freedom to the Huguenots. **1668** The poet John Dryden became the first official English poet laureate. **1860** The Pony Express made its first delivery in Sacramento, California, having left St. Joseph, Missouri, 11 days earlier. **1919** The Amritsar Massacre took place in the Punjab, India: British troops fired into a crowd of 10,000 protesting against the arrest of two Indian Congress party leaders; 379 people were killed and 1,200 wounded. **1980** Spanish golfer Severiano Ballesteros became the youngest-ever winner of the US Masters Tournament. **1983** Chicago elected its first black mayor, Harold Washington.

BIRTHS

Thomas Jefferson, 3rd US president, **1743**; Richard Trevithick, English engineer, **1771**; F.W. Woolworth, US founder of chain stores, **1852**; Howard Keel, US film actor and singer, **1917**; John Braine, English novelist, **1922**; Seamus Heaney, Irish poet who won the 1995 Nobel Prize for Literature, **1939**; Gary Kasparov, Russian chess player, **1963**.

DEATHS

Boris Godunov, Russian czar, **1605**; Jean de La Fontaine, French writer of fables, **1695**; Abdul Salam Arif, president of Iraq, **1966**.

NOTES

April 14

"Die when I may, I want it said of me by those who know me best, that I have always plucked a thistle and planted a flower where I thought a flower would grow."
—ABRAHAM LINCOLN

EVENTS

1828 US lexicographer Noah Webster published his *American Dictionary of the English Language*. **1865** President Lincoln was fatally shot by the actor John Wilkes Booth; he died the following day. **1894** Thomas Edison gave the first public demonstration of his Kinetoscope peepshow machine. **1929** The first Monaco Grand Prix was held in Monte Carlo. **1931** Spanish King Alfonso XIII fled the country after republican successes in elections. **1986** The US bombed terrorist targets in Libya in retaliation for the bombing ordered by Col. Qaddafi of a West Berlin discotheque. **1994** In skies over Iraq, two US warplanes shot down two US Army helicopters by mistake in the no-fly zone.

BIRTHS

Christiaan Huygens, Dutch astronomer and physicist, **1629**; Peter Behrens, German architect and designer, **1868**; John Gielgud, English actor, **1904**; François Duvalier, Haitian dictator, **1907**; Rod Steiger, US film actor, **1925**; Loretta Lynn, US country singer, **1935**; Steve Martin, US comic film actor, **1945**.

DEATHS

George Frederick Handel, German-born English composer, **1759**; Lazarus Zamenhof, Polish linguist who devised Esperanto, **1917**; Simone de Beauvoir, French feminist writer, **1986**; Burl Ives, US folk singer and actor, **1995**.

NOTES

April 15

"I am condemned to be free."
—JEAN-PAUL SARTRE, Being and Nothingness

EVENTS

1755 English lexicographer Dr. Samuel Johnson published his *Dictionary*; he had taken eight years to compile it. **1912** Over 1,500 people died when the passenger liner *Titanic* sank after colliding with an iceberg on its first voyage. **1922** Insulin was discovered by Canadian physician Frederick Banting and Scottish physiologist J.J.R. Macleod. **1955** McDonald's hamburger restaurants were founded in Des Plaines, Illinois, by Ray Kroc

BIRTHS

Guru Nanak, founder of Sikhism, **1469**; Henry James, US-born British novelist, **1843**; Bessie Smith, US jazz singer dubbed "the Empress of the Blues," **1898**; Jeffrey Archer, English novelist and politician, **1940**; Emma Thompson, English actress, **1959**.

DEATHS

Mme. de Pompadour, mistress of French King Louis XV, **1764**; Abraham Lincoln, 16th US president, assassinated, **1865**; Matthew Arnold, English poet and literary critic, **1888**; Father Damien, Belgian missionary to the lepers of Molokai, **1889**; Jean-Paul Sartre, French philosopher and writer, **1980**; Greta Garbo, Swedish-born Hollywood actress, **1990**.

NOTES

April 16

---

*"All I need to make a comedy is a park,
a policeman and a pretty girl."*
—CHARLIE CHAPLIN, *My Autobiography*

EVENTS

1746 Charles Edward Stuart (Bonnie Prince Charlie) was defeated at the Battle of Culloden. **1883** Paul Kruger became president of South Africa. **1912** US pilot Harriet Quimby became the first woman to fly across the English Channel. **1972** The US spacecraft *Apollo 16* was launched.

BIRTHS

John Franklin, English Arctic explorer who discovered the Northwest Passage, **1786**; Wilbur Wright, US aviator, **1867**; Charlie Chaplin, English-born film actor and director, **1889**; Peter Ustinov, English actor and novelist, **1921**; Kingsley Amis, English novelist, **1922**; Henry Mancini, US film-score composer, **1924**; Dusty Springfield, British pop singer, **1939**.

DEATHS

Francisco de Goya, Spanish painter, **1828**; Marie Tussaud, French wax-modeler, **1850**; St. Bernadette of Lourdes, French saint, **1879**; Count Basie, US jazz bandleader and musician, **1984**; David Lean, English film director, **1991**.

NOTES

April 17

"There never was a good war, or a bad peace."
—BENJAMIN FRANKLIN

The national day of Syria.

EVENTS

1521 The Diet of Worms excommunicated German church reformer Martin Luther. **1957** Archbishop Makarios returned to Greece after over a year in exile in the Seychelles. **1961** US troops and Cuban exiles failed in their attempt to invade Cuba at the Bay of Pigs. **1975** The Cambodian communist Khmer Rouge captured the capital, Pnomh Penh. **1980** Southern Rhodesia became Zimbabwe. **1993** Two Los Angeles policemen were convicted for violating the civil rights of Rodney King, a black man they had beaten while being videotaped. **1995** A US Federal Court jury awarded $19 million to Faith Pescatore, whose husband, Michael, was killed in the 1988 Lockerbie plane bombing; the award was the largest ever for a death in an airline disaster.

BIRTHS

John Ford, English playwright, **1586**; Leonard Woolley, English archeologist, **1880**; Nikita Khrushchev, Soviet leader, **1894**; Thornton Wilder, US playwright and novelist, **1897**; Sirimavo Bandaranaike, first woman prime minister of Sri Lanka, **1916**.

DEATHS

Mme. de Sévigné, French writer, **1696**; Joseph I, Holy Roman Emperor, **1711**; Benjamin Franklin, US scientist and statesman, **1790**; Kawabata Yasunari, Japanese novelist, **1972**; Scott Brady, US actor, **1985**; Turgut Ozal, Turkish politician, **1993**.

NOTES

_____

_____

_____

_____

April 18

*"I, Woodrow Wilson, President of the United States
of America, do hereby proclaim to all whom it may concern
that a state of war exists between the United States
and the Imperial German Government."*
—WOODROW WILSON, *reported on April 18, 1917*

EVENTS

1775 US patriot Paul Revere made his famous ride from Charleston to Lexington, to warn people that British troops were on their way. **1906** An earthquake and the fire that followed it destroyed most of the city of San Francisco and killed over 450 people. **1934** The first launderette, called a "washeteria," was opened in Fort Worth, Texas. **1949** Eire proclaimed itself the Republic of Ireland. **1968** The old London Bridge was sold to a US company, which shipped it, stone by stone, to Arizona, where it was reerected. **1978** The US Senate approved the return of the Panama Canal to Panama for December 31, 1999.

BIRTHS

Lucrezia Borgia, duchess of Ferrara, **1480**; Clarence Darrow, US lawyer, **1857**; Leopold Stokowski, English-born US conductor and composer, **1882**; Barbara Hayle, US film actress, **1922**; Hayley Mills, English actress, **1946**.

DEATHS

George Jeffreys, Britain's "hanging judge," **1689**; Ottorino Respighi, Italian composer, **1936**; Albert Einstein, German-born US physicist, **1955**; Benny Hill, English comedian, **1992**.

NOTES

_____

_____

_____

_____

April 19

"There are three kinds of lies: lies, damned lies, and statistics."
—BENJAMIN DISRAELI, *attributed*

EVENTS

1775 American patriots defeated the British in the first battle of the American Revolution at Lexington, Massachusetts. **1783** Congress announced the end of the Revolutionary War. **1951** The first "Miss World" contest was held in London; it was won by the Swedish contestant. **1956** US film actress Grace Kelly married Prince Rainier III of Monaco. **1995** A federal building was bombed in Oklahoma City, resulting in nearly 200 deaths.

BIRTHS

David Ricardo, English economist, **1772**; Dudley Moore, English-born comedy film actor, **1935**; Murray Perahia, US pianist and conductor, **1947**.

DEATHS

Paolo Veronese, Italian painter, **1588**; George Gordon, Lord Byron, English poet, died of malaria on his way to fight for Greek independence, **1824**; Benjamin Disraeli, British prime minister and novelist, **1881**; Charles Darwin, English biologist, **1882**; Pierre Curie, French chemist and physicist, **1906**; Konrad Adenauer, German politician, **1967**.

NOTES

_____

_____

_____

_____

April 20

"If they [artists] do see the fields blue they are deranged, and should go to an asylum. If they only pretend to see them blue, they are criminals and should go to prison."
—ADOLF HITLER

EVENTS

1526 A Mogul army led by Babur defeated an Afghan army at the Battle of Panipat, taking the cities of Delhi and Agra. **1534** French explorer Jacques Cartier arrived on the coast of Labrador, North America. **1770** English explorer James Cook reached New South Wales, Australia. **1969** Pierre Trudeau became prime minister of Canada. **1988** The US released an artist's sketch of its top-secret Stealth bomber, a project kept secret for a decade; the plane is "invisible" to radar.

BIRTHS

Adolf Hitler, German Nazi dictator, **1889**; Joan Miró, Spanish painter, **1893**; Harold Lloyd, US silent-film comedian, **1893**; Ryan O'Neal, US film actor, **1941**.

DEATHS

Jean Louis Petit, French surgeon, **1750**; Canaletto, Italian landscape painter, **1768**; Pontiac, American Indian leader, **1769**; Bram Stoker, Irish author of *Dracula*, **1912**; Christian X, king of Denmark, **1947**.

NOTES

April 21

"All you need in this life is ignorance and confidence;
then success is sure."
—MARK TWAIN

EVENTS

753 BC Traditionally, the date on which the city of Rome was founded. **1509** Henry VIII became king of England. **1836** Sam Houston led Texans to victory over Santa Anna's Mexican troops at San Jacinto, Texas. **1960** The new city of Brasília was declared the capital of Brazil, replacing Rio de Janeiro. **1967** King Constantine II of Greece was removed in an army coup, and martial law was imposed. **1989** Over 100,000 Chinese students gathered in Tiananmen Square, ignoring government warnings of severe punishment. **1994** The Red Cross estimated that some 100,000 people had been slaughtered in Rwanda during two weeks of fighting between government forces and Tutsi rebels.

BIRTHS

Anthony Quinn, US film actor, **1915**; Elizabeth II, queen of Britain, **1926**; Elaine May, US film actress and comedienne, **1932**; Andie MacDowell, US film actress, **1958**.

DEATHS

Henry VII, king of England, **1509**; Jean-Baptiste Racine, French playwright, **1699**; Mark Twain, (Samuel Clements), US humorist and novelist, **1910**; Manfred von Richtofen, "the Red Baron," German fighter pilot, **1918**; John Maynard Keynes, English economist, **1946**.

NOTES

April 22

"You only lie to two people: your girlfriend and the police. Everyone else you tell the truth to."
—JACK NICHOLSON

EVENTS

1500 Portuguese explorer Pedro Cabral claimed Brazil for Portugal. **1838** The first steamship to cross the Atlantic, the British ship *Sirius*, arrived at New York; it made the crossing in 18 days. **1889** The first Oklahoma land race saw some 50,000 homesteaders stake claims within 24 hours. **1970** The US celebrated the first Earth Day to promote ecology. **1972** The first people to row across the Pacific Ocean, Sylvia Cook and John Fairfax, arrived in Australia; they had been at sea for 362 days.

BIRTHS

Henry Fielding, English novelist, **1707**; Immanuel Kant, German philosopher, **1724**; Mme. de Staël, French writer, **1766**; Robert Oppenheimer, US physicist who developed the atomic bomb, **1904**; Eddie Albert, US film actor, **1908**; Yehudi Menuhin, US-born British violinist, **1916**; Glen Campbell, US singer, **1936**; Jack Nicholson, US film actor, **1937**.

DEATHS

James Hargreaves, English inventor of the spinning jenny, **1778**; John Crome, English landscape painter, **1821**; Richard Nixon, 37th US president, **1994**.

NOTES

_____

_____

_____

_____

April 23

"To be, or not to be: that is the question:
Whether 'tis nobler in the mind to suffer
The slings and arrows of outrageous fortune,
Or to take arms against a sea of troubles,
And by opposing end them?"
—WILLIAM SHAKESPEARE, Hamlet

The national day of England.

EVENTS

1661 Charles II was crowned king of Great Britain and Ireland. **1662** Connecticut was declared a British colony. **1896** Thomas Edison first publicly projected his moving pictures on a screen at the Koster and Bials' Music Hall in New York. **1984** Identification of a virus thought to cause acquired immune deficiency syndrome (AIDS) was announced by US researchers.

BIRTHS

William Shakespeare, English playwright and poet, **1564**; J.M.W. Turner, English painter, **1775**; James Buchanan, 15th US president, **1791**; Max Planck, German physicist, **1899**; Roy Orbison, US singer, **1936**; Sandra Dee, US film actress, **1942**.

DEATHS

William Shakespeare, **1616**; Miguel de Cervantes Saavedra, Spanish author of *Don Quixote,* **1616**; William Wordsworth, English poet, **1850**; Otto Preminger, Austrian-born US film director, **1986**; Satyajit Ray, Indian film director, **1992**.

NOTES

April 24

*"The history of every country begins in the
heart of a man or woman."*
—WILLA CATHER, O Pioneers!

EVENTS

1558 Mary, Queen of Scots, married the French dauphin. **1800**
The Library of Congress was established in Washington, DC; it
now holds more than 80 million items. **1895** US sailor Joshua
Slocum set off from Boston to sail single-handed around the
world; the voyage took just over three years. **1898** US declared
war on Spain, having blockaded Cuba two days earlier. **1916** The
Easter Rising, an Irish Republican protest against British rule,
took place in Dublin. **1970** The Gambia was declared a republic.
1980 Eight Americans were killed when a helicopter collided
with a transport plane in an unsuccessful mission to rescue US
hostages held in the US Embassy in Teheran, Iran.

BIRTHS

Anthony Trollope, English novelist, **1815**; Henri-Philippe Pétain,
French politician and soldier, **1856**; Shirley MacLaine, US actress,
1934; John Williams, Australian guitarist, **1941**; Barbra Streisand,
US film actress and singer, **1942**.

DEATHS

Daniel Defoe, English author, **1731**; Willa Cather, US novelist,
1947; Bud Abbott, straight man in the US comic team of Abbott
and Costello, **1974**; Wallis Simpson, the duchess of Windsor,
1986.

NOTES

_____

_____

_____

_____

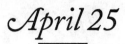

April 25

"A few honest men are better than numbers."
—OLIVER CROMWELL

Anzac Day in Australia.

EVENTS

1792 The guillotine was first used in Paris. **1859** Work began on the Suez Canal, supervised by the French engineer Ferdinand de Lesseps, who designed it. **1925** Paul von Hindenburg was elected president of Germany. **1959** The St. Lawrence Seaway was officially opened by Queen Elizabeth II and President Eisenhower, linking the Atlantic with ports on the Great Lakes. **1975** The first free elections for 50 years were held in Portugal, resulting in a precarious Socialist government. **1993** A gay-rights demonstration in Washington, DC, drew hundreds of thousands of participants.

BIRTHS

Oliver Cromwell, Puritan leader in the English Civil War, **1599**; Mark Isambard Brunel, French-born British engineer, **1769**; Guglielmo Marconi, Italian inventor and pioneer in the development of radio, **1874**; Ella Fitzgerald, US jazz singer, **1918**; Al Pacino, US film actor, **1940**.

DEATHS

Torquato Tasso, Italian poet, **1595**; Anders Celsius, Swedish astronomer who invented the centigrade thermometer, **1744**; William Cowper, English poet, **1800**; Clifford Simak, US journalist and science-fiction writer, **1988**.

NOTES

_____

_____

_____

_____

April 26

EVENTS

1865 John Wilkes Booth, who had fatally wounded Abraham Lincoln 12 days earlier, died in a blazing barn near Bowling Green, Virginia. **1937** The Spanish town of Guernica was almost destroyed by German bombers acting in support of the nationalists in the Spanish Civil War. **1968** The largest underground nuclear device ever to be tested in the US was exploded in Nevada. **1986** A major accident at the Chernobyl nuclear power station near Kiev, USSR, was announced after high radiation levels were reported in Sweden, Denmark, and Finland. **1994** Voting began in South Africa's first non-racial general election, resulting in an overwhelming victory for the African National Congress.

BIRTHS

Marcus Aurelius, Roman emperor, **121**; John James Audubon, US naturalist and painter, **1785**; Eugène Delacroix, French painter, **1798**; Michel Fokine, Russian ballet dancer and choreographer, **1880**; Ludwig Wittgenstein, Austrian philosopher, **1889**; Rudolf Hess, German Nazi leader, **1894**; Charles Francis Richter, US seismologist for whom the Richter Scale is named.

DEATHS

Karl Bosch, German metallurgist and chemist, **1940**; Gypsy Rose Lee, US dancer and striptease artist, **1970**; Count Basie, US bandleader, **1984**; Broderick Crawford, US film actor, **1986**; Lucille Ball, US comedienne, **1989**.

NOTES

April 27

"Every hero becomes a bore at last."
—RALPH WALDO EMERSON, Representative Men

EVENTS

1749 The first official performance of Handel's *Music for the Royal Fireworks* finished early due to the outbreak of fire. **1947** Norwegian anthropologist Thor Heyerdahl set off from Callao, Peru, heading for Polynesia to prove his theory that the original Polynesian islanders could have come from Peru. **1960** French Togoland became independent as the Republic of Togo. **1967** Expo 67 opened in Montreal, Canada. **1995** Timothy Spencer was executed in Virginia for raping and killing four women; he was the first man executed due to DNA evidence.

BIRTHS

Edward Gibbon, English historian who wrote *The Decline and Fall of the Roman Empire*, **1737**; Mary Wollstonecraft Godwin, English feminist author, **1759**; Samuel Morse, US inventor of Morse code, **1791**; Ulysses S. Grant, general and 18th US president, **1822**; Jack Klugman, US TV and film actor, **1922**; Coretta Scott King, US civil rights worker, wife of Martin Luther King, **1927**; Anouk Aimée, French film actress, **1932**; Sandy Dennis, US film actress, **1937**.

DEATHS

Ferdinand Magellan, Portuguese navigator, murdered by islanders in the Philippines, **1521**; Ralph Waldo Emerson, US poet and essayist, **1882**; Alexander Scriabin, Russian composer, **1915**; Harold Hart Crane, US poet, **1932**; Kwame Nkrumah, president of Ghana, **1972**.

NOTES

April 28

EVENTS

1770 English navigator Captain James Cook and his crew, including the botanist Joseph Banks, landed in Australia, at the place which was later named Botany Bay. **1788** Maryland became the 7th state. **1789** The crew of the ship *Bounty*, led by Fletcher Christian, mutinied against their captain, William Bligh. **1919** The League of Nations was founded. **1965** US Marines intervened in an attempted communist coup in the Dominican Republic. **1969** French President General de Gaulle resigned. **1994** Aldrich Ames, former head of the CIA's Soviet Counterintelligence Division, was sentenced to life imprisonment for spying.

BIRTHS

James Monroe, 5th US president, **1758**; Lionel Barrymore, US actor, **1878**; Kenneth Kaunda, president of Zambia, **1924**; James Baker, US Secretary of State, **1930**; Ann-Margret, Swedish-born US actress, **1941**.

DEATHS

Gavrilo Princip, Bosnian revolutionary assassin who caused World War I by killing Archduke Franz Ferdinand and his wife, **1918**; King Fuad I of Egypt, **1936**; Benito Mussolini, Italian Fascist dictator, **1945**; Francis Bacon, Irish-born painter, **1992**; Olivier Messiaen, French composer, **1992**.

NOTES

April 29

"Here you have a different kind of poverty. A poverty of spirit, of loneliness and being unwanted. And that is the worst disease in the world: not tuberculosis or leprosy."
—MOTHER TERESA, *reported on April 29, 1973*

The national day of Japan.

EVENTS

1429 The siege of Orléans was lifted by a French army led by Joan of Arc. **1884** England's Oxford University agreed to admit female students to examinations. **1913** Swedish-born US inventor Gideon Sundback patented the zipper in its modern form—earlier versions were unsuccessful. **1945** The German army in Italy surrendered to the Allies. **1957** Congress passed a civil-rights bill to assure voting rights for blacks. **1994** Nelson Mandela was elected as South Africa's first black president.

BIRTHS

William Randolph Hearst, US newspaper tycoon, **1863**; Duke Ellington, US composer and bandleader, **1899**; Emperor Hirohito of Japan, **1901**; Fred Zinneman, US film director, **1907**; Celeste Holm, US actress, **1919**; Carol Burnett, US TV comedienne, **1933**; Zubin Mehta, Indian conductor, **1936**; Saddam Hussein, president of Iraq, **1937**; Michelle Pfeiffer, US film actress, **1957**.

DEATHS

George Farquhar, Irish playwright, **1707**; Constantinos Cavafy, Greek poet, **1933**; Wallace Carothers, US chemist who patented nylon, **1937**; Alfred Hitchcock, British-born US film director, **1980**.

NOTES

April 30

"All my life, I was having trouble with women ... I've done a lot of writing about women. Then, after I quit having trouble with them, I could feel in my heart that somebody would always have trouble with them, so I kept writing those blues."
—MUDDY WATERS

The national day of the Netherlands.

EVENTS

1789 George Washington became the first president of the US. **1812** Louisiana became the 18th state. **1902** Debussy's opera *Pelléas et Mélisande* was first performed, in Paris. **1939** The New York World's Fair opened. **1948** The Organization of American States was established by 21 republics meeting in Bogotá, Colombia. **1975** The Vietnam War ended, with the South surrendering unconditionally to the North. **1980** Queen Juliana of the Netherlands abdicated and was succeeded by her daughter, Beatrix.

BIRTHS

Karl Gauss, German mathematician and astronomer, **1777**; Franz Lehár, Hungarian composer, **1870**; Jaroslav Hašek, Czech novelist, **1883**; Queen Juliana of the Netherlands, **1909**; Jill Clayburgh, US film actress, **1944**; Carl XVI Gustaf, king of Sweden, **1946**.

DEATHS

Edouard Manet, French painter, **1883**; "Casey" Jones, US railroad engineer and hero, **1900**; Adolf Hitler, German Nazi dictator, **1945**; Muddy Waters, US blues singer, **1983**; George Balanchine, Russian-born US choreographer, **1983**.

NOTES

May 1

"There was only one catch and that was Catch-22."
—JOSEPH HELLER, Catch-22

EVENTS

1707 The Union of England and Scotland was proclaimed. **1786** The first performance of Mozart's opera *The Marriage of Figaro* was given, in Vienna. **1873** The first US postcard was issued. **1931** The Empire State Building was opened by President Hoover; it had cost $41 million to build. **1960** A US U-2 reconnaisance aircraft, piloted by Gary Powers, was shot down as it flew over the USSR.

BIRTHS

Arthur Wellesley, duke of Wellington, English general and politician, **1769**; Mark Clark, US 5th Army commanding general in World War II, **1896**; Glenn Ford, US film actor, **1916**; Jack Paar, US TV talkshow host, **1918**; Joseph Heller, US novelist, **1923**; Rita Coolidge, US country rock singer and pianist, **1945**.

DEATHS

John Dryden, English poet, **1700**; David Livingstone, Scottish missionary, **1873**; Antonín Dvořák, Czech composer, **1904**; Joseph Goebbels, German Nazi propaganda minister, **1945**; William Fox, US film producer, **1952**; Ayrton Senna, Brazilian Formula One driver, in a crash during the San Marino Grand Prix, **1994**.

NOTES

May 2

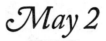

"Whatever exists in the universe, whether in essence, in act, or in the imagination, the painter has first in his mind and then in his hands."
—LEONARDO DA VINCI, *Notebooks*

EVENTS

1536 Queen Anne Boleyn, second wife of Henry VIII of England, was sent to the Tower of London and later beheaded. **1611** The Authorized Version of the Bible (King James Version) was first published. **1670** The Hudson Bay Company was incorporated. **1776** France and Spain agreed to supply arms to colonial troops in the American Revolution. **1945** In World War II, Germany surrendered to Allied forces. **1969** The passenger liner *Queen Elizabeth II* set off from Southampton, England, on its first voyage. **1970** Diane Crump was the first woman to ride in the Kentucky Derby—she finished 12th. **1989** Martial law was imposed in China as the government took a hard line against pro-democracy demonstrators in Tiananmen Square.

BIRTHS

Catherine II (the Great), empress of Russia, **1729**; Theodor Herzl, Hungarian founder of Zionism, **1860**; Benjamin Spock, US child-care specialist, **1903**; Bing Crosby, US singer, **1904**.

DEATHS

Leonardo da Vinci, Florentine artist and scientist, **1519**; Joseph McCarthy, US politician and anticommunist campaigner, **1957**; J. Edgar Hoover, US director of the FBI, **1972**.

NOTES

May 3

"We only want that which is given naturally to all peoples of the world: to be masters of our own fate, only of our fate, not of others, and in cooperation and friendship with others."
—GOLDA MEIR

EVENTS

1381 The weavers of Ghent, led by Philip van Artevelde, took Bruges; other Flemish towns revolted. **1493** Pope Alexander VI published the first bull, *Inter cetera*, dividing the New World between Spain and Portugal. **1808** A duel was fought from two hot-air balloons over Paris, the first of its kind. **1841** New Zealand was declared a British colony. **1937** Margaret Mitchell was awarded the Pulitzer Prize in fiction for *Gone with the Wind*. **1958** US President Eisenhower proposed the demilitarization of Antarctica, subsequently accepted by the countries concerned.

BIRTHS

Niccolò Machiavelli, Italian political philosopher, **1469**; John Scott Haldane, Scottish physiologist, **1860**; Golda Meir, Russian-born Israeli prime minister, **1898**; Pete Seeger, US folk singer, **1919**; Sugar Ray Robinson, US boxer, **1920**; James Brown, US singer, **1933**; Wynonna Judd, US country singer, **1964**.

DEATHS

Eglon van der Neer, Dutch painter, **1703**; Thomas Hood, English poet, **1845**; Henry Cornelius, South African-born British film director, **1958**; Karl Freund, Czech-born US film cameraman and photographer, **1969**; Bruce Cabot, US film actor, **1972**.

NOTES

May 4

"Politics is the art of acquiring, holding, and wielding power."
—INDIRA GANDHI, *reported on May 4, 1975*

EVENTS

1471 The Battle of Tewkesbury, the last battle in England's Wars of the Roses, took place; the Yorkists defeated the Lancastrians. **1904** Work began on the Panama Canal. **1970** Ohio National Guardsmen killed four Kent State University students who were protesting against the Vietnam War. **1973** The world's tallest building, Sears Tower, Chicago, was completed. **1979** Margaret Thatcher became prime minister of Britain. **1988** On the deadline for US amnesty, nearly 1.4 million illegal aliens applied, about half of these in California. **1989** Col. Oliver North, a former member of the National Security Council, was convicted of involvement in the Iran-Contra scandal; the convictions were later overturned.

BIRTHS

William Hickling Prescott, US historian, **1796**; John Speke, English explorer who discovered the source of the Nile, **1827**; Alice Liddell, the girl for whom Lewis Carroll wrote *Alice in Wonderland*, **1852**; Sylvia Pankhurst, English suffragist, **1882**; Audrey Hepburn, Dutch-born US film actress, **1929**; Randy Travis, US country singer, **1959**.

DEATHS

William Rose Benét, US poet, **1950**; Georges Enesco, Romanian composer, **1955**; Marshal Tito (Josip Broz), Yugoslavian soldier and president, **1980**.

NOTES

May 5

EVENTS

1494 Christopher Columbus discovered Jamaica, naming it Santa Gloria. **1863** In the Civil War, Confederate troops defeated Union forces at the Battle of Chancellorsville in Virginia, but "Stonewall" Jackson died of his wounds five days later. **1864** The indecisive Battle of the Wilderness, in Virginia, occurred between Union troops under Ulysses S. Grant and Confederate troops under Robert E. Lee. **1865** The first recorded US train robbery took place near North Bend, Ohio. **1865** A revolt in Santo Domingo forced Spain to renounce sovereignty. **1921** Chanel No. 5 perfume was launched. **1961** Alan B. Shepard, Jr., made the first US suborbital manned space flight.

BIRTHS

Gerardus Mercator (Gerhard Kremer), German cartographer, **1512**; Leopold III, Holy Roman Emperor, **1747**; Sören Kierkegaard, Danish philosopher, **1813**; Karl Marx, German philosopher and author, **1818**; John Stetson, US hat manufacturer who created the Stetson cowboy hat, **1830**; Tammy Wynette, US country singer, **1942**.

DEATHS

Charles, duke of Bourbon, **1527**; Napoleon Bonaparte, French emperor, **1821**; Francis Bret Harte, US author, **1902**, James Branch Cabell, US novelist, **1958**.

NOTES

_____

_____

_____

_____

May 6

"Analogies prove nothing, that is quite true,
but they can make one feel more at home."
—SIGMUND FREUD

EVENTS

1527 The Sack of Rome, when imperialist troops under Charles, duke of Bourbon (who was killed), mutinied, pillaging the city and killing some 4,000 of the inhabitants. **1626** Dutch settler Peter Minuit bought the island of Manhattan from Native Americans for trinkets worth about $25. **1910** George V became king of the United Kingdom on the death of Edward VII. **1937** The German zeppelin *Hindenburg* caught fire at Lakehurst, New Jersey, killing 36 passengers. **1994** The Channel Tunnel, the first direct link between Britain and France, opened.

BIRTHS

Maximilien François Robespierre, French revolutionary leader, **1758**; Sigmund Freud, Austrian psychoanalyst, **1856**; Robert Edwin Peary, US Arctic explorer, **1861**; Rudolph Valentino, Italian-born US film actor famed as the screen's "Great Lover," **1895**; Orson Welles, US actor, director, and writer, **1915**.

DEATHS

Juan Luis Vives, Spanish philosopher, **1540**; Cornelius Jansen, Dutch theologian, **1638**; Alexander von Humboldt, German explorer, **1859**; Henry David Thoreau, US essayist and poet, **1862**; Marlene Dietrich, German-born US actress and singer, **1992**.

NOTES

_____

_____

_____

_____

May 7

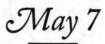

"He said true things, but called them by wrong names."
—ROBERT BROWNING, *"Bishop Blougram's Apology"*

EVENTS

1832 Greece became an independent kingdom. **1888** George Eastman launched his Kodak camera in New York, saying "You push the button, we do the rest." **1915** German forces sank the British liner *Lusitania* off the Irish coast, with the loss of 1,198 lives (including 128 Americans); the US was brought to the verge of war with Germany. **1945** Germany surrendered unconditionally to Allied forces, ending World War II in Europe. **1954** Dien Bien Phu fell to Communist Vietnamese. **1960** Leonid Brezhnev replaced Marshal Voroshilov as president of the USSR. **1984** Seven chemical companies agreed to pay Vietnam veterans $180 million for health problems arising from exposure to Agent Orange.

BIRTHS

David Hume, Scottish philosopher and historian, **1711**; Robert Browning, English poet, **1812**; Johannes Brahms, German composer, **1833**; Peter Ilyich Tchaikovsky, Russian composer, **1840**; Gary Cooper, US film actor, **1901**; Teresa Brewer, US singer, **1931**.

DEATHS

Jacques de Thou, French historian and politician, **1617**; Mary of Modena, consort of James II of England and Scotland, **1868**; Paul Doumer, French president, assassinated, **1932**; James George Frazer, Scottish anthropologist, **1941**; Eliot Ness, US FBI agent who headed the investigation of Al Capone, **1957**.

NOTES

May 8

*"It's a recession when your neighbor loses his job;
it's a depression when you lose yours."*
—HARRY S. TRUMAN

EVENTS

1886 A new Presidential succession law was passed in the US, providing for succession to the presidency in the event of the deaths of both the president and the vice president. **1902** On the Caribbean island of Martinique, the volcano Mount Pelée erupted, killing 30,000 people. **1915** Regret became the first filly to win the Kentucky Derby. **1945** V-E Day, Victory in Europe Day, when the surrender of Germany was announced to end the European conflict in World War II. **1950** Douglas MacArthur was appointed commander of UN forces in Korea. **1972** President Nixon announced the mining of North Vietnamese ports. **1990** Estonia declared its independence from the USSR.

BIRTHS

Peter Martyr (Pieto Martire Vermigli), Italian religious reformer, **1500**; Ruggiero Leoncavallo, Italian composer, **1858**; Harry S. Truman, 33rd US president, **1884**.

DEATHS

Antoine Laurent Lavoisier, French chemist, guillotined, **1794**; John Stuart Mill, English philosopher, **1873**; Gustave Flaubert, French novelist, **1880**; Paul Gauguin, French painter, **1903**; Oswald Spengler, German philosopher, **1936**; Henry Gordon Selfridge, US-born British store owner, **1947**; George Peppard, US actor, **1994**.

NOTES

May 9

"Watergate is water under the bridge."
—RICHARD NIXON, *in September 1973,
a year before his forced resignation.*

EVENTS

1926 The US explorer-aviators Richard Byrd and Floyd Bennett made the first flight over the North Pole. **1940** The British air force began night bombing raids on German cities. **1940** Romania placed itself under German protection. **1945** Russian troops took Prague. **1946** Victor Emmanuel III of Italy abdicated and Umberto II proclaimed himself king. **1974** The US House Judiciary Committee began impeachment proceedings against President Richard Nixon over the Watergate conspiracy. **1978** Italian statesman Aldo Moro was found dead in Rome after the government had refused to make concessions to his captors.

BIRTHS

Giovanni Paisiello, Italian composer, **1741**; John Brown, US abolitionist, **1800**; J.M. Barrie, Scottish novelist and dramatist who wrote *Peter Pan*, **1860**; Howard Carter, British Egyptologist, **1873**; Hank Snow, US country singer, **1914**; Mike Wallace, US TV newsman, **1918**; Alan Bennett, English actor and playwright, **1934**; Glenda Jackson, English actress, **1936**; Candice Bergen, US film actress, **1946**; Billy Joel, US pop singer, **1949**.

DEATHS

William Bradford, English-born American colonist, **1657**; Dietrich Buxtehude, Danish organist and composer, **1707**; Louis-Joseph Gay-Lussac, French physicist and chemist, **1850**; Helena Blavatsky, Russian founder of the Theosophical Society, **1891**.

NOTES

May 10

"I just put my feet in the air and move them around."
—FRED ASTAIRE

EVENTS

1775 Fort Ticonderoga was captured by Col. Ethan Allen's small American force during the American Revolution. **1869** America's transcontinental railroad was completed with the link-up of the Union Pacific and Central Pacific railroads near Ogden, Utah. **1916** Irish explorer Ernest Shackleton and companions reached South Georgia after sailing 800 mi/1,300 km in 16 days in an open boat to seek help for the remaining members of their party, marooned on Elephant Island, Antarctica. **1941** The House of Commons was destroyed in London's heaviest air raid. **1994** John Wayne Gacy was executed by lethal injection at Stateville Correctional Center, Illinois, for killing 33 men and boys in 1972–78.

BIRTHS

John Wilkes Booth, US actor and assassin of Abraham Lincoln, **1838**; Karl Barth, Swiss theologian and author, **1886**; Fred Astaire, US film actor and dancer, **1899**; David O. Selznick, US film producer who made *Gone with the Wind*, **1902**.

DEATHS

Leonhard Fuchs, German physician and botanist, **1566**; Paul Revere, American Revolution hero, **1818**; Katsushuka Hokusai, Japanese artist, **1849**; Thomas "Stonewall" Jackson, Confederate general, **1863**; Henry Morton Stanley, Welsh-born US journalist and explorer, **1904**; Joan Crawford, US film actress, **1977**.

NOTES

_____

_____

_____

_____

May 11

*"You cannot govern nations without a
mailed fist and an iron will."*
—BENITO MUSSOLINI, *reported on May 11, 1924*

EVENTS

973 Edgar was crowned at Bath as "King of all England." **1709** The first mass immigration of Germans from the Palatinate to North America began. **1811** The original Siamese twins, Chang and Eng Bunker, who were joined at the chest, were born in Siam. They settled in the US, married, and raised families. **1812** British Prime Minister Spencer Perceval was assassinated in the House of Commons. **1858** Minnesota became the 32nd state. **1949** Siam changed its name to Thailand. **1949** Israel was admitted to the United Nations. **1981** The musical *Cats* opened in London.

BIRTHS

Irving Berlin, Russian-born US composer, **1888**; Paul Nash, English painter, **1889**; Salvador Dali, Spanish Surrealist painter, **1904**; Mikhail Sholokhov, Russian novelist, **1905**; Phil Silvers, US comedy film actor, **1912**; Natasha Richardson, British actress, **1963**.

DEATHS

'Abd-al-Mu'min, Almohad ruler of Muslim Spain and NW Africa, **1163**; William Pitt, earl of Chatham, British statesman, **1778**; John Herschel, English astronomer, **1871**; William Dean Howells, US novelist and critic, **1920**; Bob Marley, Jamaican reggae artist, **1981**; Chester Gould, US cartoonist, **1985**; Kim Philby, English-born Soviet spy, **1988**.

NOTES

May 12

"I must go down to the seas again, to the lonely sea and the sky,
And all I ask is a tall ship and a star to steer her by."
—JOHN MASEFIELD, *"Sea Fever"*

EVENTS

1780 The British captured Charleston, South Carolina, and 5,000 American troops during the American Revolution. **1881** Tunisia became a French protectorate. **1935** Alcoholics Anonymous was founded by William Wilson in Akron, Ohio. **1949** The USSR lifted the Berlin blockade. **1961** The United States of the Congo was founded, with Léopoldville the federal capital. **1965** West Germany established diplomatic relations with Israel; Arab states broke off relations with Bonn.

BIRTHS

Claudio Monteverdi, Italian composer, **1567**; Joseph Nicolas Delisle, French astronomer, **1688**; Justus von Liebig, German chemist, **1803**; Florence Nightingale, English nursing pioneer, **1820**; Dante Gabriel Rossetti, English painter and poet, **1828**; Jules Massenet, French composer, **1842**; Burt Bacharach, US composer, **1929**; Emilio Estevez, US film actor, **1962**.

DEATHS

George Chapman, English playwright, **1634**; Bedřich Smetana, Czech composer, **1884**; Joris Karl Huysmans, French novelist, **1925**; Erich von Stroheim, Austrian-born US silent-film actor and director, **1957**; John Masefield, English poet, **1967**; Robert Reed, US film actor, **1992**.

NOTES

May 13

*"In Westerns you were permitted to kiss
your horse but never your girl."*
—GARY COOPER

EVENTS

1203 Byzantine emperor Alexius Comnenus seized Trebizond and established a new Greek empire there. **1643** Oliver Cromwell defeated Royalists at Grantham, England. **1846** Formal declaration of war by the US against Mexico. **1888** Serfdom was abolished in Brazil. **1927** "Black Friday" saw the collapse of Germany's economic system. **1993** The US abandoned work on its Strategic Defense Initiative (SDI), a proposed space shield against ballistic missile attack; it had been initiated in 1983 by President Ronald Reagan.

BIRTHS

Dante Alighieri, Italian poet, **1265**; Lazare Nicolas Marguerite Carnot, French revolutionary leader, **1753**; Alphonse Daudet, French novelist, **1840**; Arthur Sullivan, English composer, **1842**; Daphne du Maurier, English novelist, **1907**; Joe Louis, US heavyweight boxing champion, **1914**; Stevie Wonder, US singer, **1950**.

DEATHS

Johan van Oldenbarneveldt, Dutch lawyer and politician, **1619**; Georges Cuvier, French zoologist, **1832**; John Nash, English architect, **1835**; Friedrich Henle, German anatomist, **1885**; Fridtjof Nansen, Norwegian Arctic explorer, **1930**; Gary Cooper, US film actor, **1961**.

NOTES

_____

_____

_____

_____

May 14

*"A room is a place where you hide from the wolves
outside and that's all any room is."*
—JEAN RHYS

EVENTS

1264 The English barons under Simon de Montfort defeated
Henry III at the Battle of Lewes. **1607** Jamestown was founded in
Virginia by Capt. John Smith and colonists as the first permanent
English settlement in the New World. **1921** Twenty-nine Fascists
won office in Italian elections. **1942** Sugar rationing was introduced in the US. **1946** An anti-Jewish pogrom took place in
Kielce, Poland. **1948** As the British mandate in Palestine came to
an end, a Jewish provisional government was formed in Israel
with Chaim Weizmann as president and David Ben-Gurion as
prime minister.

BIRTHS

Gabriel Daniel Fahrenheit, German physicist, the first to use mercury in thermometers, **1686**; Robert Owen, Welsh social reformer,
1771; Otto Klemperer, German conductor, **1885**; Hastings Banda,
president of Malawi, **1905**; Constance Cummings, US film
actress, **1910**; Bobby Darin, US singer, **1936**.

DEATHS

Jean Grolier, French diplomat and bibliophile, **1565**; Henry IV,
king of France, assassinated, **1610**; Daniel Auber, French composer, **1871**; August Strindberg, Swedish playwright, **1912**; Jean
Rhys, British novelist, **1979**.

NOTES

May 15

"This is my letter to the world,
That never wrote to me."
—EMILY DICKINSON

EVENTS

1848 A communist rising began in Paris; workers overturned the government and set up a provisional administration which immediately collapsed. **1902** Portugal declared itself bankrupt. **1911** The Standard Oil Company monopoly was broken up into 34 independent companies by the US Supreme Court. **1918** The US Post Office began the world's first regular airmail service, between Washington, DC, and New York City. **1946** US President Harry Truman signed a bill of credit for $3.75 billion for Britain. **1948** Egyptian troops intervened in Palestine on the side of the Arabs. **1988** The USSR began evacuating its troops from Afghanistan.

BIRTHS

Clemens Prince Metternich, Austrian politician, **1773**; Frank L. Baum, US author of *The Wizard of Oz* and 13 sequels, **1856**; Pierre Curie, French physicist, **1859**; Arthur Schnitzler, Austrian novelist and playwright, **1862**; James Mason, British-born Hollywood film actor, **1909**; Joseph Cotton, US film actor, **1905**; Pierce Brosnan, Irish-born Hollywood actor, **1953**; Lee Horsley, US film actor, **1955**; Janet Jackson, US singer, **1966**.

DEATHS

Ephraim Chambers, English encyclopedist, **1740**; Richard Wilson, Welsh landscape painter, **1782**; Daniel O'Connell, Irish Catholic leader, **1847**; Emily Dickinson, US poet, **1886**; Rita Hayworth, US film actress, **1987**.

NOTES

May 16

EVENTS

1770 The dauphin of France (later Louis XVI) married Marie Antoinette, daughter of the Empress Maria Theresa of Austria. **1804** Napoleon was declared emperor of France. **1875** The first Kentucky Derby at Churchill Downs in Louisville was won by Oliver Lewis riding Aristides. **1929** At the first Academy Awards ceremony in Hollywood, *Wings* won as best picture. **1949** Chinese nationalists organized a Supreme Council under Chiang Kai-shek, which began to remove forces to Formosa. **1990** A Japanese businessman paid $82.5 million for Van Gogh's *Portrait of Dr. Gachet* at auction at Christies, New York.

BIRTHS

Charles IV, Holy Roman Emperor, 1316; Claude Joseph Rouget de Lisle, French soldier who wrote the "Marseillaise," 1760; Henry Fonda, US film actor, 1905; Studs Terkel, US writer and broadcaster, 1912; Woody Herman, US jazz clarinetist and bandleader, 1913.

DEATHS

Héloise, French abbess, pupil of and secretly married to Peter Abélard, 1164; Peter the Lombard, Bishop of Paris, 1164; Charles Perrault, French writer of fairy tales, 1703; Bronislaw Malinowski, Polish anthropologist, 1942; Irwin Shaw, US author, 1984; Sammy Davis, Jr., US entertainer, 1990.

NOTES

May 17

EVENTS

1215 The English barons in revolt against King John took possession of London. **1673** Louis Joliet and Father Jacques Marquette set out on an epic journey to explore the Mississippi. **1742** Frederick II of Prussia defeated the Austrians at Chotusitz. **1885** Germany annexed northern New Guinea and the Bismarck archipelago. **1939** Sweden, Norway, and Finland rejected Germany's offer of nonaggression pacts, but Denmark, Estonia, and Latvia accepted. **1954** The US Supreme Court declared racial segregation in public schools to be unconstitutional. **1987** Thirty-eight US sailors died on the frigate USS *Sark* after an Iraqi warplane accidentally fired a missile in the Persian Gulf during the Iran-Iraq war.

BIRTHS

Maria Theresa, empress of Austria, **1717**; Edward Jenner, English pioneer of vaccination, **1749**; Timothy Healy, Irish nationalist leader, **1855**; Erik Satie, French composer, **1866**; Maureen O'Sullivan, Irish-born US actress, **1911**; Dennis Hopper, US film actor, **1936**; Sugar Ray Leonard, US boxing world champion, **1956**.

DEATHS

Sandro Botticelli, Italian painter, **1510**; Charles de Talleyrand-Périgord, French politician, **1838**; Cass Gilbert, US architect, **1934**; Margaret Hamilton, US actress, **1985**.

NOTES

May 18

"Boredom is therefore a vital problem for the moralist, since half the sins of mankind are caused by the fear of it."
—BERTRAND RUSSELL

EVENTS

1302 A French garrison was massacred in the "Matins of Bruges," when the Flemings revolted against the French occupation. **1878** Colombia granted a French company a nine-year concession to build the Panama Canal. **1936** An army revolt under Emilio Mola and Francisco Franco began the Spanish Civil War. **1944** In World War II, Monte Cassino, Italy, was taken by Allied forces. **1980** Mount St. Helens in Washington state erupted for the first time since 1857, devastating an area of 230 sq mi/600 sq km.

BIRTHS

Pieter Brueghel, Flemish painter, **1525**; George Gascoigne, English poet and playwright, **1525**; Bertrand Russell, English philosopher, **1872**; Walter Gropius, German-born US architect, **1883**; Frank Capra, US screenwriter and director, **1897**; Perry Como, US singer, **1912**; Pierre Balmain, French fashion designer, **1914**.

DEATHS

Pierre Augustin Caron de Beaumarchais, French playwright, **1799**; Johann Gottfried von Herder, German critic and poet, **1803**; George Meredith, English novelist, **1909**; Gustav Mahler, Austrian composer and conductor, **1911**; Paul Dukas, French composer, **1935**; Werner Sombart, German economist, **1941**; William Saroyan, US author, **1981**.

NOTES

May 19

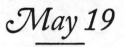

"The Bronx? No thonx."
—OGDEN NASH

EVENTS

1643 The Confederation of New England was formed by Connecticut, New Haven, Plymouth, and Massachusetts Bay. **1649** England was declared a Commonwealth. **1921** The US imposed immigration quotas. **1930** White women were enfranchised in South Africa. **1964** The US complained to Moscow about microphones concealed in its Moscow embassy.

BIRTHS

Johann Gottlieb Fichte, German philosopher, **1762**; Nellie Melba, Australian operatic soprano, **1861**; Ho Chi Minh, Vietnamese leader, **1890**; Malcolm X (Malcolm Little), US militant black civil rights leader, **1925**.

DEATHS

James Boswell, Scottish biographer and diarist, **1795**; Nathaniel Hawthorne, US novelist, **1864**; William Ewart Gladstone, British politician, **1898**; T.E. Lawrence (Lawrence of Arabia), English soldier and writer, **1935**; Charles Ives, US composer, **1954**; Ogden Nash, US poet, **1971**; John Betjeman, English poet, **1984**; Jacqueline Kennedy Onassis, US first lady, **1994**.

NOTES

May 20

*"Man is neither good nor bad; he is born
with instincts and abilities."*
—HONORÉ DE BALZAC

EVENTS

1631 Flemish commander Count Tilly's imperialist army sacked Magdeburg; terrible carnage ensued and the city caught fire, leaving only the cathedral standing. **1941** German forces invaded Crete. **1944** Nazi officers attempted to assassinate Hitler at a staff meeting. **1950** A US Senate committee denied Senator Joseph McCarthy's charges of communist infiltration of the State Department. **1956** The US tested a hydrogen bomb over Bikini atoll. **1994** President Clinton signed a law making it a federal offense to block access to abortion clinics.

BIRTHS

Donato d'Agnolo Bramante de Urbino, Italian architect, **1444**; Sandro Botticelli, Italian painter, **1444**; Honoré de Balzac, French novelist, **1799**; John Stuart Mill, English philosopher, **1806**; William Fargo, US cofounder of Wells Fargo, **1818**; James Stewart, US film actor, **1908**; Moshe Dayan, Israeli military leader, **1915**; Cher, US singer and film actress, **1946**.

DEATHS

Christopher Columbus, Genoese navigator, **1506**; Clara Schumann, German pianist and composer, **1896**; Max Beerbohm, English writer and caricaturist, **1956**; Barbara Hepworth, English sculptor, **1975**; Gilda Radner, US comic actress, **1989**.

NOTES

May 21

"Well, I made it."

—CHARLES A. LINDBERGH, *replying to the French crowd
mobbing him after his successful solo transatlantic flight.*

EVENTS

1674 John Sobieski was elected king of Poland as John III. **1767**
English taxes were introduced on imports of tea, glass, paper,
and dyestuffs in the American colonies to provide revenue for
the colonial administration. **1851** Gold was first discovered in
Australia. **1927** Charles Lindbergh landed at Le Bourget airfield
in Paris after making the first solo nonstop transatlantic flight;
his monoplane, *The Spirit of St. Louis*, had taken off from
Roosevelt Field, New York, $33\frac{1}{2}$ hours earlier on May 20. **1979**
Elton John became the first Western rock star to perform in the
USSR; the concert at Leningrad (now St. Petersburg) was sold
out and closed with a rendition of the Beatles' "Back in the
USSR."

BIRTHS

Philip II, king of Spain, **1527**; Alexander Pope, English poet and
satirist, **1688**; Elizabeth Fry, English prison reformer, **1780**; "Fats"
Waller, US jazz pianist and composer, **1904**; Harold Robbins, US
novelist, **1916**; Raymond Burr, US actor, **1917**.

DEATHS

Henry VI, king of England, **1471**; Tomaso Campanella, Italian
philosopher, **1639**; Karl Wilhelm Scheele, Swedish chemist, **1786**;
Geoffrey de Havilland, British aircraft designer, **1965**; Les Aspin,
US secretary of defense under President Bill Clinton, **1995**.

NOTES

May 22

"I know it was great, damn it, but I don't know how I did it, so how can I be sure I can do it again?"
—LAURENCE OLIVIER, *after being congratulated on portraying Othello*

EVENTS

1498 A death sentence was pronounced on Savonarola, former Prior of St. Mark's and effective ruler of Florence, who had been excommunicated in June 1497 for attempting to seek the deposition of Pope Alexander VI. **1872** Amnesty was granted to former Confederate citizens seven years after the Civil War ended. **1912** The Reichstag (German legislature) was adjourned following Socialist attacks on the German emperor. **1972** President Richard Nixon became the first US president to visit the USSR; he discussed arms limitations with Soviet President Brezhnev.

BIRTHS

Richard Wagner, German composer, **1813**; Arthur Conan Doyle, English novelist who created Sherlock Holmes, **1859**; Laurence Olivier, English actor, **1907**; Charles Aznavour, French singer, **1924**.

DEATHS

Thomas Southerne, Irish playwright, **1746**; Augustin Thierry, French historian, **1856**; Ernst Toller, German poet and playwright, **1939**; James Langston Hughes, US poet, **1967**; Cecil Day Lewis, English poet, **1972**; Rajiv Gandhi, Indian leader, assassinated, **1991**.

NOTES

_____

_____

_____

_____

May 23

EVENTS

1169 "The First Conquerors" landed in Ireland; they were Normans from Wales. **1430** Burgundian troops captured Joan of Arc and delivered her to the English. **1568** William of Orange with German mercenaries defeated a Spanish force under Count Aremberg at Heiligerlee, beginning the Revolt of the Netherlands. **1788** South Carolina became the 8th state. **1926** France proclaimed Lebanon a republic. **1934** The US bank robbers and murderers Bonnie Parker and Clyde Barrow ("Bonnie and Clyde") were killed in a police ambush in Louisiana. **1960** Adolf Eichmann, notorious Nazi war criminal, was captured in Argentina and flown to Israel to face trial.

BIRTHS

Tamerlane (the Great), Mongol leader, **1335**; Carl von Linné (Linnaeus), Swedish botanist, **1707**; Friedrich Mesmer, Austrian physician, **1733**; Otto Lilienthal, German aviator, **1848**; Rosemary Clooney, US singer, **1928**; Joan Collins, English-born Hollywood actress, **1933**.

DEATHS

Richard of Wallingford, abbot of St. Albans, England, **1335**; Girolamo Savonarola, Florentine priest, burned at the stake, **1498**; William Kidd ("Captain Kidd"), Scottish pirate, hanged, **1701**; Leopold von Ranke, German historian, **1886**; Henrik Ibsen, Norwegian playwright, **1906**.

NOTES

May 24

"When it sounds good, it is good."
—DUKE ELLINGTON

EVENTS

1153 Malcolm IV acceded to the Scottish throne. **1726** The first circulating library was opened by Allan Ramsay in Edinburgh. **1844** Samuel Morse sent the first public telegraph message ("What hath God wrought!"), from Washington, DC, to Baltimore. **1883** The 1,595-ft Brooklyn Bridge opened. **1948** The USSR stopped road and rail traffic between Berlin and the West, forcing Western powers to organize airlifts. **1994** The four convicted men in the 1993 bombing of New York's World Trade Center were each sentenced to 240 years without parole.

BIRTHS·

Philip III, king of France, **1245**; William Gilbert, English physician and early researcher into magnetism, **1540**; William Byrd, English composer, **1543**; Jean-Paul Marat, French revolutionary, **1743**; Victoria, queen of Britain, **1819**; J.C. Smuts, South African soldier and politician, **1870**; Bob Dylan, US singer and songwriter, **1941**; Rosanne Cash, US singer, **1955**.

DEATHS

Nicolaus Copernicus, Polish astronomer, **1543**; Robert Cecil, earl of Salisbury, English politician, **1725**; John Foster Dulles, US secretary of state, **1959**; Duke Ellington, US jazz composer and musician, **1974**; Hermione Gingold, English actress, **1987**.

NOTES

May 25

EVENTS

1911 Porfirio Diaz resigned as president of Mexico. **1914** The British House of Commons passed the Irish Home Rule bill. **1923** The independence of Transjordan under Amir Abdullah was proclaimed. **1935** US athlete Jesse Owens broke six world records in less than an hour at Ann Arbor, Michigan. **1961** US President Kennedy presented an extraordinary State of the Union message to Congress for funds urgently needed for US space, defense, and air programs. **1986** An estimated 30 million people around the world took part in Sportaid's "Race Against Time," a series of fun runs organized to raise money for the starving in Africa.

BIRTHS

Ralph Waldo Emerson, US poet and essayist, **1803**; Béla Bartók, Hungarian composer, **1881**; Igor Sikorsky, Russian-born US designer of the first successful helicopter, **1889**; Marshal Tito (Josip Broz), Yugoslavian soldier and president, **1892**; Miles Davis, US jazz trumpeter, **1926**; Robert Ludlum, US novelist, **1927**; Tom T. Hall, US country singer, **1936**.

DEATHS

Bede, English monk and historian, **735**; Gaspard Poussin, French painter, **1675**; Pedro Calderón de la Barca, Spanish playwright, **1681**; Samuel Pepys, English diarist, **1703**; Gustav Holst, English composer, **1934**.

NOTES

May 26

*"I don't go for all this realism in movies, see.
Pornography, violence, all that junk. Those goddam
sons of bitches making that stuff are ruining the business."*
—JOHN WAYNE

EVENTS

1521 The Edict of Worms imposed on Martin Luther the ban of the Empire. **1538** Protestant church reformer John Calvin was expelled from Geneva and settled in Strasbourg. **1659** Aurangzeb formally became Mogul Emperor. **1805** Napoleon Bonaparte was crowned king of Italy in Milan Cathedral. **1865** The last Confederate army surrendered at Shreveport, Louisiana. **1924** President Calvin Coolidge signed a bill limiting immigration into the US and excluding the Japanese. **1994** President Bill Clinton renewed China's "most favored nation" status for trade; it had been suspended following the Tiananmen Square massacre on June 4, 1989.

BIRTHS

Charles of Orléans, French poet, **1391**; Edmond de Goncourt, French novelist, **1822**; A.E. Housman, English poet, **1859**; Al Jolson, US singer, **1886**; John Wayne, US film actor, **1907**; Peter Cushing, British film actor, **1913**; Peggy Lee, US jazz singer, **1920**; Sally Ride, America's first woman astronaut, **1951**; Helena Bonham-Carter, British actress, **1966**.

DEATHS

St. Augustine, first archbishop of Canterbury, **604**; Charles Mayo, US surgeon, **1922**; Victor Herbert, US composer and conductor, **1924**; Lincoln Ellsworth, US scientist and polar explorer, **1951**.

NOTES

May 27

"Power is the ultimate aphrodisiac."
—HENRY KISSINGER, Guardian, *Nov. 28, 1976*

EVENTS

1199 Pope Innocent III imposed the first direct papal taxation of clergy. **1719** Emperor Charles VI founded the Oriental Company in Vienna to compete with Dutch trade in the Orient. **1813** In the War of 1812, US forces occupied Fort St. George, and the British abandoned the entire Niagara frontier. **1937** San Francisco's Golden Gate Bridge was opened. **1941** The German battleship *Bismarck* was sunk by the British Royal Navy west of Brest. **1963** Nationalist leader Jomo Kenyatta, who had been imprisoned by British authorities, was elected as Kenya's first prime minister.

BIRTHS

Amelia Bloomer, US feminist and dress reformer, **1818**; Julia Ward Howe, US antislavery campaigner who wrote the "Battle Hymn of the Republic," **1819**; John Cockcroft, English physicist, **1897**; Hubert Humphrey, US vice president, **1911**; Vincent Price, US film actor, **1911**; Herman Wouk, US novelist, **1915**; Henry Kissinger, US secretary of state, **1923**.

DEATHS

Minamoto Yoritomo, first shogun of Japan, **1199**; John Calvin, French religious reformer, **1564**; Niccolò Paganini, Italian violinist, **1840**; Robert Koch, German bacteriologist, **1910**; Jawaharlal Nehru, Indian politician, **1964**.

NOTES

_____

_____

_____

_____

May 28

*"Equality is a futile pursuit: equality
of opportunity is a noble one."*
—IAN MACLEOD, *reported on May 28, 1969*

EVENTS

1539 Spanish explorer Hernando De Soto reached Florida. **1539** Royal assent was given to an act (the Six Articles of Religion) "abolishing diversity of opinions" in England. **1932** The IJselmeer was formed in the Netherlands, by the completion of a dam which enclosed the former Zuider Zee. **1956** France ceded former French settlements in India to the Indian Union. **1961** The original "Orient Express" train made its last journey, from Paris to Bucharest; it had been in operation for 78 years.

BIRTHS

George I, king of Britain and Ireland, **1660**; Joseph Guillotin, French physician and revolutionary, **1738**; William Pitt, British politician, **1759**; Thomas Moore, Irish poet, **1779**; Ian Fleming, English novelist who created James Bond, **1908**; Dietrich Fischer-Dieskau, German baritone, **1925**; Carroll Baker, US film actress, **1931**; Gladys Knight, US singer, **1944**.

DEATHS

Edward Montagu, earl of Sandwich, English admiral, for whom the sandwich is named, **1672**; Thomas Chippendale, English cabinetmaker, **1779**; Jean Louis Rodolphe Agassiz, Swiss oceanographer and marine zoologist, **1807**; Noah Webster, US lexicographer, **1843**; Alfred Adler, Austrian psychiatrist, **1937**.

NOTES

May 29

"When we got into office, the thing that surprised me most was to find that things were just as bad as we'd been saying they were."
—JOHN F. KENNEDY, *speech May 27, 1961*

EVENTS

1453 Mohammed II, founder of the Ottoman Empire, captured Constantinople; the Byzantine Emperor Constantine XI was killed and the Greek Empire finally extinguished. Constantinople became the Ottoman capital. **1790** Rhode Island became the 13th state. **1848** Wisconsin became the 30th state. **1940** In World War II, the first British forces were evacuated from Dunkirk. **1947** The Indian constituent assembly outlawed "untouchability." **1953** New Zealand-born Edmund Hillary and Sherpa guide Tenzing Norgay reached the summit of Mt. Everest, becoming the first to conquer the world's highest mountain.

BIRTHS

Charles II, king of Britain and Ireland, **1630**; Patrick Henry, American Revolution patriot, **1736**; Léon Bourgeois, French politician, **1851**; G K Chesterton, English novelist and critic, **1874**; Bob Hope, British-born US comedian, **1903**; John F. Kennedy, 35th US president, **1917**.

DEATHS

Bartholomew Diaz de Novaes, Portuguese navigator, **1500**; Cornelius Van Tromp, Dutch sailor, **1691**; John Lothrop Motley, US historian and diplomat, **1877**; W.S. Gilbert, English playwright and librettist, **1911**; Mary Pickford, US film actress, **1979**.

NOTES

May 30

"We must cultivate our garden."
—VOLTAIRE, Candide

EVENTS

1431 Joan of Arc was burned as a heretic at Rouen, France. **1536** English King Henry VIII married Jane Seymour, his third wife. **1869** Memorial Day, or Decoration Day, was first observed in the US. **1911** The first Indianapolis 500 race was won by Ray Harroun. **1913** A peace treaty between Turkey and the Balkan states was signed in London. **1948** The British Citizenship Act conferred the status of British subjects on all Commonwealth citizens. **1977** The 800-mile Alaska oil pipeline was completed at a cost of $8 billion; the first barrel of oil arrived in Valdex, Alaska, on July 28.

BIRTHS

Peter I (the Great), czar of Russia, **1672**; Peter Carl Fabergé, Russian goldsmith and jeweler, **1846**; Howard Hawks, US film director, **1896**; Mel Blanc, US voice-over artist who was the voice of Bugs Bunny and Daffy Duck, **1908**; Benny Goodman, US bandleader, **1909**.

DEATHS

Christopher Marlowe, English playwright, **1593**; Peter Paul Rubens, Flemish painter, **1640**; Alexander Pope, English poet and satirist, **1744**; François Boucher, French painter, **1770**; Voltaire, French author and philosopher, **1778**; Wilbur Wright, US aviation pioneer, **1912**; Boris Pasternak, Russian novelist and poet, **1960**; Claude Rains, British-born Hollywood film actor, **1967**.

NOTES

_____

_____

_____

_____

May 31

"O Captain! my Captain! our fearful trip is done,
The ship has weathered every rack, the prize we sought is won."
—WALT WHITMAN, *"O Captain! My Captain"*

EVENTS

1889 The Johnstown, Pennsylvania, flood caused 2,200 deaths.
1927 The last "Tin Lizzie" rolled off the production line, its
design almost unchanged since the original Model T Ford of
1908. **1961** South Africa became an independent republic. **1962**
Nazi war criminal Adolf Eichmann, who supervised the death
camps where millions of Jews were killed, was executed in Israel.
1994 Dan Rostenkowski, Democratic chairman of the House Way
and Means Committee, was charged with 17 counts of federal
corruption, including embezzlement of public funds; he resigned
as chairman.

BIRTHS

Rudolphus Agricola, Dutch humanist, **1443**; Walt Whitman, US
poet, **1819**; Don Ameche, US film actor, **1908**; Clint Eastwood, US
film actor and director, **1930**; Terry Waite, Church envoy and former Beirut hostage, **1939**; Brooke Shields, US film actress, **1965**.

DEATHS

Jacopo Tintoretto, Italian painter, **1594**; Frederick William I, king of
Prussia, **1740**; Jean Cavalier, French Huguenot preacher and leader,
1740; Franz Joseph Haydn, Austrian composer, **1809**; Joseph
Grimaldi, English clown, **1837**; Walther Funk, German Nazi economist, **1960**; Jack Dempsey, US heavyweight boxing champion, **1983**.

NOTES

June 1

"I've been on a calendar, but never on time."
—MARILYN MONROE

The national day of Tunisia.

EVENTS

836 Viking raiders sacked London. **1485** Matthias of Hungary took Vienna in his conquest of Austria (from Frederick III) and made the city his capital. **1792** Kentucky became the 15th state. **1796** Tennessee became the 16th state. **1915** In World War I, the first Zeppelin attack on London took place. **1950** Mauna Loa, the world's most active volcano, erupted, sending lava pouring 25 miles across the island of Hawaii. **1979** Rhodesia became Zimbabwe.

BIRTHS

Nicolas Carnot, French founder of thermodynamics, **1796**; Brigham Young, US Mormon leader, **1801**; Mikhail Glinka, Russian composer, **1803**; Frank Whittle, English inventor who developed the jet engine, **1907**; Marilyn Monroe, US actress, **1926**; Andy Griffith, US TV and film actor, **1926**; Pat Boone, US singer, **1934**; Morgan Freeman, US film actor, **1937**.

DEATHS

James Buchanan, 15th US president, **1868**; Hugh Walpole, English novelist, **1941**; Leslie Howard, British film actor, **1943**; Ion Antonescu, Romanian dictator, executed, **1946**; Helen Keller, US author and campaigner for the blind and deaf, **1968**.

NOTES

_____

_____

_____

_____

June 2

The national day of Italy.

EVENTS

1619 A treaty was signed between England and Holland, regulating the trade in the East between the English and Dutch East India Companies. **1793** In France, the final overthrow of Girondins and arrest of Jacques Brissot began the Reign of Terror. **1916** The second battle of Ypres took place in World War I. **1949** Transjordan was renamed the Hashemite Kingdom of Jordan. **1953** The coronation of Queen Elizabeth II took place in Westminster Abbey, London. **1964** The Palestine Liberation Organization (PLO) was founded.

BIRTHS

John Sobieski, king of Poland, **1624**; Thomas Hardy, English novelist and poet, **1840**; Edward Elgar, English composer, **1857**; Johnny Weissmuller, US swimmer who played Tarzan, **1903**; Stacy Keach, US film actor, **1941**; Barry Levinson, US film director, **1942**; Marvin Hamlisch, US composer, **1944**.

DEATHS

Giuseppe Garibaldi, Italian nationalist, **1882**; Alexander Ostrovsky, Russian playwright, **1886**; Vita Sackville-West, English writer, **1962**; Andrés Segovia, Spanish classical guitarist, **1987**; Rex Harrison, British actor, **1990**.

NOTES

June 3

EVENTS

1098 The Crusaders took Antioch. **1162** Thomas à Becket was consecrated as archbishop of Canterbury. **1942** US and Japanese naval forces began the Battle of Midway, in the Pacific; the Japanese ultimately failed to take Midway Island. **1946** King Umberto II left Italy and Alcide de Gasperi, the premier, became provisional head of state. **1959** Singapore became self-governing. **1992** The United Nations "Earth Summit" conference on world environmental protection opened in Rio de Janeiro, Brazil.

BIRTHS

William Dampier, English navigator and adventurer, **1652**; George V, king of Britain, **1865**; Paulette Goddard, US actress who starred with and married Charlie Chaplin, **1911**; Tony Curtis, US film actor, **1925**.

DEATHS

William Harvey, English physician who described the circulation of the blood, **1657**; Georges Bizet, French composer, **1875**; Johann Strauss, Austrian composer, **1899**; Franz Kafka, Austrian novelist, **1924**; Mikhail Ivanovich Kalinin, Russian politician, **1946**.

NOTES

June 4

*"I no more thought of style or literary excellence than
the mother who rushes into the street and cries for help to
save her children from a burning house, thinks of the
teachings of the rhetorician or elocutionist."*
—HARRIET BEECHER STOWE, *on writing* Uncle Tom's Cabin

EVENTS

1520 Henry VIII and Francis I met at the Field of the Cloth of Gold, between Gravelines and Ardres; on June 6 they signed a treaty confirming the marriage contract of Mary Tudor and the Dauphin and ending French interference in Scotland. **1946** Juan Perón was elected president of Argentina. **1959** US-owned sugar mills and plantations in Cuba were expropriated. **1989** Tanks moved into Tiananmen Square, Beijing, to break up a peaceful pro-democracy demonstration; many protesters were killed.

BIRTHS

François Quesnay, French economist and physician, **1694**; George III, king of Britain and Ireland, **1738**; Stephen Foster, US songwriter, **1826**; Bruce Dern, US film actor, **1936**.

DEATHS

Giovanni Casanova, Italian adventurer, **1798**; O. Henry, US short-story writer, **1910**; Wilhelm II, German emperor, **1941**.

NOTES

June 5

*"But this long run is a misleading guide to current affairs.
In the long run we are all dead."*
—JOHN MAYNARD KEYNES

The national day of Denmark.

EVENTS

1912 US Marines landed in Cuba. **1945** The Allied Control Commission assumed control throughout Germany, which was divided into four occupation zones. **1947** US Secretary of State George Marshall called for a European Recovery Program (the Marshall Plan). **1967** The Six-Day War broke out between Israel and the Arab states. **1968** Robert F. Kennedy, campaigning for the presidency, was shot in Los Angeles by Jordanian Sirhan Sirhan; Kennedy, who had just celebrated his California primary victory, died the next day. **1975** The Suez Canal was reopened after being closed for eight years.

BIRTHS

Nicolas Poussin, French painter, **1594**; Pancho Villa, Mexican revolutionary, **1878**; John Maynard Keynes, English economist, **1883**; Federico García Lorca, Spanish playwright and poet, **1898**; Margaret Drabble, English novelist, **1939**.

DEATHS

1724; Carl Maria von Weber, German composer, **1826**; Stephen Crane, US novelist and poet, **1900**; Horatio, Lord Kitchener, English soldier, **1916**; Georges Feydeau, French dramatist, **1921**; Harry James, US bandleader and trumpeter, **1983**.

NOTES

June 6

The national day of Sweden.

EVENTS

1636 Puritan American colonist Roger Williams, banished from Massachusetts Bay Colony, founded Providence, Rhode Island, a colony with complete religious freedom. **1664** The Second Dutch War broke out between England and Holland in the colonies and at sea. **1797** Napoleon Bonaparte founded the Ligurian Republic in Genoa. **1933** The first drive-in movie opened in Camden, New Jersey. **1944** D-day, the successful Allied invasion of Normandy under General Dwight D. Eisenhower's command. **1986** The US national debt passed the $2 trillion mark.

BIRTHS

Diego Velázquez, Spanish painter, **1599**; Pierre Corneille, French playwright, **1606**; Robert Falcon Scott, English Antarctic explorer, **1868**; Thomas Mann, German novelist, **1875**; Ninette de Valois, Irish ballet dancer, **1898**; Björn Borg, Swedish tennis player, **1956**.

DEATHS

St. Norbert of Xanten, archbishop of Magdeburg, **1762**; Jeremy Bentham, English philosopher and jurist, **1832**; Louis Chevrolet, US automobile designer and racing driver, **1941**; Carl Gustav Jung, Swiss psychiatrist, **1961**; Robert F. Kennedy, US politician, assassinated, **1968**; Jean Paul Getty, US oil billionaire and art collector, **1976**.

NOTES

June 7

"One more drink and I'd have been under the host."
—DOROTHY PARKER

EVENTS

1494 By the Treaty of Tordesillas, Spain and Portugal agreed to divide the New World between themselves: Portugal was to have all lands east of a line north and south drawn 370 leagues west of Cape Verde; Spain was to have the rest. **1523** Gustavus Vasa was elected Gustav I of Sweden. **1672** Dutch Admiral de Ruyter was successful in action against the combined English and French fleets in Southwold Bay. **1905** The Norwegian parliament declared independence from Sweden (ratified by plebiscite in August).

BIRTHS

Aleksandr Pushkin, Russian novelist, playwright, and poet, **1799**; James Young Simpson, Scottish obstetrician who pioneered the use of anesthetics, **1811**; Paul Gauguin, French painter, **1848**; Pietro Annigoni, Italian painter, **1910**; James Ivory, US film director, **1928**; Tom Jones, Welsh pop singer, **1940**; Prince, US singer, **1960**.

DEATHS

Robert I (the Bruce), king of Scotland, **1329**; Jean Harlow, US film actress, **1937**; Dorothy Parker, US wit and writer, **1967**; E.M. Forster, English novelist, **1970**; Henry Miller, US novelist, **1980**.

NOTES

_____

_____

_____

_____

June 8

"Our Constitution does not contain the absurdity of giving power to make laws and another to resist them."
—ANDREW JACKSON

EVENTS

1919 Nicaragua asked the US for protection against Costa Rica. **1939** George VI visited the US at the end of his tour of Canada; he was the first British monarch to do so. **1965** US troops were authorized to engage in offensive operations in Vietnam. **1968** James Earl Ray, wanted for the murder of Martin Luther King, was arrested in London. **1978** Naomi James of New Zealand completed her voyage to become the first woman to sail solo around the world.

BIRTHS

Giovanni Cassini, Italian astronomer, **1625**; Robert Schumann, German composer, **1810**; Frank Lloyd Wright, US architect, **1869**; Joan Rivers, US comedienne, **1937**; Nancy Sinatra, US singer, **1940**.

DEATHS

Mohammed, prophet and founder of Islam, **632**; Christiaan Huygens, Dutch physicist and astronomer, **1695**; Thomas Paine, English-born American patriot and author of *The Rights of Man*, **1809**; Andrew Jackson, 7th US president, **1845**; George Sand (Amandine Dudevant, born Dupin), French novelist, **1876**; Gerard Manley Hopkins, English poet, **1889**; Gerhart Hauptmann, German novelist and playwright, **1946**; Robert Taylor, US film actor, **1969**.

NOTES

June 9

"In olden days a glimpse of stocking
Was looked on as something shocking.
Now, heaven knows,
Anything goes."
—COLE PORTER, *"Anything Goes"*

EVENTS

1572 A new Turkish fleet put to sea against Don John of Austria to complete the capture of Cyprus. **1885** The Treaty of Tientsin between France and China recognized the French protectorate in Annam. **1934** The cartoon character Donald Duck first appeared. **1959** The USS *George Washington* was launched, the first submarine to be armed with ballistic missiles.

BIRTHS

George Stephenson, English locomotive engineer, **1781**; Cole Porter, US composer, **1893**; Robert McNamara, US secretary of defense, **1916**; Michael J. Fox, Canadian-born Holywood actor, **1961**; Johnny Depp, US film actor, **1963**.

DEATHS

Charles Dickens, English novelist, **1870**; William Lilly, English astrologer, **1681**; Cochise, American Apache leader, **1874**; Maxwell William Aitken, Lord Beaverbrook, Canadian-born politician and newspaper proprietor, **1964**.

NOTES

June 10

EVENTS

1899 Congress appointed a canal commission to report on routes through Panama. **1942** The Czech village of Lidice was destroyed and every man in it killed in reprisal for the assassination of Nazi leader Richard Heydrich. **1943** The ball-point pen was patented in the US by Lazlo Biró. **1967** The Six-Day War between Israel and the Arab states ended. **1975** A special investigation headed by Vice President Nelson Rockefeller revealed illegal CIA operations against American citizens.

BIRTHS

James Francis Edward Stuart ("the Old Pretender" to the British throne), **1688**; Gustave Courbet, French painter, **1819**; Henry Morton Stanley, Welsh-born US journalist and explorer, **1840**; Frederick Loewe, US composer who joined lyricist Alan Jay Lerner to write the Broadway musical hit *My Fair Lady*, **1901**; Saul Bellow, US novelist, **1915**; Prince Philip, duke of Edinburgh, **1921**; Judy Garland, US singer and film actress, **1922**; Maurice Sendak, US illustrator, **1928**.

DEATHS

Luis Vaz de Camoens, Portuguese poet, **1580**; Alessandro Algardi, Italian sculptor, **1654**; André Ampère, French physicist, **1836**; June Haver, US film actress, **1926**; Spencer Tracey, US film actor, **1967**.

NOTES

June 11

EVENTS

1509 Henry VIII of England married Catherine of Aragon, his first wife. **1727** George I became king of Great Britain. **1955** US President Dwight Eisenhower proposed financial and technical aid to all non-communist countries to develop atomic energy. **1964** Greece rejected direct talks with Turkey over Cyprus. **1977** The colt Seattle Slew won the Belmont Stakes and racing's Triple Crown, having previously won the Kentucky Derby and the Preakness. **1990** Retired Admiral John Poindexter was sentenced to six months' imprisonment for his involvement in the Iran-Contra affair; he was acquitted on appeal in 1991.

BIRTHS

Ben Jonson, English playwright, **1572**; John Constable, English painter, **1776**; Jacques Cousteau, French oceanographer, **1910**; William Styron, US novelist, **1925**; Athol Fugard, South African dramatist and director, **1932**; Gene Wilder, US comic film actor, **1935**.

DEATHS

Louis, duc de Vendôme, French soldier, **1712**; John Franklin, English Arctic explorer, **1847**; Clemens, Prince Metternich, Austrian politician, **1859**; Alexander Kerensky, Russian politician, **1970**; John Wayne, US film actor, **1979**.

NOTES

June 12

"Read my lips—no new taxes."
—GEORGE BUSH, *unfulfilled election promise during
1988 presidential campaign*

The national day of the Philippines.

EVENTS

1683 The Rye House Plot, to assassinate King Charles II and his brother James, duke of York, was discovered. **1901** A Cuban convention making the country virtually a protectorate of the US was incorporated in the Cuban constitution as a condition of the withdrawal of US troops. **1934** Political parties were banned in Bulgaria. **1964** Nelson Mandela and seven others were sentenced to life imprisonment in South Africa for acts of sabotage. **1991** Boris Yeltsin became the first-ever Russian leader elected by democratic vote.

BIRTHS

Harriet Martineau, English writer, **1802**; Charles Kingsley, English novelist, **1819**; Anthony Eden, Viscount Avon, British politician, **1897**; George Bush, 41st US president, **1924**; Vic Damone, US singer, **1928**; Anne Frank, Jewish Dutch diarist, **1929**; Chick Corea, US jazz composer and pianist, **1941**.

DEATHS

Jimmy Dorsey, US musician and bandleader, **1957**; John Ireland, English composer, **1962**; Medgar Evers, US civil-rights leader, **1963**.

NOTES

_____

_____

_____

_____

June 13

*"A pity beyond all telling,
Is hid in the heart of love."*
—W.B. YEATS

EVENTS

1849 Communist riots in Paris were easily put down and led to repressive legislation. **1866** The US 14th Amendment guaranteed citizenship for former slaves, and due process and equal protection under the law for all citizens. **1900** The Boxer Rebellion began in China against Europeans. **1944** The first flying bomb was dropped on London. **1956** The last British troops left the Suez Canal base. **1961** Austria refused an application by Archduke Otto of Hapsburg to return as a private individual. **1971** The *New York Times* began publishing the classified "Pentagon Papers" revealing government secrets about the Vietnam War. **1993** Kim Campbell became Canada's first female prime minister.

BIRTHS

James Clerk Maxwell, Scottish physicist, **1831**; William Butler Yeats, Irish poet, **1865**; Don Budge, US tennis player who was the first to win the grand slam of major tournaments, **1915**.

DEATHS

Alexander the Great, **323 BC**; St. Antonio of Padua, **1231**; Arcangelo Corelli, Italian composer, **1713**; Benny Goodman, US bandleader, **1986**.

NOTES

June 14

"Writing is nothing more than a guided dream."
—JORGE LUIS BORGES, Dr. Brodie's Report

EVENTS

1404 Glendower, having won control of Wales, assumed the title of Prince of Wales. **1645** In the English Civil War, Oliver Cromwell defeated the Royalists at the Battle of Naseby, Northamptonshire. **1777** The Continental Congress adopted the Stars and Stripes as the official flag. **1800** Napoleon Bonaparte defeated an Austrian army at the Battle of Marengo and reconquered Italy. **1900** The Hawaiian Islands became a US territory. **1940** In World War II, German forces entered Paris. **1962** The European Space Research Organization was established at Paris. **1994** The United Nations completed its destruction of Iraq's chemical weapons, part of the agreement to end the Gulf War.

BIRTHS

Charles Augustin Coulomb, French physicist, **1736**; Harriet Beecher Stowe, US novelist who wrote *Uncle Tom's Cabin*, **1811**; Burl Ives, US film actor and singer, **1909**; Che Guevara, Argentinian communist revolutionary, **1928**; Boy George, British pop singer, **1961**; Steffi Graf, German tennis player, **1969**.

DEATHS

Gene Barry, US film actor, **1919**; Gilbert Keith Chesterton, English author, **1936**; John Logie Baird, Scottish inventor who developed television, **1946**; Jorge Luis Borges, Argentinian author, **1986**; Vincent Hamlin, US cartoonist, **1993**; Henry Mancini, US composer, **1994**.

NOTES

June 15

*"But in this world nothing can be said to
be certain, except death and taxes."*
—BENJAMIN FRANKLIN, *letter, Nov. 13, 1789*

EVENTS

1520 Pope Leo X excommunicated Martin Luther by the bull
Exsurge. **1672** The Sluices were opened in Holland to save
Amsterdam from the invading French. **1752** Benjamin Franklin
flew a kite in a thunderstorm to prove that electricity existed in
lightning. **1775** The Continental Congress appointed George
Washington as commander-in-chief of American forces. **1836**
Arkansas became the 25th state. **1869** Celluloid was patented in
the US. **1924** Congress passed an act making citizens of all Native
Americans. **1977** Spain held its first general elections since 1936.
1978 American Elizabeth Halaby, 26, wed King Hussein of
Jordan. **1993** The last Russian troops left Cuba.

BIRTHS

St. Francesco de Paolo, **1416**; Joannes Argyropoulos, Greek
scholar, **1416**; Edvard Grieg, Norwegian composer, **1843**; Harry
Langdon, US silent-film comedian, **1884**; Mario Cuomo, New
York governor, **1932**; Waylon Jennings, US country singer, **1937**.

DEATHS

Wat Tyler, English rebel leader, **1381**; Philip the Good, duke of
Burgundy, **1467**; Marguerite De Launay, Baronne Staal, French
writer, **1750**; James Knox Polk, 11th US president, **1849**.

NOTES

June 16

EVENTS

1755 Soldiers from Boston captured a French fort in Nova Scotia, Canada. **1779** Spain declared war on Britain, and the siege of Gibraltar began. **1961** Russian ballet dancer Rudolf Nureyev defected to the West at Le Bourget airport, France. **1972** Burglars were caught breaking into the Democratic party headquarters in the Watergate Building, Washington, DC. **1977** Leonid Brezhnev became president of the USSR.

BIRTHS

Gustav V, king of Sweden, **1858**; Stan Laurel, English-born US film comedian, **1890**; Giacomo Agostini, Italian motorcycle champion, **1942**.

DEATHS

Roger van der Weyden, Flemish painter, **1464**; John Churchill, duke of Marlborough, English general, **1722**; Guilio Alberoni, Italian-born Spanish politician and cardinal, **1752**; Elmer Ambrose Sperry, US inventor, **1930**.

NOTES

June 17

"Don't fire until you see the whites of their eyes."
—WILLIAM PRESCOTT, *American revolutionary,*
at the battle of Bunker Hill, 1775

The national day of Iceland.

EVENTS

1775 In the American Revolution, American troops won a victory at Bunker Hill, sustaining the siege of British-held Boston. **1928** US aviator Amelia Earhart became the first woman to fly across the Atlantic, from Newfoundland to Burry Point, Wales. **1963** The US Supreme Court ruled unconstitutional any laws requiring public school students to recite the Lord's Prayer or read Bible verses. **1994** A judge sentenced five Branch Davidian cult members to 10 years in jail for aiding voluntary manslaughter of federal officers during the 1993 seige of their compound at Waco, Texas.

BIRTHS

Pedro Calderón de la Barca, Spanish dramatist, **1600**; John Wesley, English founder of Methodism, **1703**; Igor Stravinsky, Russian composer, **1882**; Dean Martin, US singer and film actor, **1917**; Newt Gingrich, US speaker of the House of Representatives, **1943**; Barry Manilow, US singer and songwriter, **1946**.

DEATHS

Claude, duc de Villars, French soldier, **1734**; Prosper Jolyot de Crébillon, French playwright, **1762**; Imre Nagy, Hungarian prime minister, executed, **1958**.

NOTES

June 18

"No one can make you feel inferior without your consent."
—ELEANOR ROOSEVELT

EVENTS

1429 The French, led by Joan of Arc, defeated the English at the Battle of Patay. **1812** The US declared war on Great Britain, beginning the War of 1812; a major cause was the practice of British ships stopping American ones on the high seas to impress (often former) British subjects. **1815** The duke of Wellington and Gebhard von Blücher defeated Napoleon at the Battle of Waterloo. **1953** A republic was proclaimed in Egypt, with General M. Neguib as president. **1983** Sally Ride became America's first woman astronaut, launched in the space shuttle *Challenger* from Cape Canaveral, Florida.

BIRTHS

Nikolaus Horthy de Nagybánya, Hungarian politician, **1868**; Edouard Daladier, French politician, **1884**; Jeanette MacDonald, US singer and actress, **1901**; Sammy Cahn, US songwriter, **1913**; Paul McCartney, English pop singer and member of the Beatles, **1942**; Isabella Rossellini, Italian film actress, **1952**.

DEATHS

Andrew Jackson, 7th president of the US, **1845**; John Augustus Sutter, US pioneer, **1880**; Samuel Butler, English novelist, **1902**; Roald Amundsen, Norwegian polar explorer, **1928**; Maxim Gorky, Russian author, **1936**; Ethel Barrymore, US actress, **1959**; Jeff Chandler, US film actor, **1961**.

NOTES

June 19

"Some of my plays peter out, and some pan out."
—J.M. BARRIE

EVENTS

1464 An ordinance of Louis XI in France created the *poste*, organizing relays of horses on the main roads for the king's business. **1754** The French and Indian War broke out in North America when a force under George Washington skirmished with French troops near Fort Duquesne. **1867** Emperor Maximilian was executed in Mexico. **1953** Julius and Ethel Rosenberg, convicted of spying, were executed in the electric chair at Sing Sing Prison, New York. **1965** Ben Bella, President of Algeria, was deposed; Houari Boumédienne headed a revolutionary council. **1967** The Monterey Pop Festival, attended by about 50,000 people, kicked off San Francisco's "Summer of Love."

BIRTHS

Blaise Pascal, French mathematician and philosopher, 1623; Félicité Robert de Lamennais, French writer, 1783; Douglas, Earl Haig, British field-marshal, 1861; Ernst Chain, German-born British bacteriologist who helped develop penicillin, 1906; Joshua Nkomo, Zimbabwean politician, 1917; Salman Rushdie, British novelist, 1947; Kathleen Turner, US film actress, 1954.

DEATHS

J.M. Barrie, Scottish author of *Peter Pan*, 1937; John Cheever, US novelist and short-story writer, 1982.

NOTES

June 20

*"The public has always expected me to be a playboy,
and a decent chap never lets his public down."*
—ERROL FLYNN

EVENTS

840 Vikings sailed up the River Seine as far as Rouen, for the first time. **1756** In India, rebels imprisoned a large number of British subjects in a cell ("The Black Hole of Calcutta"); only 23 came out alive. **1789** In France, the third estate took the Tennis Court oath, undertaking not to depart until a constitution was drawn up. **1837** Queen Victoria succeeded to the British throne. **1837** Natal Republic was founded by Dutch settlers. **1863** West Virginia became the 35th state. **1930** *Hot Chocolates*, a hit revue by Fats Waller and Louis Armstrong, opened on Broadway. **1994** O.J. Simpson, US football star and actor, pleaded not guilty to murdering his wife, Nicole, and her friend, Ronald Goldman, on June 12.

BIRTHS

Jacques Offenbach, German-born French composer, **1819**; Errol Flynn, Australian-born US film actor, **1909**; Chet Atkins, US guitarist, **1924**; Audie Murphy, US film actor and the nation's most decorated World War II soldier, **1924**; Lionel Richie, US jazz musician, **1950**.

DEATHS

Willem Barents, Dutch explorer, **1597**; Emmanuel Joseph Sieyès, French revolutionary leader, **1836**; Nikolai Rimsky-Korsakov, Russian composer, **1908**; Bernard Baruch, US financier, **1965**.

NOTES

_____

_____

_____

_____

June 21

EVENTS

1661 The Peace of Kardis was signed between Russia and Sweden. **1788** The US Constitution came into force, when ratified by the 9th state, New Hampshire. **1798** British General Gerard Lake defeated Irish rebels, ending the Irish Rebellion. **1813** The duke of Wellington routed the French at Vittoria. **1919** The German fleet was scuttled in Scapa Flow, in Britain's Orkney Islands. **1942** German forces under Field-Marshal Rommel captured Tobruk. **1943** Race riots caused 34 deaths in Detroit and six in New York City. **1948** Dr. Peter Goldmark of Columbia Records demonstrated the first successful long-playing record.

BIRTHS

Increase Mather, American clergyman and president of Harvard, **1639**; Jean-Paul Sartre, French philosopher, novelist, and playwright, **1905**; Jane Russell, US film actress, **1921**; Françoise Sagan, French novelist, **1935**.

DEATHS

Sebastiano del Piombo, Italian painter, **1547**; John Smith, Virginia colonist, **1631**; Inigo Jones, English architect and stage designer, **1652**; George Hepplewhite, English cabinetmaker, **1786**; Friedrich Froebel, German educator, **1852**; Antonio López de Santa Anna, Mexican revolutionary, **1876**; Jean-Edouard Vuillard, French painter, **1940**; Maureen Connolly ("Little Mo"), US tennis player, **1969**.

NOTES

June 22

EVENTS

1611 English navigator Henry Hudson, his son, and seven others were cast adrift in a small boat in the bay named after him when his crew muntinied; they were never seen again. **1671** Turkey declared war on Poland. **1826** The Pan-American Congress met in Panama under the influence of Simón Bolívar in an unsuccessful effort to unite the American republics. **1894** Dahomey was proclaimed a French colony. **1922** A two-day coal strike began at Herrin, Illinois, resulting in 36 deaths. **1937** Joe Louis, the "Brown Bomber," beat Jim Braddock to become world heavyweight boxing champion.

BIRTHS

Jean Chardin, French painter, **1699**; Jacques Delille, French poet, **1738**; Giuseppe Mazzini, Italian patriot, **1805**; Billy Wilder, Austrian-born US film director, **1906**; Mike Todd, US film producer, **1909**; Kris Kristofferson, US singer and actor, **1936**; Ed Bradley, US TV newsman, **1941**; Meryl Streep, US actress, **1949**.

DEATHS

Roger I, king of Sicily, **1101**; Niccolò Machiavelli, Italian political philosopher, **1527**; Fred Astaire, US dancer and film actor, **1987**; David O. Selznick, US film producer who made *Gone with the Wind*, **1965**; Judy Garland, US singer and film actress, **1969**.

NOTES

June 23

*"I submit to you that if a man hasn't discovered
something he will die for, he isn't fit to live."*
—MARTIN LUTHER KING, *speech June 23, 1963*

The national day of Luxembourg.

EVENTS

1683 William Penn signed a friendship treaty with the Delaware Indians and paid for land in Pennsylvania. **1757** British troops under Robert Clive captured Plassey, in Bengal, and recovered Calcutta. **1934** Saudi Arabia and Yemen signed a peace agreement after a war of six weeks. **1951** Britain's Guy Burgess and Donald Maclean, "missing diplomats," fled to the USSR as spies. **1952** The US Air Force bombed hydroelectric plants in North Korea. **1987** The Supreme Court accepted the use of hypnosis to obtain testimony.

BIRTHS

John Banér, Swedish general, **1596**; Giovanni Battista Vico, Italian philosopher, **1668**; Josephine de Beauharnais, French wife of Napoleon, **1763**; Anna Akhmatova, Russian poet, **1889**; Dr. Alfred Kinsey, US zoologist and sex researcher, **1894**; Jean Anouilh, French playwright, **1910**; William Rogers, US secretary of state, **1913**; Bob Fosse, US actor, choreographer, and director, **1927**.

DEATHS

Vespasian, Roman emperor, **79**; Pedro de Mendoza, Spanish explorer, **1537**; Jonas Salk, who developed the first successful vaccine against polio, **1995**.

NOTES

_____

_____

_____

_____

June 24

*"I am scarcely less free than I was before, for
have I not been a prisoner all my life?"*
—NICHOLAS II, CZAR OF RUSSIA, *reported on June 24, 1917*

EVENTS

1535 Charles V of Spain led an expedition to conquer Tunis from
Barbarossa; Charles restored the Bey, Mulai Hassan (deposed by
the Turks in 1534), and completed the Spanish conquest of the
North African coast. **1812** Napoleon crossed the River Niemen and
entered Russian territory. **1917** The Russian Black Sea fleet
mutinied at Sebastopol. **1948** The Berlin Blockade began when the
USSR stopped all traffic from the Western zone of Germany into
Berlin; the West launched a massive airlift of food and supplies
into the city two days later. **1956** Gamal Abdel Nasser became the
first president of Egypt.

BIRTHS

St. John of the Cross (Juan de Yepez y Alvarez), Spanish mystic,
1542; John Churchill, duke of Marlborough, English general,
1650; Horatio, Lord Kitchener, British soldier, **1850**; Jack
Dempsey, US world heavyweight boxing champion, **1895**; Juan
Fangio, Argentinian racing driver, **1911**; Fred Hoyle, English
astronomer, **1915**; Jack Carson, US film actor, **1923**; Claude
Chabrol, French film director, **1930**.

DEATHS

Ferdinand I, king of Castile and Leon, **1065**; Lucrezia Borgia,
duchess of Ferrara, **1519**; Grover Cleveland, 22nd and 24th US
president, **1908**.

NOTES

_____

_____

_____

_____

June 25

EVENTS

1524 The Peasants' Revolt in southern Germany began; rebels demanded the abolition of enclosures and feudal services. **1646** The surrender of Oxford to the Roundheads virtually signified the end of the English Civil War. **1788** Virginia became the 10th state. **1867** The first patent for barbed wire was taken out in Ohio. **1876** Gen. George Custer and his 264 men were killed by Sioux Indians at the Battle of the Little Bighorn, in Montana ("Custer's Last Stand.") **1938** The US minimum wage law was enacted. **1950** The Korean War began when North Korean troops invaded South Korea. **1975** Mozambique achieved independence from Portugal. **1991** Croatia and Slovenia declared independence from Yugoslavia.

BIRTHS

George Orwell, English essayist and novelist, **1903**; Sidney Lumet, US film director, **1924**; June Lockhart, US film actress, **1925**; Carly Simon, US singer and songwriter, **1945**; George Michael, English singer and songwriter, **1963**.

DEATHS

George Armstrong Custer, US soldier, **1876**; Johnny Mercer, US composer, lyricist, and singer, **1976**; Warren Burger, chief justice of the US Supreme Court, **1995**.

NOTES

June 26

"Children have never been very good at listening to their elders, but they have never failed to imitate them."
—JAMES BALDWIN

EVENTS

1519 Church reformer Martin Luther's public disputation with Johann Eck on doctrine began at Leipzig. **1917** The first US troops arrived in France during World War I. **1945** The United Nations Charter was signed by 50 nations in San Francisco. **1993** The US launched a missile attack on Iraqi intelligence headquarters, Baghdad, after revelations of an alleged plot by Iraq to murder former President George Bush. **1994** Russia joined the NATO Partnership for Peace program, allowing them to participate in joint military exercises.

BIRTHS

William Thomson, Lord Kelvin, English physicist, **1824**; Pearl S. Buck, US novelist, **1892**; Peter Lorre, Hungarian-born US film actor, **1904**; Laurie Lee, English poet and author, **1914**; "Colonel" Tom Parker, US impresario and Elvis Presley's manager, **1919**; Claudio Abbado, Italian conductor, **1933**.

DEATHS

Francisco Pizarro, Spanish explorer who conquered Peru, assassinated, **1541**; Joseph-Michel Montgolfier, French balloonist, **1810**; George IV, king of Britain, **1830**; Carl Foreman, US film director and producer, **1984**; George Horace Gallup, US journalist and statistician who devised the Gallup Poll, **1984**.

NOTES

June 27

EVENTS

1771 Russia completed its conquest of the Crimea. **1801** Cairo fell to English forces. **1932** A constitution was proclaimed in Siam (now Thailand), replacing the absolute ruler with a consitutional monarchy. **1940** The USSR invaded Romania on the refusal of King Carol to cede Bessarabia and Bukovina; Romania appealed for German aid in vain. **1941** Hungary declared war on Russia. **1944** Allied forces took Cherbourg. **1954** The first nuclear power station was opened at Obninsk, near Moscow, in the USSR. **1976** Palestinian terrorists hijacked an Air France airplane and forced it to fly to Entebbe, Uganda.

BIRTHS

Louis XII, king of France, **1462**; Charles Stewart Parnell, Irish nationalist leader, **1846**; John Monash, Australian civil engineer, **1865**; Helen Keller, US blind and deaf author and teacher, **1880**; H. Ross Perot, US businessman and independent presidential candidate, **1930**.

DEATHS

Giorgio Vasari, Italian painter and art historian, **1742**; Samuel Hood, British admiral, **1816**; James Smithson, English scientist, **1829**; Joseph Smith, founder of the Mormons, **1844**; Malcolm Lowry, British novelist, **1957**.

NOTES

_____

_____

_____

_____

June 28

"Never exceed your rights, and they will soon become unlimited."
—JEAN JACQUES ROUSSEAU

EVENTS

1519 Charles I of Spain, Sicily, and Sardinia was elected Holy Roman Emperor as Charles V. **1778** In the American Revolution, the indecisive Battle of Monmouth, New Jersey, took place between the troops of General George Washington and Sir Henry Clinton. **1895** Union of Nicaragua, Honduras, and El Salvador (ended in 1898 by El Salvador's opposition.) **1914** Archduke Francis Ferdinand of Austria and his wife were assassinated at Sarajevo by Gavrilo Princip, a Bosnian revolutionary, starting World War I. **1948** Yugoslavia was expelled from Cominform for hostility to the USSR. **1950** The novice US soccer team beat England 1-0 in the first round of the World Cup in Brazil. **1956** Labor riots at Poznan, Poland, were put down with heavy loss of life.

BIRTHS

Sigismund of Luxembourg, Holy Roman Emperor, **1368**; Henry VIII, king of England, **1491**; Jean Jacques Rousseau, French philosopher and writer, **1712**; Luigi Pirandello, Italian playwright, **1867**; Richard Rodgers, US composer, **1902**; Mel Brooks, US comic film actor, director, and producer, **1926**.

DEATHS

James Madison, 4th US president, **1836**; Robert Burke, Irish explorer of Australia, **1861**; William Wyler, US film director, **1961**; Boris Christoff, Bulgarian operatic bass, **1993**.

NOTES

June 29

*"Too often the strong silent man is silent only because
he does not know what to say and is reputed strong
only because he has remained silent."*
—WINSTON CHURCHILL, *reported on June 29, 1924*

EVENTS

1949 The US completed its withdrawal of occupying forces from South Korea. **1949** The South African Citizenship Act imposed a ban on mixed marriages between Europeans and non-Europeans, the beginning of the apartheid program. **1954** Following the meeting of President Eisenhower and Winston Churchill in Washington, the Potomac Charter, or six-point declaration of Western policy, was issued. **1956** Dramatist Arthur Miller married Marilyn Monroe in London. **1995** Francisco Duran was sentenced to 40 years' imprisonment for shooting at the White House in October 1994.

BIRTHS

Peter Paul Rubens, Flemish painter, **1577**; Giacomo Leopardi, Italian poet, **1798**; George Ellery Hale, US astronomer, **1868**; Antoine de Saint-Exupéry, French author and aviator, **1900**; Nelson Eddy, US singer and film actor, **1901**; Frank Loesser, US composer, **1910**; Prince Bernhard of the Netherlands, **1911**.

DEATHS

Elizabeth Barrett Browning, English poet, **1861**; T.H. Huxley, English biologist, **1895**; Albert Sorel, French historian, **1906**; Paul Klee, Swiss painter, **1940**; Ignaz Paderewski, Polish musician and politician, **1941**; Jayne Mansfield, US film actress, **1967**.

NOTES

June 30

---

*"I cannot and will not cut my conscience to
fit this year's fashions."*
—LILLIAN HELLMAN, *letter to the House
Un-American Activities Committee, May 1952*

EVENTS

1782 Spain completed its conquest of British-held Florida. **1846**
The Mormons under Brigham Young left Nauvoo, Illinois, for the
Great Salt Lake. **1859** Charles Blondin crossed Niagara Falls by
tightrope in just eight minutes. **1906** The US Pure Food and Drug
Act was passed. **1934** A Nazi purge—the Night of the Long
Knives—took place in Germany with summary executions of
Kurt von Schleicher, Ernst Roehm, and other party leaders for an
alleged plot against Hitler. **1960** Alfred Hitchcock's *Psycho* pre-
miered in New York. **1965** An India-Pakistan cease-fire was
signed, ending the conflict over the Rann of Cutch.

BIRTHS

Charles VIII, king of France, **1469**; Georges Duhamel, French
novelist and poet, **1884**; Stanley Spencer, English painter, **1891**;
Lena Horne, US singer and actress, **1917**; Buddy Rich, US jazz
drummer, **1917**; Mike Tyson, US world heavyweight boxing
champion, **1966**.

DEATHS

Montezuma II, Aztec ruler, assassinated, **1520**; Johann Reuchlin,
German humanist and Hebrew scholar, **1522**; Willem Barents,
Dutch explorer, **1597**; William Oughtred, English mathematician,
1660; Lillian Hellman, US playwright, **1984**.

NOTES

July 1

*"We cannot tear out a single page of our life,
but we can throw the whole book in the fire."*
—GEORGE SAND

The national day of Canada.

EVENTS

1751 The first volume of Diderot's *Encyclopédie* was published in Paris. **1847** First US adhesive postage stamps sold. **1863** The Battle of Gettysburg began in the Civil War. **1916** The first Battle of the Somme began in World War I; more than 21,000 men were killed on the first day. **1963** ZIP codes were introduced by the US Post Office. **1990** A state treaty establishing a unified economy and monetary system for East and West Germany went into effect. **1991** The Warsaw Pact was formally disbanded. **1994** A new currency, the real, was introduced in Brazil.

BIRTHS

George Sand, (Amandine Dudevant, born Dupin), French novelist, **1804**; Louis Blériot, French aviator, **1872**; Olivia de Havilland, US film actress, **1916**; Sydney Pollack, US film director, **1934**; Karen Black, US film actress, **1942**; Diana, the Princess of Wales, **1961**; Carl Lewis, US athlete, **1961**.

DEATHS

Charles Goodyear, US inventor who developed vulcanized rubber, **1860**; Allan Pinkerton, US founder of the detective agency, **1884**; Harriet Beecher Stowe, US author, **1896**; Erik Satie, French composer, **1925**; Juan Perón, Argentinian politician, **1974**.

NOTES

July 2

"All good books have one thing in common—they are truer than if they had really happened."
—ERNEST HEMINGWAY

EVENTS

1644 Oliver Cromwell defeated Prince Rupert at the Battle of Marston Moor, his first victory over the Royalists in the English Civil War. **1865** At a revivalist meeting at Whitechapel, London, William Booth formed the Salvation Army. **1881** President James Garfield was shot by a disappointed office-seeker in a railroad station in Washington, DC; he died on September 19. **1900** The 2nd Olympic Games opened in Paris. **1926** The US Army Air Corps was established. **1937** Amelia Earhart, US aviator, disappeared over the Pacific. **1956** Elvis Presley recorded "Hound Dog" and "Don't Be Cruel" in New York. **1964** President Johnson signed the US Civil Rights Bill prohibiting racial discrimination. **1990** Over a thousand Muslim pilgrims were killed when a stampede occurred in a pedestrian tunnel leading to the holy city of Mecca.

BIRTHS

Thomas Cranmer, archbishop of Canterbury, **1489**; Christoph Gluck, German composer, **1714**; William Henry Bragg, English physicist, **1862**; Hermann Hesse, German poet and novelist, **1877**.

DEATHS

Nostradamus, French physician and astrologer, **1566**; Jean Jacques Rousseau, French philosopher and writer, **1778**; Ernest Hemingway, US novelist, suicide, **1961**; Betty Grable, US film actress, **1973**; Vladimir Nabokov, Russian novelist, **1977**.

NOTES

July 3

"I'm a one-key piano player, and as a playwright, most of my plays have been presented in two acts for the simple reason that I could seldom think of an idea for a third act."
—GEORGE M. COHAN

EVENTS

1608 French explorer Samuel Champlain founded Québec. **1863** The Union forces, under General George Meade, defeated the Confederates, under General Robert E. Lee, at the Battle of Gettysburg. **1890** Idaho became the 43rd state. **1976** An Israeli commando force rescued 103 hostages from a hijacked aircraft, who were being held at Entebbe airport, Uganda. **1988** The USS *Vincennes*, patrolling the Persian Gulf during the Iran–Iraq conflict, mistook an Iranian civil airliner for a bomber and shot it down, killing all 290 people on board.

BIRTHS

Robert Adam, Scottish architect and designer, **1728**; Leoš Janáček, Czech composer, **1854**; George M. Cohan, US songwriter and performer, **1878**; Franz Kafka, Czech-born Austrian writer, **1883**; Ken Russell, British film director, **1927**; Tom Cruise, US film actor, **1962**.

DEATHS

Marie de' Medici, queen of France, **1642**; Joel Chandler Harris, US author, **1908**; Brian Jones, English rock guitarist, **1961**; Jim Morrison, US singer, **1971**; Rudy Vallee, US singer, **1986**; Joe De Rita, US comedian, **1993**.

NOTES

_____

_____

_____

_____

July 4

*"We hold these Truths to be self-evident, that all
Men are created equal, that they are endowed by their
Creator with certain unalienable Rights, that among these are Life,
Liberty and the Pursuit of Happiness."*
—DECLARATION OF INDEPENDENCE, *1776*

Independence Day.

EVENTS

1776 The Declaration of Independence was approved by Congress. **1828** The Baltimore & Ohio, America's first passenger railroad, began operations. **1848** The Communist Manifesto was published by Karl Marx and Friedrich Engels. **1883** The people of France presented the Statue of Liberty to the US; it was dedicated in 1886. **1976** The US celebrated its bicentennial, highlighted by a gathering of tall ships in New York's harbor. **1991** Colombia's President Cesar Gaviria Trujillo lifted a state of siege, in effect since 1984.

BIRTHS

Nathaniel Hawthorne, US author, **1804**; Giuseppe Garibaldi, Italian soldier and patriot, **1807**; Calvin Coolidge, 30th US president, **1872**; Louis "Satchmo" Armstrong, US jazz musician, **1900**; Neil Simon, US dramatist, **1927**.

DEATHS

Thomas Jefferson, 3rd US president, **1826**; John Adams, 2nd US president, **1826**; James Monroe, 5th US president, **1831**; Marie Curie, Polish scientist, **1934**.

NOTES

_____

_____

_____

_____

July 5

"Making money ain't nothing exciting to me. You might be able to buy a little better booze than the wino on the corner. But you get sick just like the next cat and when you die you're just as graveyard dead."
—LOUIS ARMSTRONG, *reported on July 5, 1970*

The national day of Venezuela.

EVENTS

1946 A swimsuit designed by Louis Reard, called "bikini," was first modeled at a Paris fashion show. **1965** Maria Callas, US operatic soprano, gave her last stage performance at the age of 41, singing Tosca at Covent Garden, London. **1967** Israel annexed Gaza. **1980** Sweden's Björn Borg won the Wimbledon tennis singles championship for a record fifth consecutive time. **1989** Jailed African National Congress leader Nelson Mandela met secretly with South African President Pieter W. Botha in Capetown.

BIRTHS

Phineas T. Barnum, US showman, **1810**; Cecil Rhodes, South African statesman, **1853**; Dwight Davis, US statesman, **1879**; Jean Cocteau, French poet, novelist, artist, and film director, **1889**; Georges Pompidou, French statesman, **1911**.

DEATHS

1894; Georges Bernanos, French author, **1948**; Thomas Joseph Mboya, Kenyan statesman, **1969**; Walter Adolph Gropius, German-born US architect, **1969**; Georgette Heyer, English novelist, **1974**.

NOTES

July 6

"The last sound on the worthless earth will be two human beings trying to launch a homemade spaceship and already quarreling about where they are going next."
—WILLIAM FAULKNER

The national day of Malawi.

EVENTS

1535 Sir Thomas More was beheaded on London's Tower Hill for treason. **1553** Mary I acceded to the throne, becoming the first queen to rule England in her own right. **1928** The first all-talking feature film, *Lights of New York*, was presented at the Strand Theater in New York City. **1988** An explosion aboard the North Sea oil rig *Piper Alpha* resulted in the loss of 166 lives. **1994** Forest fires killed 14 firefighters near Greenwood Springs, Colorado; others died as fires swept over 240,000 acres in 11 Western states.

BIRTHS

John Paul Jones, Scottish-born US naval hero, **1747**; Nancy Reagan, US first lady, **1923**; Bill Haley, US rock 'n' roll pioneer, **1925**; Janet Leigh, US film actress, **1927**; Tenzin Gyatso, the Dalai Lama, Tibetan spiritual leader, **1935**; Vladimir Ashkenazy, Russian pianist, **1937**; Sylvester Stallone, US film actor, **1946**.

DEATHS

Guy de Maupassant, French writer, **1893**; William Faulkner, US novelist, **1962**; Louis Armstrong, US jazz musician, **1971**; Otto Klemperer, German conductor, **1973**.

NOTES

July 7

"Where there is no imagination there is no horror."
—SIR ARTHUR CONAN DOYLE

EVENTS

1853 US naval officer Commodore Matthew Perry arrived in Japan and persuaded the country to open trade contacts with the West. **1862** US Land Grant Act was passed and eventually helped found state universities. **1896** William Jennings Bryan delivered his "Cross of Gold" speech (advocating unlimited silver coinage) at the Democratic National Convention in Chicago. **1898** Hawaii was annexed by the US. **1929** The Vatican City State, with the pope as its sovereign, came into being through the Lateran Treaty. **1990** Martina Navratilova won a record ninth Wimbledon singles title.

BIRTHS

Marc Chagall, Russian painter and designer, **1887**; George Cukor, US film director, **1899**; Vittorio de Sica, Italian film director, **1901**; Pierre Cardin, French fashion designer, **1922**; Ringo Starr, English drummer for the Beatles, **1940**; Dan Aykroyd, Canadian-born US comic actor, **1952**.

DEATHS

Edward I, king of England, **1307**; Giacomo da Vignola, Italian architect, **1573**; R.B. Sheridan, Irish dramatist and politician, **1816**; Georg Ohm, German physicist, **1854**; Arthur Conan Doyle, British author who created Sherlock Holmes, **1930**.

NOTES

July 8

EVENTS

1497 Portuguese navigator Vasco da Gama left Lisbon for a voyage on which he discovered the Cape route to India. **1907** The *Ziegfeld Follies* opened for the first time, on Broadway. **1943** Jean Moulin, the French Resistance leader known as "Max," was executed by the Gestapo. **1978** Reinhold Messner and Peter Habeler became the first to climb Mt. Everest entirely without supplemental oxygen. **1991** Iraq admitted to the UN that it had been conducting clandestine programs to produce enriched uranium, a key element in nuclear weapons.

BIRTHS

Jean de la Fontaine, French writer, **1621**; Joseph Chamberlain, British statesman, **1836**; John D. Rockefeller, US oil millionaire, **1839**; Nelson Rockefeller, US vice president, **1908**; Billy Eckstine, US singer, **1915**; Steve Lawrence, US singer, **1935**; Anjelica Huston, US film actress, **1951**.

DEATHS

Percy Bysshe Shelley, English poet, **1822**; Henry Havelock Ellis, English physician and author, **1939**; Vivien Leigh, English film actress, **1967**; Fred Weick, US aeronautical engineer, **1993**.

NOTES

July 9

"Riots are the language of the unheard."
—MARTIN LUTHER KING, *reported on July 9, 1969*

The national day of Argentina.

EVENTS

1810 Napoleon annexed Holland, making his brother, Louis, its king. **1816** Argentina declared independence from Spain at the Congress of Tucuman. **1877** The first Wimbledon Lawn Tennis championship was held. **1922** Johnny Weissmuller, aged· 18, swam the 100 meters in under a minute (58.6 sec). **1979** In Nicaragua, General Somoza was overthrown by the Sandinista rebels. **1991** The International Olympic Committee lifted a 21-year-old boycott on South Africa.

BIRTHS

Elias Howe, US inventor of the sewing machine in 1846, **1819**; Edward Heath, British politician, **1916**; David Hockney, English painter, **1937**; Tom Hanks, US film actor **1956**.

DEATHS

Jan van Eyck, Flemish painter, **1440**; Edmund Burke, British statesman, **1797**; Gilbert Stuart, US painter, **1828**; Zachary Taylor, 12th US president, **1850**; King Camp Gilette, US safety-razor inventor, **1932**; Randall Thompson, US composer, **1984**.

NOTES

_____

_____

_____

_____

July 10

"It is seldom indeed that one parts on good terms, because if one were on good terms one would not part."
—MARCEL PROUST, Remembrance of Things Past

EVENTS

1553 Following the death of Edward VI, Lady Jane Grey was proclaimed queen of England. **1890** Wyoming became the 44th state. **1900** The Paris subway, the Metro, was opened. **1962** The US launched its first communications satellite, *Telstar*, which would inaugurate live television between America and Europe. **1976** Seveso, in northern Italy, was covered by a cloud of toxic weedkiller leaked from a chemical factory. **1985** The Greenpeace campaign ship *Rainbow Warrior* sank in Auckland, New Zealand, after two explosions tore its hull.

BIRTHS

John Calvin, French religious reformer, **1509**; Camille Pissarro, French painter, **1830**; James McNeill Whistler, US painter, **1834**; Marcel Proust, French author, **1871**; Jimmy McHugh, US songwriter, **1894**; Carl Orff, German composer, **1895**; David Brinkley, US TV newsman, **1920**; Arthur Ashe, US tennis player, **1943**; Arlo Guthrie, US folk singer, **1947**.

DEATHS

Hadrian, Roman emperor, **138**; El Cid, Spanish hero, **1099**; Louis Jacques Mandé Daguerre, French photographic pioneer, **1851**; Karl Richard Lepsius, German Egyptologist, **1884**; "Jelly Roll" Morton, US ragtime pianist and composer, **1941**; Giorgio de Chirico, Italian painter, **1978**; Masuji Ibuse, Japanese writer, **1993**.

NOTES

July 11

*"Freedom is a bourgeois notion devised as a cloak
for the specter of economic slavery."*
—V.I. LENIN, *reported on July 11, 1920*

The national day of Mongolia.

EVENTS

1804 US Vice President Aaron Burr shot his political rival Alexander Hamilton, former secretary of the treasury, in a duel in Weehawken, New Jersey; Hamilton died the following day. **1975** Excavations at the tomb of Emperor Qin Shi Huangdi, near the ancient Chinese capital of Xi'an, uncovered an army of 8,000 life-size terracotta warriors dating to about 206 BC. **1979** America's *Skylab I* returned to earth after 34,981 orbits and six years in space.

BIRTHS

Robert (the Bruce), king of Scotland, **1274**; Frederick I, king of Prussia, **1657**; John Quincy Adams, 6th US president, **1767**; Yul Brynner, US film actor, **1915**; Tab Hunter, US film actor, **1931**; Leon Spinks, US heavyweight champion, **1953**.

DEATHS

Alfred Dreyfus, French soldier, **1935**; George Gershwin, US composer, **1937**; Paul Nash, English painter, **1946**; Buddy DeSylva, US lyricist and film director, **1950**; Laurence Olivier, English actor and director, **1989**.

NOTES

July 12

"Most people would sooner die than think: in fact they do so."
—BERTRAND RUSSELL, *reported on July 12, 1925*

Orangeman's Day in Northern Ireland.

EVENTS

1543 Henry VIII married Catherine Parr, his sixth and last wife. **1794** British Admiral Horatio Nelson lost his right eye at the siege of Calvi, in Corsica. **1878** Cyprus was ceded to British administration by Turkey. **1920** US President Woodrow Wilson opened the Panama Canal. **1970** Thor Heyerdahl and his crew crossed the Atlantic in 57 days, in a papyrus boat.

BIRTHS

Gaius Julius Caesar, Roman general and dictator, **100 BC**; Henry Thoreau, US author, **1817**; George Eastman, US photographic pioneer, **1854**; Amadeo Modigliani, Italian painter and sculptor, **1884**; Oscar Hammerstein II, US lyricist who teamed with Richard Rodgers, **1895**; Milton Berle, US comedian, **1908**; Van Cliburn, US pianist, **1934**; Bill Cosby, US comedian and actor, **1937**.

DEATHS

Desiderius Erasmus, Dutch scholar, **1536**; Charles Stewart Rolls, British engineer and aviator, **1910**; Mazo de la Roche, Canadian novelist, **1961**.

NOTES

July 13

"I have done my task, let others do theirs."
—CHARLOTTE CORDAY, *on being interrogated*
for the murder of Jean-Paul Marat

EVENTS

1793 Jean-Paul Marat, French revolutionary leader, was stabbed to death in his bath by Charlotte Corday. **1837** Queen Victoria became the first sovereign to move into the newly constructed Buckingham Palace. **1863** Four days of draft riots began in New York City; some 1,000 were killed or wounded. **1878** The Treaty of Berlin was signed, granting Bosnia-Herzegovina to Austria-Hungary and securing the independence of Romania, Serbia, and Montenegro from Turkey. **1930** The soccer World Cup was first held in Uruguay; the hosts beat the 13 other competing countries. **1985** Two simultaneous "Live Aid" concerts, one in London and one in Philadelphia, raised over $75 million for famine victims in Africa. **1995** The US announced the closure of 79 military bases.

BIRTHS

David Storey, English novelist and dramatist, **1933**; Harrison Ford, US film actor, **1942**.

DEATHS

Richard Cromwell, lord protector of England, **1712**; John Charles Frémont, US explorer, **1890**; Arnold Schoenberg, Austrian composer, **1951**; Seretse Khama, Botswanan politician, **1980**.

NOTES

July 14

"Our constitution works. Our great republic is a government of laws, not of men."
—GERALD FORD

The national days of France (Bastille Day) and of Iraq.

EVENTS

1789 The Bastille was stormed by the citizens of Paris and razed to the ground as the French Revolution began. **1823** During a visit to Britain, King Kamehameha II of Hawaii and his queen died of measles. **1867** Alfred Nobel demonstrated dynamite for the first time. **1881** US outlaw William "Billy the Kid" Bonney was fatally shot by Sheriff Pat Garrett, his former friend. **1958** In a military coup led by General Kassem, King Faisal of Iraq was assassinated and a republic proclaimed. **1959** The USS *Long Beach*, the first nuclear warship, was launched. **1989** Over 300,000 Siberian coalminers went on strike, for better pay and conditions.

BIRTHS

Emmeline Pankhurst, English suffragist, **1858**; Isaac Bashevis Singer, Polish-born US author, **1904**; Woody Guthrie, US folk singer, **1912**; Gerald Ford, 38th US president, **1913**; Ingmar Bergman, Swedish film director, **1918**; John Chancellor, US TV anchorman, **1927**.

DEATHS

Alfred Krupp, German industrialist, **1887**; Paul Kruger, Boer leader, **1904**; Grock, Swiss clown, **1959**; Adlai Stevenson, US statesman, **1965**.

NOTES

July 15

"A diplomat is a man who can make his guests feel at home when he wishes they were at home."
—WALTER GIFFORD, *reported on July 15, 1951*

EVENTS

1099 Jerusalem was captured by the Crusaders. **1795** The "Marseillaise," written by Rouget de Lisle in 1792, was officially adopted as the French national anthem. **1869** Margarine was patented by Hippolyte Mège-Mouriès in Paris. **1965** The US space probe *Mariner* transmitted the first close-up pictures of Mars. **1990** In an ongoing campaign of violence, separatist Tamil Tigers massacred 168 Muslims in Colombo, the Sri Lankan capital.

BIRTHS

Inigo Jones, English architect, **1573**; Rembrandt (van Rijn), Dutch painter, **1606**; Iris Murdoch, Irish novelist, **1919**; Linda Ronstadt, US singer, **1946**.

DEATHS

General Tom Thumb, US circus midget, **1883**; Anton Chekhov, Russian dramatist and short-story writer, **1904**; Hugo von Hofmannsthal, Austrian dramatist and poet, **1929**; John Pershing, US general in World War I, **1948**; Paul William Gallico, US writer, **1976**.

NOTES

July 16

"You'd be surprised how much it costs to look this cheap."
—DOLLY PARTON

EVENTS

622 Traditionally, the beginning of the Islamic Era, when Mohammed began his flight (the Hejira) from Mecca to Medina. **1782** Mozart's opera *The Abduction from the Seraglio* was first performed, in Vienna. **1790** Site of the District of Columbia was established for US capital. **1918** The last czar of Russia, Nicholas II, along with his family, doctor, servants, and even the pet dog, was murdered by Bolsheviks at Ekaterinburg. **1945** The first atomic bomb developed by Robert Oppenheimer and his team at Los Alamos was exploded in New Mexico. **1965** The Mont Blanc road tunnel, linking France with Italy, was opened. **1990** An earthquake struck the main Philippine island of Luzon, killing over 1,500 people.

BIRTHS

Andrea del Sarto, Italian painter, 1486; Joshua Reynolds, English painter, 1723; Mary Baker Eddy, US founder of the Christian Science Church, 1821; Roald Amundsen, Norwegian polar explorer, 1872; Barbara Stanwyck, US film actress, 1907; Ginger Rogers, US film actress and dancer, 1911.

DEATHS

Anne of Cleves, fourth wife of Henry VIII of England, 1557; Josiah Spode, English potter, 1827; John Phillips Marquand, US writer, 1960; Herbert von Karajan, Austrian conductor, 1989.

NOTES

July 17

*"Cleaning your house while your kids are still growing
is like shoveling the walk before it stops snowing."*
—PHYLLIS DILLER

EVENTS

1453 With the defeat of the English at the Battle of Castillon, the Hundred Years' War between France and England came to an end. **1917** The British royal family changed their name from "House of Saxe-Coburg-Gotha" to "House of Windsor." **1945** The Potsdam Conference of Allied leaders Truman, Stalin, and Churchill (later replaced by Attlee) began. **1975** The US *Apollo* spacecraft and the Russian *Soyuz* craft successfully docked while in orbit. **1981** The Humber Estuary Bridge in northeast England, the world's longest single-span structure, was officially opened. **1990** Iraqi President Saddam Hussein threatened to use force against Kuwait and the United Arab Emirates, to stop their driving oil prices down by overproduction.

BIRTHS

Erle Stanley Gardner, US mystery writer, **1889**; James Cagney, US film actor, **1899**; Art Linkletter, Canadian-born US TV host, **1912**; Phyllis Diller, US comedienne, **1917**; Donald Sutherland, Canadian-born Hollywood actor, **1934**.

DEATHS

Charlotte Corday, murderess of Marat, executed, **1793**; James McNeill Whistler, US painter, **1903**; Dragolub Mihajlovic, Serbian nationalist, executed, **1946**; Billie Holiday, US jazz singer, **1959**.

NOTES

_____

_____

_____

_____

July 18

"It is a truth universally acknowledged, that a single man in possession of a good fortune, must be in want of a wife."
—JANE AUSTEN, Pride and Prejudice

The national day of Spain.

EVENTS

64 The great fire began in Rome and lasted for nine days. **1870** The Vatican Council proclaimed the dogma of papal infallibility in matters of faith and morals. **1923** Under the Matrimonial Causes Bill, British women were given equal divorce rights with men. **1925** *Mein Kampf*, Hitler's political testament, was published. **1936** The Spanish Civil War began with an army revolt led by Francisco Franco against the republican government. **1955** Disneyland, the 160-acre amusement park, opened near Anaheim, California.

BIRTHS

W.M. Thackeray, English novelist and poet, **1811**; Red Skelton, US comedian, **1913**; Nelson Mandela, South African politician, **1918**; John Glenn, US astronaut and Ohio senator, **1921**; Richard Branson, British entrepreneur, **1950**; Nick Faldo, English golfer, **1957**.

DEATHS

Michelangelo Merisi da Caravaggio, Italian painter, **1610**; Antoine Watteau, French painter, **1721**; Peter III, czar of Russia, murdered, **1762**; Jane Austen, English novelist, **1817**; Jean Negulesco, Romanian-born US film director, **1993**.

NOTES

_____

_____

_____

_____

July 19

*"I don't want to achieve immortality through my work ...
I want to achieve it through not dying."*
—WOODY ALLEN

EVENTS

1545 The *Mary Rose*, the pride of Henry VIII's battle fleet, sank in the Solent with the loss of 700 lives. (The ship was raised October 11, 1982, and is now on display in Portsmouth, England.) **1848** At a convention in Seneca Falls, New York, female rights campaigner Amelia Bloomer introduced "bloomers" to the world. **1903** The first Tour de France cycle race was won by Maurice Garin. **1949** Laos gained independence. **1991** A political scandal erupted in South Africa after the government admitted that it had made secret payments to the Zulu-based Inkatha Freedom party. **1993** President Clinton announced that homosexuals could serve in the US military, though restrictions were imposed.

BIRTHS

Samuel Colt, US firearm inventor, **1814**; Edgar Degas, French painter, **1834**; Lizzie Borden, alleged US ax murderess, **1860**; Charles Horace Mayo, US physician, **1865**; A.J. Cronin, Scottish novelist, **1896**; George McGovern, Democratic presidental candidate, **1922**; Ilie Nastase, Romanian tennis player, **1946**.

DEATHS

Petrarch, Italian poet, **1374**; Syngman Rhee, South Korean politician, **1965**; Clarence White, US pop guitarist, **1973**; Szymon Goldberg, Polish-born violinist and conductor, **1993**.

NOTES

July 20

"That's one small step for man, one giant leap for mankind."
—NEIL ARMSTRONG, *reported on July 20, 1969*

The national day of Colombia.

EVENTS

1845 Charles Sturt became the first European to enter Simpson's Desert in central Australia. **1940** In the US, *Billboard* published the first singles-record charts. **1944** German staff officer Colonel von Stauffenberg attempted to assassinate Hitler, in Rastenburg, Germany. **1969** The US lunar module *Eagle* of the Apollo 11 space mission landed on the Moon, and astronaut Neil Armstrong was the first man to set foot on the surface, followed by Edwin "Buzz" Aldrin. **1975** After an 11-month journey, the US unmanned *Viking 1* made a soft landing on Mars. **1993** Vincent Foster, deputy White House counsel, was found shot to death in a Virginia park, an apparent suicide.

BIRTHS

Petrarch, Italian poet, **1304**; Alberto Santos-Dumont, Brazilian aviator, **1873**; John Reith, Scottish engineer and first director general of the BBC, **1889**; Edmund Hillary, New Zealand mountaineer, **1919**; Jacques Delors, French politician, **1925**; Diana Rigg, English actress, **1938**.

DEATHS

Pope Leo XIII, **1903**; Guglielmo Marconi, Italian inventor, **1937**; Ian Macleod, British statesman, **1970**; Bruce Lee, US martial-arts film actor, **1973**.

NOTES

July 21

"Grace under pressure."
—ERNEST HEMINGWAY, *defining "guts" in* The New Yorker

The national day of Belgium.

EVENTS

1798 The Battle of the Pyramids took place, in which Napoleon defeated an army of some 60,000 Mamelukes. **1861** The Confederates defeated the Union troops in the first Battle of Bull Run (also called the Battle of Manassas) at Manassas, Virginia; Confederate General Thomas Jonathan Jackson earned the name "Stonewall" for holding his brigade's position. **1944** Guam was retaken by US Marines. **1960** Sirimavo Bandaranaike replaced her murdered husband as prime minister of Sri Lanka, becoming the first woman to hold this office. **1976** American Legion members began a four-day convention in Philadelphia; 29 died from a mysterious sickness later labeled "legionnaire's disease." **1990** Over 150,000 people attended "The Wall," a rock concert in East Berlin to celebrate the dismantling of the Berlin Wall.

BIRTHS

Paul Julius von Reuter, German news agency founder, **1816**; Ernest Hemingway, US novelist, **1899**; Kay Starr, US singer, **1922**; Norman Jewison, Canadian film director, **1926**; Cat Stevens, English rock singer and songwriter, **1948**.

DEATHS

Robert Burns, Scottish poet, **1796**; Albert Luthuli, South African politician, **1967**; Basil Rathbone, British-born Hollywood actor, **1967**.

NOTES

_____

_____

_____

_____

July 22

The national day of Poland.

EVENTS

1812 The duke of Wellington defeated the French in the Battle of Salamanca, in Spain. **1847** Brigham Young led the Mormons into the Valley of the Great Salt Lake. **1933** American pioneer aviator Wiley Post completed the first around-the-world solo airplane flight; the journey took 7 days, 18 hrs, and 49.5 min. **1934** US bank robber and "public enemy no. 1," John Dillinger, was gunned down by an FBI squad in Chicago. **1946** Bread rationing started in Britain.

BIRTHS

Philip I, king of Spain, **1478**; Gregor Mendel, Austrian monk and botanist, **1822**; Selman Abraham Waksman, US biochemist, **1888**; Alexander Calder, US sculptor, **1898**; Terence Stamp, British actor, **1938**.

DEATHS

Marie François Xavier Bichat, French anatomist, **1802**; Florenz Ziegfeld, US theatrical producer, **1932**; Mackenzie King, Canadian statesman, **1950**; Carl Sandburg, US poet and biographer of Abraham Lincoln, **1967**.

NOTES

July 23

"I know no method to secure the repeal of bad or obnoxious laws so effective as their stringent execution."
—ULYSSES S. GRANT, *inaugural address, March 4, 1869*

The national days of Ethiopia and of the United Arab Republic.

EVENTS

1745 Charles Stuart, the "Young Pretender" to the British throne, landed in the Hebrides. **1952** King Farouk of Egypt was deposed by General Neguib. **1967** An eight-day riot by blacks began in Detroit, eventually causing 40 deaths with some 2,000 injured; the violence was suppressed by 4,700 paratroopers and 8,000 National Guardsmen. **1986** Prince Andrew married Lady Sarah Ferguson in Westminster Abbey and was created duke of York.

BIRTHS

Raymond Chandler, US detective writer who created private eye Philip Marlowe, **1888**; Haile Selassie, Ethiopian emperor, **1892**; Gloria DeHaven, US film actress, **1925**.

DEATHS

Domenico Scarlatti, Italian composer, **1757**; Isaac Singer, US inventor, **1875**; Ulysses S. Grant, general and 18th US president, **1885**; D.W. Griffith, US film director, **1948**; Montgomery Clift, US film actor, **1966**; Eddie Rickenbacker, US World War I fighter pilot, **1973**; Raul Gardini, Italian businessman, **1993**.

NOTES

July 24

"Failure must be but a challenge to others."
—AMELIA EARHART

EVENTS

1534 Jacques Cartier landed at Gaspé in Canada and claimed the territory for France. **1704** British Admiral Sir George Rooke captured Gibraltar from the Spaniards. **1824** The result of the world's first public opinion poll, on voters' intentions in the 1824 US presidential election, was published in the *Harrisburg Pennsylvanian*. **1925** John T. Scopes, a high school science teacher in Dayton, Tennessee, was found guilty of teaching evolution in violation of state law and fined $100. **1925** A six-year-old girl became the first patient to be successfully treated with insulin, at Guy's Hospital, London.

BIRTHS

Simón Bolívar, South American liberator, **1783**; Alexandre Dumas *père*, French author, **1802**; Frank Wedekind, German dramatist, **1864**; Amelia Earhart, US aviator, **1898**; Lynda Carter, US actress and singer, **1951**.

DEATHS

Martin van Buren, 8th US president, **1862**; Sacha Guitry, French actor and dramatist, **1957**; Constance Bennett, US film actress, **1965**; James Chadwick, English physicist, discoverer of the neutron, **1974**; Peter Sellers, English comic film actor, **1980**.

NOTES

July 25

EVENTS

1139 Alfonso I of Portugal defeated the Moors at Ourique. **1581** A confederation of the northern provinces of the Netherlands proclaimed their independence from Spain. **1909** French aviator Louis Blériot made the first Channel crossing in an airplane, which he had designed. **1917** Margaretha Zelle, the Dutch spy known as Mata Hari, was sentenced to death. **1943** Benito Mussolini was forced to resign as dictator of Italy, bringing an end to the Fascist regime. **1948** Bread rationing in Britain ended. **1952** The European Coal and Steel Community, established by the Treaty of Paris in 1951, was ratified. **1978** The first test-tube baby in Britain was born.

BIRTHS

Arthur James Balfour, British statesman, **1848**; Walter Brennan, US film actor, **1894**; Johnny "Rabbit" Hodges, US jazz saxophonist, **1907**; Steve Goodman, US songwriter, **1948**.

DEATHS

Constantine I (the Great), Roman emperor, **337**; Samuel Taylor Coleridge, English poet, **1834**; Engelbert Dolfuss, Austrian statesman, **1934**.

NOTES

July 26

---

*"When a stupid man is doing something he is ashamed of,
he always declares that it is his duty."*
—GEORGE BERNARD SHAW

The national day of Liberia.

EVENTS

1788 New York became the 11th state. **1847** Liberia became the first African colony to secure independence. **1908** The Federal Bureau of Investigation (FBI) was founded. **1956** President Nasser of Egypt nationalized the Suez Canal, leading to confrontation with Britain, France, and Israel.

BIRTHS

George Bernard Shaw, Irish dramatist, **1856**; Serge Koussevitsky, Russian-born US conductor, **1874**; Carl Jung, Swiss psychologist, **1875**; Aldous Huxley, English novelist, **1894**; Blake Edwards, US film director and screenwriter, **1922**; Jason Robards, Jr., US actor, **1922**; Stanley Kubrick, US film director, **1928**; Mick Jagger, British rock singer, **1943**; Vitas Gerulaitis, US tennis player, **1954**.

DEATHS

Sam Houston, US general and president of the Republic of Texas, **1863**; Eva Perón, Argentinian political figure, **1952**; Averell Harriman, US diplomat and chief negotiator for the Vietnam peace talks, **1986**.

NOTES

July 27

EVENTS

1694 The Bank of England was founded by act of Parliament. **1866** The *Great Eastern* arrived at Heart's Content in Newfoundland, having successfully laid the transatlantic telegraph cable. **1942** The Battle of El Alamein ended after 17 days, with the British having prevented the German and Italian advance into Egypt. **1953** The Korean armistice was signed at Panmujom, ending three years of war. **1985** Ugandan President Milton Obote was overthrown for a second time, this time by Brigadier Tito Okello.

BIRTHS

Alexandre Dumas *fils*, French dramatist, **1824**; Hilaire Belloc, English poet and author, **1870**; Norman Lear, US TV producer, **1922**; Bobbie Gentry, US singer, **1942**.

DEATHS

John Dalton, English physicist and chemist, **1844**; William Matthew Flinders Petrie, English Egyptologist, **1942**; Gertude Stein, US novelist and poet, **1946**; Mohammad Reza Pahlavi, shah of Iran, **1980**; James Mason, English actor, **1984**.

NOTES

July 28

The national day of Peru.

EVENTS

1794 Maximilien Robespierre and 19 other French revolutionaries went to the guillotine. **1821** San Martin and his forces liberated Peru and proclaimed its independence from Spain. **1868** The 14th Amendment to the US Constitution, concerning equal rights, was ratified. **1914** Austria-Hungary declared war on Serbia, beginning World War I. **1915** US troops invaded Haiti to end political violence and stayed until 1934. **1976** The Tian Shan area of China was struck by an earthquake which caused over 800,000 deaths.

BIRTHS

Beatrix Potter, English author and illustrator who created Peter Rabbit, **1866**; Marcel Duchamp, French painter, **1887**; Rudy Vallee, US singer, **1901**; Jacqueline Onassis, the widow of President Kennedy and of Greek millionaire Aristotle Onassis, **1929**; Riccardo Muti, Italian conductor, **1941**.

DEATHS

Thomas Cromwell, chancellor to Henry VIII of England, executed, **1540**; Cyrano de Bergerac, French poet and soldier, **1655**; Antonio Vivaldi, Italian composer, **1741**; Johann Sebastian Bach, German composer, **1750**; Nathan Mayer Rothschild, British banker, **1836**; Otto Hahn, German nuclear physicist, **1944.**

NOTES

July 29

"I have 14 other grandchildren and if I pay one penny now,
then I'll have 14 kidnapped grandchildren."
—J. PAUL GETTY, *reported on July 29, 1973*

EVENTS

1588 The Spanish Armada was defeated by the English fleet under Howard and Drake, off Plymouth. **1900** King Umberto I of Italy was assassinated by an anarchist and succeeded by Victor Emmanuel. **1948** The 14th Olympic Games opened in London, the first in 12 years due to World War II. **1968** Pope Paul VI reaffirmed the Church's traditional teaching on (and condemnation of) birth control. **1981** The Prince of Wales married Lady Diana Spencer at London's St. Paul's Cathedral; the televised ceremony was watched by over 700 million viewers around the world.

BIRTHS

Alexis de Tocqueville, French historian and politician, **1805**; Booth Tarkington, US author, **1869**; Benito Mussolini, Italian Fascist leader, **1883**; Sigmund Romberg, Hungarian-born US composer, **1887**; Dag Hammarskjöld, Swedish UN secretary-general, **1905**; Mikis Theodorakis, Greek composer, **1925**.

DEATHS

Robert Schumann, German composer, **1833**; Vincent van Gogh, Dutch painter, **1890**; John Barbirolli, English conductor, **1970**; Raymond Massey, Canadian actor, **1983**; David Niven, Scottish-born US film actor, **1983**; Luis Buñuel, Spanish film director, **1983**.

NOTES

July 30

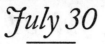

"History is bunk."
—HENRY FORD

EVENTS

1619 Colonists at Jamestown, Virginia, established the New World's first representative assembly, the House of Burgesses. **1793** Toronto (known as York until 1834) was founded by General John Simcoe. **1935** Penguin paperback books, founded by Allen Lane, went on sale in Britain. **1963** Kim Philby, British intelligence officer from 1940 and Soviet agent from 1933, fled to the USSR. **1974** The House Judiciary Committee completed its three recommendations of impeachment against President Nixon.

BIRTHS

Giorgio Vasari, Italian painter, architect, and writer, **1511**; Emily Brontë, English novelist, **1818**; Henry Ford, US automobile manufacturer, **1863**; Henry Moore, English sculptor, **1898**; Peter Bogdanovich, US film director, **1939**; Paul Anka, Canadian rock singer and songwriter, **1941**.

DEATHS

William Penn, English Quaker leader who founded Pennsylvania colony, **1718**; Otto von Bismarck, German chancellor, **1898**; Lynn Fontanne, US actress, **1983**; Howard Dietz, US lyricist, **1983**.

NOTES

_____

_____

_____

_____

July 31

*"Sometimes ... when you stand face-to-face with
someone, you cannot see his face."*
—MIKHAIL GORBACHEV, *after the unsuccessful
Icelandic summit meeting with President Reagan, Oct. 12, 1986*

EVENTS

1498 Columbus arrrived at Trinidad on his third voyage. **1919**
The Weimar Republic was established in postwar Germany. **1954**
Mount Godwin-Austin (K2) in the Himalayas was first climbed
by an Italian expedition, led by Ardito Desio. **1971** US astronauts
David Scott and James Irwin entered their Lunar Roving Vehicle
and went for a ride on the Moon. **1991** Presidents Bush and
Gorbachev signed the Strategic Arms Reduction Treaty (START)
in Moscow.

BIRTHS

George Henry Thomas, Union general known as "the Rock of
Chickamauga," **1816**; Milton Friedman, US economist, **1912**; Curt
Gowdy, US sportscaster, **1919**; Geraldine Chaplin, US film
actress, **1944**; Evonne Cawley, Australian tennis player, **1951**;
Wesley Snipes, US film actor, **1963**.

DEATHS

Ignatius of Loyola, Spanish founder of the Jesuits, **1556**; Andrew
Johnson, 17th US president, **1875**; Franz Liszt, Hungarian pianist
and composer, **1886**; Jim Reeves, US country singer, **1964**;
Baudouin I, king of the Belgians, **1993**.

NOTES

August 1

*"The Swiss are not a people so much as a neat,
clean, quite solvent business."*
—WILLIAM FAULKNER, Intruder in the Dust

The national day of Switzerland.

EVENTS

1498 Christopher Columbus reached the American mainland and named it Santa Isla, believing it to be an island. **1774** English chemist Joseph Priestley identified oxygen, which he called "a new species of air." **1876** Colorado became the 38th state. **1903** The first US transcontinental automobile trip ended; the journey from San Francisco to New York City began May 23. **1936** The 11th Olympic Games, the last for 12 years due to World War II, opened in Berlin. **1975** Thirty-five nations, including the US and the USSR, signed the Helsinki Agreement on cooperation in human rights and other global issues.

BIRTHS

Claudius, Roman emperor, **10 BC**; Francis Scott Key, US lawyer who wrote "The Star-Spangled Banner," **1779**; Herman Melville, US novelist, **1819**; Jack Kramer, US tennis champion, **1921**; Dom DeLuise, US comic film actor, **1933**; Yves Saint-Laurent, French couturier, **1936**.

DEATHS

Louis VI, king of France, **1137**; Anne, queen of Britain and Ireland, **1714**; Theodore Roethke, US poet, **1963**; Walter Ulbricht, East German politician, **1973**; Alfred Manessier, French painter, **1993**.

NOTES

_____

_____

_____

_____

August 2

---

*"One of the reasons people cling to their hates so
stubbornly is because they seem to sense once hate is gone
that they will be forced to deal with pain."*
—JAMES BALDWIN, Notes of a Native Son

EVENTS

1858 The rule of the East India Company, which was established
throughout India, was transferred to the British government.
1945 The Potsdam Conference, establishing the initial postwar
treatment of Germany and demanding unconditional Japanese
surrender, ended. **1980** Right-wing terrorists exploded a bomb in
the crowded Bologna railroad station, northern Italy, killing 84
people. **1985** Montgomery Ward announced it was closing its
mail-order business; the Ward catalog (older than Sear's) was to
be discontinued after 113 years of publication. **1990** Iraq invaded
and annexed Kuwait, precipitating an international crisis.

BIRTHS

John Tyndall, Irish physicist, **1820**; Arthur Bliss, English composer, **1891**; Myrna Loy, US film actress, **1905**; James Baldwin, US
writer, **1924**; Peter O'Toole, Irish actor, **1932**.

DEATHS

Thomas Gainsborough, English painter, **1788**; Enrico Caruso,
Italian operatic tenor, **1921**; Warren G. Harding, 29th US presi-
dent, **1923**; Louis Blériot, French aviator, **1936**; Fritz Lang,
Austrian-born Hollywood film director, **1976**; Carlos Chavez,
Mexican composer, **1978**.

NOTES

August 3

*"If I should die, think only this of me: that there's
some corner of a foreign field that is for ever England."*
—RUPERT BROOKE, *"The Soldier"*

EVENTS

1492 Christopher Columbus left Spain, on his first voyage of discovery. **1778** La Scala opera house opened in Milan, Italy. **1858** Lake Victoria, the source of the Nile, was discovered by the English explorer John Speke. **1904** Members of a British expedition became the first Westerners to enter the "Forbidden City" of Lhasa, Tibet. **1914** Germany declared war on France. **1914** The first ships passed through the completed Panama Canal. **1940** Latvia was incorporated into the USSR as a constituent republic. **1958** The USS *Nautilus*, the first nuclear submarine, passed under the North Pole. **1981** Some 13,000 federal air-traffic controllers began an illegal strike for more pay; President Reagan fired most of them on August 5.

BIRTHS

Joseph Paxton, English architect, **1801**; Stanley Baldwin, British prime minister, **1867**; Rupert Brooke, English poet, **1887**; Tony Bennett, US singer, **1926**; Martin Sheen, US actor, **1940**; Osvaldo Ardiles, Argentinian soccer player, **1953**.

DEATHS

James II, king of Scotland, **1460**; Richard Arkwright, English inventor, **1792**; Joseph Conrad, Polish-born British novelist, **1924**; Colette, French novelist, **1954**; Lenny Bruce, US comedian, **1966**.

NOTES

_____

_____

_____

_____

August 4

"If the state is strong, it crushes us. If it is weak, we perish."
—PAUL VALÉRY

EVENTS

1265 During the Barons' War in England, the Battle of Evesham took place, in which Simon de Montfort was defeated by Royalist forces led by the future King Edward I. **1578** The Portuguese were defeated by the Berbers at the Battle of Alcazarquivir. **1914** Britain declared war on Germany after the Germans had violated the Treaty of London, and World War I began. **1917** The US bought the Virgin Islands from Denmark for $25 million. **1918** The Second Battle of the Marne ended. **1940** Italy invaded Kenya, the Sudan, and British Somaliland. **1966** In a US radio interview, John Lennon claimed that the Beatles were probably more popular than Jesus Christ; Beatles records were consequently banned in many US states and in South Africa. **1977** The US Energy Department was established.

BIRTHS

Percy Bysshe Shelley, English poet, **1792**; Knut Hamsun, Norwegian novelist, **1859**; Queen Elizabeth, the Queen Mother, **1900**.

DEATHS

Henry I, king of France, **1060**; Hans Christian Andersen, Danish fairy tale writer, **1875**; James Cruze, US film director, **1942**.

NOTES

_____

_____

_____

_____

August 5

---

*"I cannot and will not give my undertaking at a time when I,
and you, the people, are not free. Your freedom and mine
cannot be separated."*
—NELSON MANDELA, *message read by his daughter
to a rally in Soweto, Feb. 10, 1985*

EVENTS

1858 The first transatlantic cable service was opened when Queen Victoria exchanged greetings with President Buchanan. **1864** The Battle of Mobile Bay was a Union naval success in the Civil War. **1891** The first American Express traveler's check was cashed. **1924** The Turkish government abolished polygamy. **1962** ANC leader Nelson Mandela was arrested and given a life sentence on charges of attempting to overthrow the South African government. **1963** The Test Ban Agreement was signed by the US, the USSR, and the UK, contracting to test nuclear weapons only underground.

BIRTHS

Niels Henrik Abel, Norwegian mathematician, **1802**; Guy de Maupassant, French author, **1850**; John Huston, US film director, **1906**; Neil Armstrong, US astronaut, **1930**; Bob Geldof, Irish musician, **1951**.

DEATHS

Frederick North, British prime minister during the American Revolution, **1792**; Friedrich Engels, German political writer, **1895**; Marilyn Monroe, US film actress, **1962**; Richard Burton, Welsh actor, **1984**; Eugen Suchon, Slovakian composer, **1993**.

NOTES

August 6

"I am become death, the destroyer of worlds."
—ROBERT J. OPPENHEIMER, *US nuclear physicist
who developed the atomic bomb, quoting Vishnu*

The national day of Bolivia.

EVENTS

1890 William Kemmler, a murderer, became the first to be executed in the electric chair, in Auburn Prison, Auburn, New York. **1926** US swimmer Gertrude Ederle became the first woman to swim the English Channel, in 14 hr., 34 min. **1934** US troops left Haiti after 19 years of occupation. **1945** An atomic bomb was dropped on the Japanese city of Hiroshima from a US Boeing B29 bomber. **1962** Jamaica became independent after being a British colony for 300 years. **1988** Russian ballerina Natalia Makarova danced again with the Kirov Ballet in London, 18 years after she had defected to the West. **1994** Fourteen firefighters were killed battling a forest fire near Glenwood Springs, Colorado.

BIRTHS

Daniel O'Connell, Irish politician, **1775**; Alfred, Lord Tennyson, English poet, **1809**; Paul Claudel, French poet, **1868**; Alexander Fleming, Scottish bacteriologist who discovered penicillin, **1881**; Robert Mitchum, US film actor, **1917**.

DEATHS

Anne Hathaway, wife of William Shakespeare, **1623**; Diego Velázquez, Spanish painter, **1660**; Fulgencio Batista y Zaldivar, Cuban dictator, **1973**; Pope Paul VI, **1978**.

NOTES

August 7

"The funniest line in English is 'Get it?'
When you say that, everyone chortles."
—GARRISON KEILLOR, We Are Still Married

EVENTS

1830 Louis Philippe was proclaimed French "Citizen King" (Philippe Egalité), for his support of the 1792 Revolution. **1858** Ottawa became the capital of the Dominion of Canada. **1942** Guadalcanal, in the southern Solomon Islands, was assaulted by the US Marines in one of the most costly campaigns of World War II. **1960** The Ivory Coast (Côte d'Ivoire) achieved independence from France. **1990** President Bush sent US forces to Saudi Arabia to prevent Iraqi invasion.

BIRTHS

Mata Hari (Margaretha Geertruida Zelle), Dutch courtesan, dancer, and probable spy, **1876**; Louis Leakey, British archeologist, **1903**; Ralph Bunche, US diplomat and the first black to head a Department of State division, **1904**; Garrison Keillor, US humorist, **1942**.

DEATHS

Robert Blake, British admiral, **1657**; Bix Beiderbecke, US jazz musician and composer, **1931**; Konstantin Stanislavsky, Russian theater director, **1938**; Rabindranath Tagore, Indian writer, **1941**; Oliver Hardy, US film comedian, **1957**.

NOTES

August 8

"When the President does it, that means that it is not illegal."
—RICHARD NIXON, *in David Frost's* I Gave Them a Sword

EVENTS

117 Hadrian became emperor of Rome following the death of his father, Trajan. **1786** Mont Blanc, Europe's tallest peak, was climbed for the first time; Swiss scientist Horace Saussure had offered a prize for the accomplishment of this feat. **1940** The Battle of Britain, which would continue into the following October, began. **1945** The USSR declared war on Germany. **1963** England's "Great Train Robbery," in which over £2.5 million (over $3.5 million) was stolen, took place near Bletchley, Buckinghamshire. **1974** Richard Nixon became the first US president to resign from office in face of threats to impeach him for his implication in the Watergate scandal. **1988** The luckiest day of the decade, according to the Chinese, because the date 8.8.88 is a palindrome.

BIRTHS

Godfrey Kneller, German painter, **1646**; Ernest O. Lawrence, US physicist, **1901**; Dino De Laurentis, Italian film producer, **1919**; Esther Williams, US swimmer and film actress, **1923**; Dustin Hoffman, US actor, **1937**; Connie Stevens, US actress and singer, **1938**; Nigel Mansell, British racing driver, **1953**.

DEATHS

Girolamo Fracastoro, Italian physician and writer, **1553**; James Tissot, French painter, **1902**; Frank Winfield Woolworth, founder of the "five-and-dime" stores, **1919**; James Gould Cozzens, US novelist, **1978**; Louise Brooks, US actress, **1985**.

NOTES

August 9

"There's that famous saying about whores and ugly buildings: If you stay around long enough, eventually you get respectable."
—JERRY GARCIA, *on The Grateful Dead band.*

EVENTS

1842 The US-Canadian border was defined for Maine and Minnesota by the Webster-Ashburton treaty, signed by the US and Britain. **1912** An earthquake struck Turkey, in the area of Istanbul, killing 6,000 people and rendering 40,000 homeless. **1945** The second atomic bomb of World War II was dropped on the Japanese city of Nagasaki. **1965** Singapore gained independence from Britain. **1974** Gerald Ford was sworn in as the 38th president, succeeding Richard Nixon. **1989** President Bush signed a bill to rescue the savings and loan industry at the cost of $400 billion over 30 years.

BIRTHS

Izaak Walton, English author, **1593**; Thomas Telford, Scottish civil engineer, **1757**; Léonide Massine, Russian dancer and choreographer, **1869**; Leonid Nikolayevich Andreyev, Russian author, **1871**; Philip Larkin, English poet, **1922**; Rod Laver, Australian tennis player, **1938**; Melanie Griffith, US film actress, **1957**.

DEATHS

Maarten Harpertszoon Tromp, Dutch admiral, **1653**; Ruggiero Leoncavallo, Italian composer, **1919**; Hermann Hesse, German author, **1962**; Joe Orton, English playwright, **1967**; Dmitri Shostakovich, Russian composer, **1975**; Jerry Garcia, US rock musician, **1995**.

NOTES

August 10

The national day of Ecuador.

EVENTS

1787 Wolfgang Amadeus Mozart completed his popular *Eine Kleine Nachtmusik.* **1821** Missouri became the 24th state. **1846** The Smithsonian Institution was established in Washington, DC, to foster scientific research. **1889** The screw bottletop was patented **1904** In the Russo-Japanese War, Japan inflicted heavy losses on the Russian fleet at the Battle of the Yellow Sea, off Port Arthur **1966** *Orbiter I,* the first US lunar satellite, was launched. **1989** US Army General Colin Powell became the first black to be chairman of the Joint Chiefs of Staff. **1993** President Clinton signed a bill to reduce the federal budget deficit by $496 billion over five years.

BIRTHS

Camillo Benso, Count Cavour, Italian nationalist politician, **1810**; Herbert Hoover, 31st US president, **1874**; Rhonda Fleming, US film actress, **1923**; Eddie Fisher, US singer, **1928**.

DEATHS

Allan Ramsay, Scottish portrait painter, **1784**; Otto Lillienthal, German aviator, **1896**.

NOTES

_____

_____

_____

_____

August 11

"Abstract painting is abstract. It confronts you. There was a reviewer a while back who wrote that my pictures didn't have any beginning or any end. He didn't mean it as a compliment, but it was. It was a fine compliment."
—JACKSON POLLOCK

EVENTS

1576 English navigator Martin Frobisher, on his search for the Northwest Passage, entered the bay in Canada now named for him. **1810** Severe earthquakes struck the Azores, causing the village of São Miguel to sink. **1877** Phobos and Deimos, the satellites, or "moons," of Mars were discovered by US astronomer Asaph Hall. **1941** President Franklin Roosevelt and Prime Minister Winston Churchill signed the Atlantic Charter. **1964** Congress passed the War on Poverty bill. **1994** US major league baseball players went on strike over salary caps, and the season and World Series were canceled.

BIRTHS

Jean Victor Marie Moreau, French general, **1772**; Hugh MacDiarmid, Scottish poet, **1892**; Arlene Dahl, US film actress, **1928**; Jerry Falwell, US TV evangelist, **1933**.

DEATHS

Hans Memling, Flemish painter, **1495**; John Henry Newman, English Roman Catholic theologian and cardinal, **1890**; Andrew Carnegie, Scottish-born US industrialist and philanthropist, **1919**; Jackson Pollock, US painter, **1956**.

NOTES

August 12

"What I have crossed out I didn't like. What I haven't crossed out I'm dissatisfied with."
—CECIL B. DE MILLE, *attributed remark on a script*

EVENTS

1851 The US schooner *America* won a race around the Isle of Wight, giving rise to the later America's Cup trophy. **1883** The quagga in Amsterdam Zoo died, the last of this species in the world. **1898** The US annexed the republic of Hawaii. **1898** Spain and the US concluded an armistice over Cuba and other possessions. **1944** PLUTO ("pipe line under the ocean") began operating beneath the English Channel, supplying gasoline to Allied forces in France. **1969** The world's first communications satellite was launched—*America's Echo*. **1970** The US Postal Service became independent of the government.

BIRTHS

George IV, king of Britain, **1762**; Robert Southey, English poet, **1774**; Cecil B. De Mille, US film director and producer, **1881**; Buck Owens, US country singer, **1929**; George Hamilton, US film actor, **1939**.

DEATHS

Giovanni Gabrieli, Italian composer, **1612**; William Blake, English poet, **1827**; George Stephenson, English engineer, **1848**; Thomas Mann, German novelist, **1955**; Ian Fleming, English novelist who created James Bond, **1964**; Henry Fonda, US film actor, **1982**; John Cage, US composer, **1992**.

NOTES

August 13

"A revolution is not a bed of roses. A revolution is a struggle to the death between the future and the past."
—FIDEL CASTRO, *speech given Jan. 1961
on the second anniversary of the Cuban revolution*

EVENTS

1521 Spanish conquistador Hernándo Cortés recaptured Tenochtitlán (Mexico City) and overthrew the Aztec empire. **1705** The Battle of Blenheim took place in southern Germany, in which the Anglo-Austrian army inflicted a decisive defeat on the French armies. **1868** Earthquakes killed over 25,000 people and destroyed four cities in Peru and Ecuador. **1923** Kemal Atatürk was elected the first president of Turkey. **1961** The border between East and West Berlin was sealed off by East Germany. **1991** Prosecutors announced the discovery of one of the largest bank frauds in Japan's history, involving $2.5 billion in fraudulently obtained loans.

BIRTHS

Annie Oakley (Phoebe Anne Moses), US entertainer and markswoman, **1860**; John Baird, Scottish television pioneer, **1888**; Alfred Hitchcock, English film director, **1899**; Ben Hogan, US golfer, **1912**; Fidel Castro, Cuban leader, **1927**.

DEATHS

René Laënnec, French physician, **1826**; Eugéne Delacroix, French painter, **1863**; Florence Nightingale, English nurse, **1910**; H.G. Wells, English writer, **1946**.

NOTES

August 14

"Damn the torpedoes—full speed ahead."
—ADMIRAL DAVID FARRAGUT, *as his
Union fleet entered Mobile Bay.*

EVENTS

1678 The French repulsed William of Orange at the Battle of Mons in Belgium. **1842** The eight-year US war with the Seminole Indians in Florida ended; they were moved to Oklahoma. **1880** Cologne Cathedral was completed; it had been started in the 13th century. **1893** France became the first country to introduce license plates. **1900** The Boxer Rebellion against European influence in China ended. **1935** Congress passed the Social Security Act. **1945** Japan accepted Allied terms of surrender, ending World War II. **1947** Pakistan became an independent country. **1969** British troops were deployed in Northern Ireland to restore order. **1986** Pakistani politician Benazir Bhutto was arrested by President Zia and detained in prison for 30 days.

BIRTHS

Samuel Wesley, English organist and composer, **1810**; John Galsworthy, English novelist and playwright, **1867**.

DEATHS

David Farragut, Union admiral during the Civil War, **1870**; William Randolph Hearst, US newspaper tycoon, **1951**; Bertolt Brecht, German writer, **1956**; J.B. Priestley, English novelist and playwright, **1984**; Enzo Ferrari, Italian automobile manufacturer, **1988**.

NOTES

_____

_____

_____

_____

August 15

"Not tonight, Josephine."
—NAPOLEON BONAPARTE, *attributed*

EVENTS

1543 The Jesuit order (Society of Jesus) was founded by Ignatius de Loyola in Paris. **1914** The Panama Canal formally opened after 10 years of construction by US engineers. **1935** US humorist Will Rogers and aviation pioneer Wiley Post were killed in an airplane crash in Alaska. **1945** V-J Day, Victory over Japan Day, when Japan surrendered to end World War II (September 2, 1945, when Japan signed the surrender document, is sometimes called V-J Day.) **1948** The republic of South Korea was proclaimed. **1965** The National Guard was called in to quell race riots in Watts, Los Angeles, which left 28 dead and 676 injured. **1969** The Woodstock Music and Arts Fair began on a dairy farm in upstate New York. In the three days it lasted, 400,000 attended, two children were born, and three people died.

BIRTHS

Napoleon Bonaparte, French emperor, **1769**; Sir Walter Scott, Scottish novelist, **1771**; Edna Ferber, US novelist, **1887**; T.E. Lawrence, English soldier and writer, **1888**; Mike Connors, US actor, **1925**; Princess Anne, **1950**.

DEATHS

Macbeth, king of Scotland, **1057**; Joseph Joachim, Hungarian violinist and composer, **1907**; Paul Signac, French painter, **1935**; René Magritte, Belgian painter, **1967**; John Cameron Swayze, US broadcaster, **1995**.

NOTES

_____

_____

_____

_____

August 16

"I can throw a fit, I'm master at it."
—MADONNA

EVENTS

1513 King Henry VIII and his English troops defeated the French in the Battle of the Spurs, at Guinigatte, NW France. **1779** The battle of Camden, South Carolina, in the American Revolution resulted in a British victory by General Charles Cornwallis. **1934** US explorer Charles Beebe and engineer Otis Barton made a record-breaking dive to 3028 ft/923 m in their bathysphere (a spherical diving vessel) near Bermuda. **1960** Cyprus became an independent republic, with Archbishop Makarios as president. **1974** Turkish forces called a cease-fire in Cyprus, after having taken control of the northern part of the island.

BIRTHS

Johan Siegwald Dahl, Norwegian painter, **1827**; Menachem Begin, Israeli prime minister, **1913**; Ann Blyth, US film actress, **1928**; Robert Culp, US film actor, **1930**; Edie Gorme, US singer, **1932**; Madonna (Ciccone), US rock singer, **1958**.

DEATHS

Joe Miller, English comedian, **1738**; Robert Wilhelm Bunsen, German chemist and inventor, **1899**; Umberto Boccioni, Italian sculptor, **1916**; Margaret Mitchell, US author of *Gone with the Wind*, **1949**; Bela Lugosi, Hungarian-born US horror-film actor, **1956**; Elvis Presley, US rock 'n' roll legend, **1977**; Irene Sharaff, US film-set and costume designer, **1993**; Stewart Granger, English-born US actor, **1993**.

NOTES

August 17

"Virtue has its own reward, but no sale at the box office."
—MAE WEST

The national day of Indonesia.

EVENTS

1833 The Canadian *Royal William*, the first steamship to cross the Atlantic entirely under power, set off from Nova Scotia. **1876** The first performance of Wagner's opera *Götterdämmerung* was given, in Bayreuth, Germany. **1896** Gold was discovered at Bonanza Creek in Canada's Yukon Territory, leading to the great gold rush of 1898. **1976** Earthquakes and tidal waves in the Philippines resulted in the deaths of over 6,000 people. **1978** Three Americans—Ben Abruzzo, Maxie Anderson, and Larry Newman—made the first successful Atlantic crossing in a balloon, taking six days in their *Double Eagle II* from Presque Isle, Maine, to Miserey, France.

BIRTHS

David ("Davy") Crockett, US frontiersman, **1786**; Mae West, US film actress, **1892**; V.S. Naipaul, Trinidadian novelist, **1932**; Robert De Niro, US film actor, **1943**; Sean Penn, US film actor, **1960**.

DEATHS

Frederick II (the Great), king of Prussia, **1786**; Honoré de Balzac, French novelist, **1850**; Fernand Léger, French painter, **1955**; Ludwig Mies van der Rohe, German-born US architect, **1973**; Ira Gershwin, US lyricist, **1983**; Mohammad Zia ul-Haq, Pakistani general, **1988**.

NOTES

August 18

*"I did a picture in England one winter
and it was so cold I almost got married."*
—SHELLEY WINTERS

EVENTS

1812 Napoleon's forces defeated the Russians at the Battle of Smolensk. **1866** The Treaty of Alliance forming the North German Confederation, under the leadership of Prussia, was signed. **1920** The 19th Amendment to the US Constitution was ratified, giving women the right to vote. **1960** The first oral contraceptive was marketed by the Searle Drug Company in the US. **1964** South Africa was banned from participating in the Olympics because of its racial policies. **1967** Long Beach, California, purchased the liner *Queen Mary*.

BIRTHS

Virginia Dare, first English child born in America, at Roanoke Island, North Carolina, **1587**; Antonio Salieri, Italian composer, **1750**; Franz Josef I, Austro-Hungarian emperor, **1830**; Moura Lympany, English concert pianist, **1916**; Shelley Winters, US film actress, **1922**; Roman Polanski, Polish film director, **1933**; Robert Redford, US film actor, **1937**; Patrick Swayze, US film actor, **1954**.

DEATHS

Genghis Khan, Mongol conqueror, **1227**; Guido Reni, Italian painter, **1642**; André Jacques Garnerin, French balloonist, **1823**; William Henry Hudson, US writer, **1922**; Anita Loos, US writer, **1981**.

NOTES

August 19

*"I never forget a face but in your case
I'll be glad to make an exception."*
—GROUCHO MARX, *in Leo Rosten's* People I
Have Loved, Known or Admired

EVENTS

1861 The US began requiring passports. **1934** A plebiscite was held in Germany, giving sole power to Adolf Hitler, the Führer. **1942** British and Canadian troops raided the port of Dieppe, suffering heavy casualties. **1958** The US launched the largest submarine ever built, the nuclear-powered *Triton*. **1989** Poland became the first Eastern European country to end one-party rule, when a coalition government was formed with Tadeuz Mazowiecki as prime minister. **1994** President Clinton announced the US was ending its 28-year policy of accepting refugees from Cuba; US ships intercepted over 7,000 boat refugees within a week for return to Cuba or US internment.

BIRTHS

John Dryden, English poet, **1631**; Orville Wright, US aviation pioneer, **1871**; Gabrielle (Coco) Chanel, French couturier, **1883**; Ogden Nash, US humorist, **1902**; Bill Clinton, 42nd US president, **1946**; Jill St. John, US film actress, **1969**.

DEATHS

Augustus, first Roman emperor, **14**; Blaise Pascal, French philosopher and mathematician, **1662**; Sergei Diaghilev, Russian choreographer, **1929**; Federico Garcia Lorca, Spanish poet and playwright, **1936**; Julius "Groucho" Marx, US comedian, **1977**.

NOTES

August 20

EVENTS

1710 The French were defeated by the Austrians at the Battle of Saragossa. **1914** In World War I, German forces occupied Brussels. **1960** Senegal gained independence from France. **1968** Russian troops invaded Czechoslovakia. **1977** The US *Voyager I* spacecraft was launched on its journey via Jupiter and Saturn to become the first artificial object to leave the solar system.

BIRTHS

Thomas Corneille, French playwright, **1625**; Benjamin Harrison, 23rd US president, **1833**; Raymond Poincaré, French statesman, **1860**; H.P. Lovecraft, US writer, **1890**; Jack Teagarden, US jazz trombonist, **1905**; Jim Reeves, US country singer, **1924**.

DEATHS

Friedrich Wilhelm Joseph von Schelling, German philosopher, **1854**; Adolphe William Bouguereau, French painter, **1905**; William Booth, English founder of the Salvation Army, **1912**; Paul Ehrlich, German biochemist, **1915**; Leon Trotsky, Russian politician, **1940**.

NOTES

_____

_____

_____

_____

August 21

*"There is a sweeping crisis that threatens our civilization.
The most profound need is to move away from a technology-centered
to a culture-centered way of living."*
—MIKHAIL GORBACHEV, *San Francisco speech, Oct. 1995*

EVENTS

1808 French forces, under General Junot, were defeated by England's commander Wellington at the Battle of Vimiero. **1901** The Cadillac Motor Company was formed in Detroit, Michigan, named for the French explorer, Antoine Cadillac. **1911** Leonardo da Vinci's painting the *Mona Lisa* was stolen from the Louvre in Paris; it was recovered two years later. **1959** Hawaii became the 50th state. **1991** An attempted coup d'état in the USSR failed; faced with international condemnation and popular protests led by Boris Yeltsin, the junta stepped down and Gorbachev was reinstated.

BIRTHS

William IV, king of Britain and Ireland, **1765**; Aubrey Beardsley, English illustrator, **1872**; Count Basie, US jazz pianist and bandleader, **1904**; Princess Margaret, of the UK, **1930**; Janet Baker, English operatic mezzo-soprano, **1933**; Matthew Broderick, US film actor, **1962**.

DEATHS

Richard Crashaw, English poet, **1649**; Benigno Aquino, Filipino politician, assassinated, **1983**; Tatiana Troyanos, US operatic mezzo-soprano, **1993**.

NOTES

August 22

*"I don't know much about being a millionaire, but I'll bet
I'd be darling at it."*
—DOROTHY PARKER

EVENTS

1642 The English Civil War began, between the supporters of
Charles I and of Parliament. **1788** The British settlement in Sierra
Leone was founded, the purpose of which was to secure a home
in Africa for freed slaves from England. **1846** New Mexico was
annexed by the US. **1864** The International Red Cross was
founded by the Geneva Convention to assist the wounded and
prisoners of war. **1910** Korea was annexed by Japan.

BIRTHS

Claude Debussy, French composer, **1862**; Jacques Lipchitz, US
sculptor and painter, **1891**; Dorothy Parker, US humorist and
writer, **1893**; Henri Cartier-Bresson, French photographer, **1908**;
Ray Bradbury, US science-fiction writer, **1920**; Karlheinz
Stockhausen, German composer, **1928**; H. Norman Schwarzkopf,
US general who was commander-in-chief of the Gulf War, **1934**.

DEATHS

Jean Honoré Fragonard, French painter, **1806**; Michael Collins,
Irish nationalist, **1922**; Michael Fokine, Russian dancer and
choreographer, **1942**.

NOTES

_____

_____

_____

_____

August 23

*"I suppose they like me because I bring romance
into their lives for a few moments."*
—RUDOLPH VALENTINO

The national day of Romania.

EVENTS

1839 Hong Kong was taken by the British. **1914** The British Expeditionary Force fought its first battle at Mons, in World War I. **1921** Faisal I was crowned as King of Iraq. **1927** Nicola Sacco and Bartolomeo Vanzetti, two Italian-American anarchists, were convicted of murder on dubious evidence and executed in the electric chair; many still believe in their innocence. **1940** The Blitz began as German bombers began an all-night raid on London. **1948** The World Council of Churches was founded.

BIRTHS

Edgar Lee Masters, US poet and novelist, **1869**; Gene Kelly, US dancer and singer, **1912**; Peter Thomson, Australian golfer, **1929**; Vera Miles, US film actress, **1929**; Barbara Eden, US actress, **1934**; Keith Moon, British rock drummer with The Who, **1947**; River Phoenix, US film actor, **1971**.

DEATHS

Charles Auguste de Coulomb, French physicist, **1806**; Rudolph Valentino, Italian-born Hollywood film actor and cult figure, **1926**; Oscar Hammerstein II, US lyricist, **1960**; Didier Peroni, French racing driver, **1987**.

NOTES

August 24

*"Good sense about trivialities is better than
nonsense about things that matter."*
—MAX BEERBOHM

EVENTS

79 Mount Vesuvius erupted and buried the cities of Pompeii and
Herculaneum in hot volcanic ash. **410** The Visigoths, led by
Alaric, sacked Rome. **1572** Charles IX ordered the massacre of the
Huguenots throughout France; in Paris thousands were killed in
what became known as the St Bartholomew's Day Massacre.
1704 The French were defeated by the English and Dutch fleets at
the Battle of Malaga. **1814** British forces captured Washington,
DC, and burned the Capitol and White House. **1921** The Turkish
army, led by Mustafa Kemal, drove back the Greeks at the Battle
of the Sakkaria River. **1949** The North Atlantic Treaty
Organization (NATO) was formed by the US, Canada, and 10
Western European countries.

BIRTHS

William Wilberforce, English philanthropist, **1759**; Max
Beerbohm, English writer and caricaturist, **1872**.

DEATHS

Pliny the Elder, Roman naturalist and writer, **79**; Alaric I, king of
the Visigoths, **410**; Thomas Blood, Irish adventurer, **1680**;
Thomas Chatterton, English poet, **1770**; Nicolas Léonard Sadi
Carnot, French physicist, **1832**.

NOTES

August 25

"Beggars should be abolished. It annoys one to give them,
and it annoys one not to give them."
—F.W. NIETZSCHE

The national day of Uruguay.

EVENTS

325 The Council of Nicaea set the rules for the computation of Easter. **1830** A revolution against the Netherlands union erupted in Brussels. **1914** Louvain was sacked by the Germans. **1940** The RAF made the first air raid on Berlin. **1944** The Allies liberated Paris. **1960** The 17th Olympic Games opened in Rome. **1989** The US space probe *Voyager* reached Neptune; pictures of Triton, its moon, revealed the existence of two additional moons.

BIRTHS

Ivan IV ("the Terrible"), czar of Russia, **1530**; Allan Pinkerton, founder of the US detective agency, **1819**; Van Johnson, US film actor, **1916**; Mel Ferrer, US film actor, **1917**; Leonard Bernstein, US conductor and composer, **1918**; George Wallace, Alabama governor and independent presidential candidate, **1919**; Sean Connery, Scottish actor, **1930**; Martin Amis, English novelist, **1949**.

DEATHS

Jan Vermeer, Dutch painter, **1691**; David Hume, Scottish philosopher, **1776**; William Herschel, English astronomer, **1822**; Michael Faraday, English chemist and physicist, **1867**; Friedrich Wilhelm Nietzsche, German philosopher, **1900**; Truman Capote, US author, **1984**.

NOTES

_____

_____

_____

_____

August 26

"Veni, vidi, vici. (I came, I saw, I conquered.)"
—JULIUS CAESAR

EVENTS

55 BC Julius Caesar landed in Britain. **1789** The French Assembly adopted the Declaration of the Rights of Man. **1846** Mendelssohn's oratorio *Elijah* was first performed in Birmingham, England. **1883** Krakatoa, the island volcano, began erupting, killing thousands. **1920** The 19th Amendment to the US Constitution came into effect, and women could now vote. **1972** The 20th Olympic Games opened in Munich. **1978** Albino Cardinal Luciani was elected Pope John Paul I. **1994** Congressional hearings began on the Whitewater property failure of the 1980s involving President Bill Clinton and his wife, Hillary.

BIRTHS

Sir Robert Walpole, effectively Britain's first prime minister, **1676**; Lee De Forest, US physicist known as "the father of radio," **1873**; Jules Romains, French novelist, playwright, and poet, **1885**; Christopher Isherwood, English novelist, **1904**; Geraldine Ferraro, America's only woman vice-presidential candidate, **1935**; Macaulay Culkin, US child actor, **1980**.

DEATHS

Frans Hals, Dutch painter, **1666**; Anton van Leeuwenhoek, Dutch naturalist and microscopist, **1723**; Louis Philippe, "Citizen King" of France, **1850**; Charles Lindbergh, US pioneer aviator, **1974**; Charles Boyer, French actor, **1978**.

NOTES

_____

_____

_____

_____

August 27

"What you do not want done to yourself do not do to others."
—CONFUCIUS

EVENTS

1776 The British won the Battle of Long Island in the American Revolution; General George Washington evacuated New York. **1859** Edwin Drake was the first in the US to strike oil, at Titusville, Pennsylvania. **1913** A Russian pilot, Lieutenant Peter Nesterov, became the first to perform the loop-the-loop. **1928** The antiwar Kellogg-Briand Pact was signed by 15 nations. **1939** The first jet-propelled aircraft, the Heinkel 178, made its first flight. **1958** The USSR launched *Sputnik 3*, carrying two dogs. **1994** Congress approved a crime bill costing more than $30 billion over six years and adding 100,000 new police.

BIRTHS

Confucius, Chinese philosopher, 551 BC; Georg Wilhelm Friedrich Hegel, German philosopher, 1770; Samuel Goldwyn, US film magnate, 1882; Lyndon B. Johnson, 36th US President, 1908; Lester "Prez" Young, US jazz saxophonist, 1909; Mother Teresa, Albanian-born Indian missionary, 1910; Tuesday Weld, US film actress, 1940.

DEATHS

Titian, Italian painter, 1576; Louis Botha, South African statesman, 1919; Le Corbusier, Swiss architect, 1965; Haile Selassie, deposed emperor of Ethiopia, 1975; Earl Mountbatten of Burma, assassinated by the IRA, 1979; Gracie Allen, English comedienne partner of husband George Burns, 1964.

NOTES

August 28

*"I have a dream that my four little children will one day
live in a nation where they will not be judged by the color
of their skin but by the content of their character."*
—MARTIN LUTHER KING

EVENTS

1849 Venice was taken by the Austrians after a siege. **1850** The English Channel telegraph cable was laid between Dover and Cap Gris Nez. **1914** The Battle of Heligoland Bight, the first major naval battle of World War I, was fought. **1945** US forces under General George Marshall landed in Japan. **1963** The massive (200,000 people) civil-rights march from the South ended in Washington, DC, where Martin Luther King delivered his famous "I have a dream" speech. **1995** The Chemical Banking Corporation and Chase Manhattan Corporation announced their merger, creating the largest US commercial bank.

BIRTHS

Johann Wolfgang Goethe, German poet, novelist and dramatist, **1749**; Edward Burne-Jones, British painter, **1833**; Godfrey Hounsfield, British inventor of the CAT-scan prototype, **1919**; Donald O'Connor, US film actor, singer, and dancer, **1925**; Ben Gazzara, US actor, **1930**.

DEATHS

Hugo Grotius, Dutch jurist and politician, **1645**; Ernest Orlando Lawrence, US physicist, **1958**; John Huston, US film director, **1987**.

NOTES

_____

_____

_____

_____

August 29

"In Casablanca *there was often nothing in my face. But the audience put into my face what they thought I was giving."*
—INGRID BERGMAN, My Story

EVENTS

1831 Michael Faraday successfully demonstrated the first electrical transformer. **1835** The city of Melbourne, Australia, was founded. **1842** The Treaty of Nanking was signed between the British and the Chinese, ending the Opium War and leasing the Hong Kong territories to Britain. **1904** The 3rd Olympic Games opened at St. Louis. **1953** The USSR exploded a hydrogen bomb. **1966** At Candlestick Park, San Francisco, the Beatles played their last live concert. **1991** The Supreme Soviet voted to suspend formally all activities of the Communist party.

BIRTHS

John Locke, English philosopher, **1632**; Jean Auguste Dominique Ingres, French painter, **1780**; Ingrid Bergman, Swedish actress, **1915**; Charlie "Bird" Parker, US jazz saxophonist, **1920**; Richard Attenborough, English actor and director, **1923**; Elliott Gould, US film actor, **1938**; Peter Jennings, Canadian-born US TV news anchorman, **1938**; Richard Gere, US film actor, **1949**; Michael Jackson, US pop singer, **1958**.

DEATHS

Brigham Young, US Mormon leader, **1877**; Éamon de Valera, Irish nationalist politician, **1975**; Ingrid Bergman, Swedish-born Hollywood actress, **1982**; Lee Marvin, US actor, **1987**.

NOTES

August 30

"I trust that God will grant us a great victory."
—"STONEWALL" JACKSON, *at Chancellorsville, Virginia,*
nine hours before his own troops accidentally wounded
him mortally while winning a great victory

EVENTS

1862 "Stonewall" Jackson led the Confederates to victory at the second Battle of Bull Run, in Virginia, during the American Civil War. **1881** The first stereo system, for a telephonic broadcasting service, was patented in Germany by Clement Adler. **1941** The siege of Leningrad by German forces began (ended January 1943). **1963** To reduce the risk of accidental nuclear war, the "hotline" between the US president and the Soviet premier was established. **1991** At the World Athletics Championships in Tokyo, Mike Powell leapt 29 ft 4.5 in/9.95 m in the long jump, beating the record set by Bob Beamon in 1968.

BIRTHS

Jacques Louis David, French painter, **1748**; Mary Wollstonecraft Shelley, English writer who created Frankenstein, **1797**; Ernest Rutherford, New Zealand physicist, **1871**; Raymond Massey, Canadian-born US film actor, **1896**; Fred MacMurray, US film actor, **1908**; Jean Claude Killy, French ski champion, **1943**.

DEATHS

Cleopatra, queen of Egypt, **30 BC**; Louis XI, king of France, **1483**; John Ross, Scottish explorer, **1856**; Georges Sorel, French socialist philosopher, **1922**; J.J. Thomson, English physicist, **1940**.

NOTES

_____

_____

_____

_____

August 31

"Would that the Roman people had but one neck!"
—CALIGULA

The national day of Malaysia.

EVENTS

1942 The German offensive was halted by the British at the Battle of Alam al-Halfa, marking the turning point in the North African campaign. **1972** US swimmer Mark Spitz won five of the seven gold medals he achieved in total at the Munich Olympics. **1983** The USSR shot down a South Korean airliner, killing 269 people aboard. **1994** The Irish Republican Party (IRA) announced a cease-fire in Northern Ireland; more than 3,000 people had been killed by IRA and rival Protestant terrorists in 25 years.

BIRTHS

Caligula, Roman emperor, **12**; Maria Montessori, Italian educator, **1870**; Fredric March, US actor, **1897**; William Saroyan, US novelist, **1908**; Bernard Lovell, British astronomer, **1913**; Alan Jay Lerner, US lyricist who teamed with composer Frederick Loewe to write *My Fair Lady*, **1918**; Buddy Hackett, US comic film actor, **1924**; James Coburn, US film actor, **1928**; Van Morrison, Irish musician, **1945**; Edwin Moses, US track star, **1955**.

DEATHS

John Bunyan, English author, **1688**; Charles Pierre Baudelaire, French poet, **1867**; Georges Braque, French painter, **1963**; Rocky Marciano, US heavyweight champion, **1969**; John Ford, US film director, **1973**; Henry Moore, British sculptor, **1986**.

NOTES

September 1

"Thank God kids never mean well."
—LILY TOMLIN

The national day of Libya.

EVENTS

70 The destruction of Jerusalem under Titus took place. **1853** The world's first triangular postage stamps were issued by the Cape of Good Hope. **1864** General Sherman's Union forces took Atlanta. **1920** The state of Lebanon was created by the French. **1923** Nearly 200,000 people were killed in earthquakes in Tokyo and Yokohama. **1939** Germany invaded Poland, starting World War II. **1969** Colonel Qaddafi seized power in Libya, after overthrowing King Idris I. **1972** Bobby Fischer defeated Boris Spassky at Reykjavik, becoming the first US world chess champion.

BIRTHS

Roger David Casement, Irish nationalist, **1864**; Edgar Rice Burroughs, US novelist and creator of Tarzan, **1875**; Estee Lauder, cosmetics executive, **1908**; Yvonne DeCarlo, US film actress, **1922**; Rocky Marciano, US world heavyweight boxing champion, **1923**; Lily Tomlin, US comedienne, **1939**; Leonard Slatkin, US conductor, **1954**.

DEATHS

Pope Adrian IV, the only English pope, **1159**; Jacques Cartier, French explorer, **1557**; Louis XIV, the "Sun King" of France, **1715**; Siegfried Sassoon, English writer, **1967**; François Mauriac, French novelist, **1970**.

NOTES

September 2

EVENTS

31 BC Emperor Augustus (Octavian) defeated Antony at the Battle of Actium. **1666** The Great Fire of London started; it destroyed 13,000 buildings in four days. **1752** The Julian calendar was used in Europe officially for the last time; the following day became September 14 in the Gregorian calendar. **1898** The British, led by Lord Kitchener, defeated the Sudanese at the Battle of Omdurman and reoccupied Khartoum, the capital. **1906** Roald Amundsen completed his sailing around Canada's Northwest Passage. **1923** The Irish Free State held its first elections. **1958** China's first television station opened in Beijing. **1987** The CD-video, combining digital sound with high-definition video, was launched by Philips.

BIRTHS

Giovanni Verga, Italian novelist and dramatist, **1840**; Wilhelm Ostwald, German chemist, **1853**; Jimmy Connors, US tennis player, **1952**; Keanu Reeves, US film actor, **1964**.

DEATHS

José Ribera ("Lo Spagnoletto"), Spanish painter, **1652**; Henri Rousseau, French painter, **1910**; Pierre de Coubertin, founder of the modern Olympics, **1937**; J.R.R. Tolkein, English writer, **1973**.

NOTES

September 3

"I'm the most insecure guy in Hollywood."
—ALAN LADD, *who stood 5 ft 5 in*

EVENTS

1651 Royalist troops under Charles II were defeated by Cromwell at the second Battle of Worcester. **1783** Britain recognized US independence with the signing of a treaty in Paris. **1916** In World War I, the first Zeppelin was shot down over England. **1930** Santo Domingo, in the Dominican Republic, was destroyed by a hurricane which killed 5,000 people. **1935** Britain's Malcolm Campbell reached a new world land speed record of 301.13 mph in *Bluebird* on Bonneville Salt Flats, Utah. **1939** Britain, New Zealand, Australia, and France declared war on Germany. **1943** The Allies landed at Salerno, on mainland Italy, and the Italian government surrendered. **1967** Sweden changed from driving on the left to the right. **1976** The US spacecraft *Viking 2* landed on Mars and began sending pictures of the red planet to earth.

BIRTHS

Louis Henry Sullivan, US architect, **1856**; Jean-Léon Jaurès, French socialist politician, **1859**; Macfarlane Burnet, Australian immunologist, **1899**; Alan Ladd, US film actor, **1913**; Charlie Sheen, US film actor, **1965**.

DEATHS

Oliver Cromwell, lord protector of England, **1658**; Ivan Sergeyevich Turgenev, Russian novelist, **1883**; e e cummings, US poet, **1962**; Ho Chi Minh, president of North Vietnam, **1969**; Frank Capra, US film director, **1991**.

NOTES

September 4

"Poor people always lean forward when they speak because they want people to listen to them. Rich people can sit back."
—MICHAEL CAINE, *reported on Sept. 4, 1966*

EVENTS

1260 The Battle of Montaperti, between the rival Guelphs and Ghibellines, was fought in central Italy. **1870** Emperor Napoleon III, Bonaparte's nephew, was deposed and the Third Republic was proclaimed. **1886** Geronimo, the Apache chief, surrendered to the US Army. **1909** The first Boy Scout rally was held at Crystal Palace, near London, England. **1940** The Columbia Broadcasting System (CBS) gave a demonstration of color TV on station WXAB. **1944** The Allies liberated Antwerp, Belgium. **1970** Natalia Makarova, of the Kirov Ballet, defected to the West. **1985** The wreck of the *Titanic* on the Atlantic seabed was photographed by remote sensing.

BIRTHS

Vicomte François René de Chateaubriand, French author, **1768**; Anton Bruckner, Austrian composer, **1824**; Antonin Artaud, French dramatist and director, **1896**; Mary Renault, English novelist, **1905**; Paul Harvey, US radio and TV news commentator, **1918**; Mitzi Gaynor, US film actress and singer, **1930**; Dawn Fraser, Australian swimmer, **1937**; Tom Watson, US golfer, **1949**.

DEATHS

Robert Schuman, French statesman, **1963**; Albert Schweitzer, French organist and missionary surgeon, **1965**; Georges Simenon, Belgian crime writer, **1989**.

NOTES

September 5

*"A writer's ambition should be to trade a hundred
contemporary readers for ten readers in ten years' time
and for one reader in a hundred years' time."*
—ARTHUR KOESTLER

EVENTS

1774 The first Continental Congress in America opened in Philadelphia; it remained in session until October 26. **1914** The first Battle of the Marne, during World War I, began. **1922** US aviator James Doolittle made the first US coast-to-coast flight in 21 hrs, 19 min. **1972** At the Olympic Games in Munich, Arab terrorists of the Black September group seized Israeli athletes as hostages; nine of the Israelis, four of the terrorists, and one German policeman were killed. **1980** The world's longest road tunnel, the St. Gotthard, was opened running 10 mi/16 km from Goschenen, Switzerland to Airolo, Italy.

BIRTHS

Louis XIV, the "Sun King" of France, **1638**; Giacomo Meyerbeer, German composer, **1791**; Jesse James, US outlaw, **1847**; Darryl Zanuck, US film producer, **1902**; Arthur Koestler, Hungarian author, **1905**; Raquel Welch, US actress, **1940**.

DEATHS

Pieter Brueghel the Elder, Flemish painter, **1569**; Auguste Comte, French philosopher, **1857**; Charles Péguy, French poet, **1914**; Josh White, US blues singer, **1969**.

NOTES

_____

_____

_____

_____

September 6

EVENTS

1522 Ferdinand Magellan's 17 surviving crew members reached the Spanish coast aboard the *Vittoria*, having completed the first circumnavigation of the world. **1901** US President William McKinley was shot and fatally wounded by an anarchist in Buffalo, New York. **1941** Nazi Germany made the wearing of the yellow Star of David badges compulsory for all its Jewish citizens. **1965** India invaded West Pakistan. **1975** A massive earthquake centered on Lice, Turkey, caused nearly 3,000 deaths. **1989** Due to a computer error, 41,000 Parisians received letters charging them with murder, extortion, and organized prostitution instead of traffic violations.

BIRTHS

The Marquis de Lafayette, French soldier and statesman, **1757**; John Dalton, British chemist, **1766**; Jane Addams, US social worker and writer, **1860**; Edward Appleton, British physicist, **1892**; Britt Ekland, Swedish film actress, **1943**.

DEATHS

Suleiman I, sultan of Turkey, **1566**; Jean-Baptiste Colbert, French politician, **1683**; Gertrude Lawrence, English actress and singer, **1952**; Hendrik Verwoerd, South African prime minister, assassinated, **1966**.

NOTES

_____

_____

_____

_____

September 7

"Anger makes dull men witty, but it keeps them poor."
—QUEEN ELIZABETH I, *attributed*

The national day of Brazil.

EVENTS

1812 The Russians were defeated by Napoleon's forces at the Battle of Borodino, 70 miles west of Moscow. **1901** The Peace of Peking was signed, ending the Boxer Rebellion in China. **1904** Francis Younghusband led a British expedition to Tibet, where a treaty was signed with the Dalai Lama. **1920** The first "Miss America" beauty contest was held in Atlantic City, New Jersey. **1986** Bishop Desmond Tutu was appointed archbishop of Capetown, the first black head of South African Anglicans. **1991** Peace talks on the Yugoslav civil war opened in The Hague, the Netherlands, under European Union sponsorship.

BIRTHS

Elizabeth I, queen of England, **1533**; Anna Mary "Grandma" Moses, US primitive artist who began painting at the age of about 75, **1860**; Elia Kazan, US stage and film director, **1909**; James Van Allen, US physicist who discovered the two radiation belts around the Earth that bear his name, **1914**; Sonny Rollins, US saxophonist, **1929**; Buddy Holly, US rock 'n' roll singer, **1936**.

DEATHS

Catherine Parr, sixth wife of Henry VIII of England, **1548**; Armand Sully-Prudhomme, French poet, **1907**; Keith Moon, English rock drummer with The Who, **1978**.

NOTES

September 8

*"Mr. Nixon was the 37th president of the United States.
He had been preceded by 36 others."*
—GERALD FORD

EVENTS

1664 The Dutch colony of New Amsterdam was surrendered to the British, who renamed it New York. **1886** Johannesburg, South Africa, was founded after the discovery of gold there. **1900** Parts of Texas were hit by a tornado and tidal waves, which caused over 6,000 deaths near Galveston. **1935** Louisiana Senator Huey Long was shot by Dr. Carl Weiss, who was killed by Long's bodyguards; Long died two days later. **1944** The first German V2 flying bombs fell on Britain. **1951** The Treaty of Peace with Japan was signed by 49 nations in San Francisco. **1954** The Southeast Asia Treaty Organization (SEATO) was established by the US and seven other nations. **1974** US President Ford fully pardoned Richard Nixon for his part in the Watergate affair.

BIRTHS

Richard I (the Lion-Hearted), king of England, **1157**; Ludovico Ariosto, Italian poet, **1474**; Antonín Dvořák, Czech composer, **1841**; Jean-Louis Barrault, French actor and director, **1910**; Sid Caesar, US TV comedian, **1922**; Peter Sellers, English actor and comedian, **1925**.

DEATHS

Francisco Gomez de Quevedo y Villegas, Spanish writer, **1645**; Richard Strauss, German composer, **1949**; André Derain, French painter, **1954**; Jean Seberg, US actress, **1979**.

NOTES

_____

_____

_____

_____

September 9

EVENTS

1513 The Scots were defeated by the English at the Battle of Flodden Field. **1850** California became the 31st state. **1850** Senator Henry Clay's "Compromise of 1850" prohibited slavery in California but strengthened the Fugitive Slave Act. **1943** Allied forces landed at Salerno, Italy. **1945** General Douglas MacArthur began supervising Japan. **1975** Czech tennis player Martina Navratilova, aged 18, defected to the West, requesting political asylum in the US. **1985** Massive earthquakes in Mexico left more than 4,700 dead and 30,000 injured.

BIRTHS

Cardinal Richelieu, French statesman, **1585**; Luigi Galvani, Italian physiologist, **1737**; Leo Tolstoy, Russian novelist, **1828**; James Hilton, English novelist, **1900**; Otis Redding, US soul singer and songwriter, **1941**.

DEATHS

William I (the Conqueror), king of England, **1087**; James IV, king of Scotland, **1513**; Giambattista Piranesi, Italian architect, **1778**; Stéphane Mallarmé, French poet, **1898**; Henri de Toulouse-Lautrec, French painter, **1901**; Mao Zedong, Chinese leader, **1976**.

NOTES

September 10

"It would have been better if the experiment had been conducted in a small country to make it clear that it was a utopian idea, although a beautiful idea."
—BORIS YELTSIN

EVENTS

1813 At the Battle of Lake Erie in the War of 1812, Commandant Oliver Perry's US fleet destroyed a British squadron. **1823** Simón Bolívar, known as "The Liberator," became the dictator of Peru. **1919** The Treaty of Saint-Germain was signed; the new boundaries it set brought about the end of the Austrian Empire. **1981** Picasso's *Guernica* was returned to Spain after 40 years in US custodianship; the artist had refused to show the painting in Spain before the restoration of democracy. **1989** Hungary opened its border to the West, allowing thousands of East Germans to leave, much to the anger of the East German government.

BIRTHS

Giovanni Domenico Tiepolo, Italian painter, **1727**; Franz Werfel, Austrian novelist and poet, **1890**; Fay Wray, Canadian-born Hollywood actress, **1907**; Robert Wise, US film director, **1914**; Arnold Palmer, US golfer, **1929**; José Feliciano, US singer, **1945**.

DEATHS

Louis IV, king of France, **954**; Mary Wollstonecraft, British feminist, **1797**; Huey Long, Louisiana governor and senator, assassinated, **1935**; Balthazar Johannes Vorster, South African Nationalist politician, **1983**.

NOTES

September 11

"I believe that Providence has chosen me for a great work."
—ADOLF HITLER, *reported on Sept. 11, 1932*

EVENTS

1709 England's duke of Marlborough and Prince Eugene of Austria defeated the French, under Marshal Villars, at the Battle of Malplaquet. **1777** American troops led by George Washington were defeated by the British at the Battle of Brandywine Creek, in the American Revolution. **1855** In the Crimean War, Sebastopol was taken by the Allies after capitulation by the Russians. **1951** Stravinsky's opera *The Rake's Progress* was performed for the first time, in Venice; the libretto was by W.H. Auden. **1973** A military junta, with US support, overthrew the elected government of Chile. **1978** Georgi Markov, a Bulgarian defector, was fatally stabbed by a poisoned umbrella point wielded by a Bulgarian secret agent in London.

BIRTHS

Pierre de Ronsard, French poet, **1524**; O. Henry, US short-story writer, **1862**; James Hopwood Jeans, British mathematician and scientist, **1877**; D.H. Lawrence, English writer, **1885**; Kristy McNichol, US film actress, **1962**; Harry Connick, Jr., US singer, pianist, and songwriter, **1967**.

DEATHS

Giovanni Domenico Cassini, Italian-French astronomer, **1712**; Jan Christian Smuts, South African statesman, **1950**; Nikita Khrushchev, Russian leader, **1971**; Salvador Allende Gossens, Chilean politician, **1973**; Peter Tosh, Jamaican reggae star, **1987**.

NOTES

September 12

EVENTS

1609 Henry Hudson sailed the sloop *Half Moon* into New York Harbor and up to Albany to discover the river later named for him. **1910** Alice Stebbins Wells, a former social worker, became the world's first policewoman, appointed by the Los Angeles Police Department. **1940** The Lascaux Caves, France, containing prehistoric wall paintings, were discovered. **1943** Benito Mussolini, imprisoned by the Allies, was rescued by German parachutists. **1974** A military coup deposed Emperor Haile Selassie of Ethiopia, "the Lion of Judah." **1994** A two-seater aircraft crashed onto the White House lawn while President and Mrs. Clinton were away; the pilot, Frank Corder from Maryland, was killed.

BIRTHS

Richard Jordan Gatling, US inventor of the rapid-firing gun bearing his name, **1818**; H.L. Mencken, US journalist and linguist, **1880**; Louis MacNeice, British poet, **1907**; Jesse Owens, US athlete, **1913**; George Jones, US country singer, **1931**.

DEATHS

François Couperin, French composer, **1733**; Gebhard Leberecht von Blücher, Prussian general and field-marshal, **1819**; Steve Biko, South African civil rights leader, **1977**; Anthony Perkins, US actor, **1992**.

NOTES

September 13

*"'Tis the star-spangled banner; O long may it wave
O'er the land of the free, and the home of the brave!"*
—FRANCIS SCOTT KEY

EVENTS

1759 The British defeated the French at the Battle of Quebec, completing the British conquest of North America. **1788** New York officially became the capital of the US (until 1790). **1814** The British bombardment of Fort McHenry at Baltimore was witnessed by the American lawyer Francis Scott Key, who was inspired to write the poem "The Star-Spangled Banner." **1845** The Knickerbocker Club, the first baseball club, was founded in New York. **1989** Britain's biggest ever banking computer error gave customers an extra £2 billion (over $3 billion) in a period of 30 minutes; 99.3% of the money was reportedly returned. **1993** A peace agreement (the "Declaration of Principles") was signed in Washington, DC, between Israel and the Palestine Liberation Organization.

BIRTHS

Arnold Schoenberg, Austrian composer, **1874**; J.B. Priestley, English author, **1894**; Claudette Colbert, French-born US actress, **1905**; Jacqueline Bisset, English actress, **1944**.

DEATHS

Andrea Mantegna, Italian painter, **1506**; Charles James Fox, English statesman, **1806**; Alexis-Emmanuel Chabrier, French composer, **1894**; Leopold Stokowski, English-born US conductor, **1977**; Joe Pasternak, US film producer, **1991**.

NOTES

September 14

*"The freedom of the press works in such a way
that there is not much freedom from it."*
—PRINCESS GRACE OF MONACO

EVENTS

1812 Napoleon entered Moscow in his disastrous invasion of Russia. **1860** Niagara Falls was first illuminated. **1901** Theodore Roosevelt became the 26th US president, 12 hours after the death of President McKinley, who had been shot by an anarchist on September 6. **1923** Miguel Primo de Riviera became dictator of Spain. **1959** The Soviet *Lunik II* became the first spacecraft to land on the Moon. **1975** Elizabeth Bayley Seton became the first native-born American to become a Roman Catholic saint. **1991** The South African government, the ANC, and the Inkatha Freedom Party signed a peace accord aimed at ending the factional violence in the black townships.

BIRTHS

Peter Lely, Dutch painter, **1617**; Baron von Humboldt, German traveler and naturalist, **1769**; Margaret Sanger, US nurse who pioneered birth-control education, **1883**; Jan Garrigue Masaryk, Czech statesman, **1886**.

DEATHS

Dante Alighieri, Italian poet, **1321**; James Fenimore Cooper, US novelist, **1851**; Arthur Wellesley, first duke of Wellington, English soldier and politician, **1852**; William McKinley, 25th US president, assassinated, **1901**; Isadora Duncan, US dancer, **1927**; Princess Grace of Monaco (Grace Kelly), **1982**.

NOTES

September 15

*"I have two boys and they're the cruelest sons of bitches I've ever seen.
Violence, aggression, is part of the human structure."*
—OLIVER STONE

The national day of Costa Rica.

EVENTS

1915 Military tanks, designed by Ernest Swinton, were first used by the British Army, at Flers, in the Somme offensive. **1935** The Nuremburg laws were passed in Germany, outlawing Jews and making the swastika the country's official flag. **1950** US troops landed at Inchon, South Korea. **1974** The civil war between Christians and Muslims in Beirut began. **1985** Tony Jacklin's European golf team won the Ryder Cup from the US, which had long dominated the competition.

BIRTHS

Trajan, Roman emperor, **53**; James Fenimore Cooper, US novelist, **1789**; William Howard Taft, 27th US president, **1857**; Agatha Christie, English detective novelist, **1890**; Mel Torme, US jazz singer and songwriter, **1925**; Jessye Norman, US operatic soprano, **1945**; Oliver Stone, US film director, producer, and screenwriter, **1946**; Tommy Lee Jones, US film actor, **1946**.

DEATHS

Isambard Kingdom Brunel, British engineer, **1859**; John Hanning Speke, British explorer, **1864**; José Echegaray, Spanish dramatist and scientist, **1916**; Robert Penn Warren, US novelist, **1989**.

NOTES

September 16

*"I think your whole life shows in your face
and you should be proud of that."*
—LAUREN BACALL, *reported on March 6, 1988*

The national day of Mexico.

EVENTS

1620 The *Mayflowere* sailed from Plymouth, England, carrying 101 Pilgrims to the New World. **1906** The Buick and Oldsmobile automobile manufacturers merged to become General Motors. **1920** A bomb at New York's Wall Street killed 30 and injured 100. **1976** The Episcopal Church in the US approved the ordination of women to the priesthood. **1987** For the first time in South Africa, *Othello* was performed with a black actor, John Khani, playing the Moor. **1991** All Iran-Contra charges against Oliver North were dropped. **1994** An Alaskan jury ordered Exxon to pay $5 billion to 34,000 residents in Alaska for the 1989 *Exxon Valdez* oil spill; this was the largest award ever for a pollution case.

BIRTHS

Henry V, king of England, **1387**; Alexander Korda, British film director and producer, **1893**; Lauren Bacall, US actress, **1924**; Charles Haughey, Irish politician, **1925**; B.B. King, US blues singer and guitarist, **1926**; Peter Falk, US actor, **1927**.

DEATHS

Tomás de Torquemada, Spanish Inquisitor-General, **1498**; Gabriel Daniel Fahrenheit, German physicist, **1736**; Louis XVIII, king of France, **1824**; Maria Callas, US operatic soprano, **1977**.

NOTES

September 17

"Anyone who looks for a source of power in the transformation of the atom is talking moonshine."
—SIR ERNEST RUTHERFORD, *reported on Sept. 17, 1933*

EVENTS

1787 The US Constitution was signed. **1862** General George McClellan blocked General Robert E. Lee's Confederate invasion of the North at Antietam, Maryland, in a Civil War battle. **1908** Lt. Selfridge, on a test flight with Orville Wright, was killed when the plane crashed, the first passenger to die in an airplane crash. **1931** The first long-playing record was demonstrated in New York by RCA-Victor, but the venture failed because of the high price of the players. **1939** Poland was invaded by the USSR. **1978** Mohammed Ali beat Leon Spinks to become the first boxer to win the world heavyweight championship three times.

BIRTHS

Francisco Gomez de Quevado y Villegas, Spanish poet and satirist, **1580**; William Carlos Williams, US poet, **1883**; Stirling Moss, English racing driver, **1929**; Anne Bancroft, US actress, **1931**; Maureen "Little Mo" Connolly, US tennis player, **1934**.

DEATHS

Philip IV, king of Spain, **1665**; Tobias George Smollett, Scottish novelist, **1771**; William Henry Fox Talbot, English photographic pioneer, **1877**; Count Folke Bernadotte, Swedish diplomat, assassinated, **1948**; Laura Ashley, Welsh designer and fabric retailer, **1985**; Karl Popper, Austrian philosopher of science, **1994**.

NOTES

September 18

The national day of Chile.

EVENTS

1759 Quebec surrendered to the British after a fierce battle in which the British commander, General Wolfe, and the French commander, the Marquis de Montcalm, were both killed. **1851** The *New York Times* was first published. **1910** The Chilean revolt against Spanish rule began. **1914** The Irish Home Rule Bill went into effect. **1927** CBS, the Columbia Broadcasting System, was inaugurated. **1934** The USSR was admitted to the League of Nations. **1981** France abolished execution by guillotine. **1991** The Yugoslav navy began a blockade of seven port cities on the Adriatic coast in Dalmatia.

BIRTHS

Dr. Samuel Johnson, English writer and lexicographer, **1709**; Jean Bernard Léon Foucault, French physicist, **1819**; Greta Garbo, Swedish-born US film actress, **1905**; Frankie Avalon, US singer and actor, **1939**.

DEATHS

Leonhard Euler, Swiss mathematician, **1783**; Dag Hammarskjöld, Swedish UN secretary-general, **1961**; Sean O'Casey, Irish dramatist, **1964**; John Douglas Cockcroft, English nuclear physicist, **1967**; Jimi Hendrix, US rock guitarist, **1970**.

NOTES

_____

_____

_____

_____

September 19

*"A girl who thinks that a man will treat her
better after marriage than before is a fool."*
—WILLIAM CLARKE HALL, *reported on Sept. 19, 1920*

EVENTS

1783 The Montgolfier brothers sent up the first balloon with live creatures aboard; passengers included a sheep, a rooster, and a duck. **1796** George Washington gave his farewell speech as president and warned against creating a large federal debt. **1876** The US inventor Melville Bissell patented the first carpet sweeper. **1893** New Zealand became the first country to grant its female citizens the right to vote. **1960** A new dance craze began when Chubby Checker's "The Twist" became a hit in the US. **1989** The New York Supreme Court reversed an earlier decision to award the America's Cup to New Zealand, allowing the San Diego Yacht Club to retain the award.

BIRTHS

George Cadbury, English chocolate manufacturer and social reformer, **1839**; William Golding, English novelist, **1911**; Jeremy Irons, English actor, **1948**; Rosemary Casals, US tennis player, **1948**; Twiggy (Lesley Hornby), English model and actress, **1949**.

DEATHS

Meyer Amschel Rothschild, German banker, **1812**; James Garfield, 20th US president, **1881**; David Low, British cartoonist, **1963**; Chester Carlson, US inventor of the xerography photocopying process, **1968**.

NOTES

September 20

EVENTS

451 The Romans defeated the Huns under Attila at Châlon-sur-Marne. **1519** Ferdinand Magellan, with a fleet of five small ships, sailed from Seville on his expedition around the world. **1797** The 44-gun US frigate *Constitution* was launched at Boston; known as "Old Ironsides," it was active in the War of 1812. **1854** The Russian army was defeated by the Allied armies at the Battle of Alma in the Crimean War. **1928** The Fascist party took over the supreme legislative body in Rome, replacing the Chamber of Deputies. **1959** On a visit to the US, Soviet premier Nikita Khrushchev was refused entry to Disneyland for security reasons. **1966** The liner *Queen Elizabeth II* (QE2) was launched at Clydebank, Scotland. **1984** The US embassy in Beirut was attacked by a suicide bomber; explosives in a truck were set off, killing 40 people.

BIRTHS

Alexander the Great, king of Macedonia, **356 BC**; Upton Sinclair, US novelist, **1878**; Ferdinand Joseph La Menthe "Jelly Roll" Morton, US jazz pianist and composer, **1885**; Sophia Loren, Italian film actress, **1934**.

DEATHS

Jakob Karl Grimm, German philologist and folklorist, **1863**; Annie Besant, British socialist and feminist activist, **1933**; Jean Sibelius, Finnish composer, **1957**; George Seferis, Greek poet and diplomat, **1971**.

NOTES

September 21

"Meanwhile, Time is flying—flying never to return."
—VIRGIL

The national day of Malta.

EVENTS

1784 *The Pennsylvania Packet and General Advertiser*, the first successful US daily newspaper, was first published. **1915** Stonehenge in England was sold at auction to C.H. Chubb for £6,600; he presented it to the nation three years later. **1917** Latvia proclaimed its independence. **1938** The Anglo-French plan to cede Sudetenland to Germany was accepted by the Czech cabinet. **1974** Over 8,000 people were killed by floods caused by hurricanes in Honduras. **1981** Sandra Day O'Connor became the first woman associate justice of the US Supreme Court. **1989** Hurricane Hugo struck the US coastal states of Georgia and South Carolina, causing widespread damage and loss of life.

BIRTHS

Girolamo Savonarola, Italian political reformer and martyr, **1452**; John Loudon McAdam, Scottish engineer, **1756**; H.G. Wells, English writer, **1866**; Larry Hagman, US actor, **1931**; Stephen King, US writer of horror novels, **1948**.

DEATHS

Virgil, Roman poet, **19** BC; Sir Walter Scott, Scottish novelist, **1832**; Arthur Schopenhauer, German philosopher, **1860**; Haakon VII, king of Norway, **1957**; William Plomer, South African author, **1973**; Walter Brennan, US film actor, **1974**.

NOTES

September 22

"I only regret that I have but one life to lose for my country."
—NATHAN HALE, *American revolution hero,*
on being hanged by the British

EVENTS

1776 The American patriot Nathan Hale was hanged by the British as a spy, having been captured the previous day disguised as a Dutch schoolteacher. **1780** Benedict Arnold was identified as a traitor but escaped to the British army. **1792** France was declared a republic. **1862** President Lincoln issued the Emancipation Proclamation, ordering the freeing of slaves. **1869** Wagner's opera *Das Rheingold* was first performed, in Munich. **1955** Argentinian leader Juan Perón was deposed in a military coup. **1972** Idi Amin gave the 8,000 Asians in Uganda 48 hours to leave the country. **1980** The Solidarity movement in Poland was created, with Lech Walesa as its elected leader. **1985** A severe earthquake hit Mexico, killing 2,000 people.

BIRTHS

Anne of Cleves, fourth wife of Henry VIII of England, **1515**; Michael Faraday, English chemist and physicist, **1791**; Erich von Stroheim, Austrian-born US actor and film director, **1885**; John Houseman, US actor and producer, **1902**; Fay Weldon, British author, **1931**; Catherine Oxenberg, US film actress, **1961**.

DEATHS

Nathan Hale, American revolutionary patriot, hanged, **1776**; Axel Springer, German publisher, **1985**; Jaco Pastorius, US bass guitarist, **1987**; Irving Berlin, US composer, **1989**.

NOTES

September 23

"I have not yet begun to fight."
—JOHN PAUL JONES, *when the Battle of
Flamborough Head was in doubt*

The national day of Saudi Arabia.

EVENTS

1779 In the American Revolution, John Paul Jones in his flagship *Bon Homme Richard* captured the British frigate *Serapis*, at the Battle of Flamborough Head off Scarborough, England. **1846** German astronomer Johann Galle discovered the planet Neptune. **1848** Chewing gum was first commercially produced in the US by John Curtis in his home and was called "State of Maine Pure Spruce Gum." **1912** *Cohen Collects a Debt*, the first of US film producer Mack Sennet's silent slapstick Keystone Kops films, was released. **1973** Juan Perón was reelected president of Argentina; he had been ousted in 1955.

BIRTHS

Augustus, first Roman emperor, **63 BC**; Walter Lippman, US journalist, **1889**; Mickey Rooney, US film actor, **1920**; John Coltrane, US saxophonist, **1926**; Ray Charles, US singer, **1930**; Julio Iglesias, Spanish singer, **1943**; Bruce Springsteen, US rock star, **1949**.

DEATHS

Nicholas François Mansart, French architect, **1666**; Wilkie Collins, English novelist, **1889**; Sigmund Freud, Austrian psychoanalyst, **1939**; Pablo Neruda, Chilean poet, **1973**; Bob Fosse, US choreographer and director, **1987**.

NOTES

September 24

---

*"In the real dark night of the soul it is always
three o'clock in the morning, day after day."*
—F. SCOTT FITZGERALD, The Crack-Up

EVENTS

1852 French engineer Henri Giffaud made the first flight in a dirigible balloon, from Paris to Trappe. **1930** Noel Coward's *Private Lives* was first staged in London. **1953** *The Robe*, the first Cinemascope film, premiered in Hollywood. **1957** President Eisenhower sent federal troops to Little Rock to protect black students admitted to Central High School the previous day. **1960** The first nuclear-powered aircraft carrier, the USS *Enterprise*, was launched at Newport, Virginia. **1975** British mountaineers Dougal Haston and Doug Scott became the first to reach Mt. Everest's summit via the southwest face. **1980** The Iraqis blew up the Abadan oil refinery, turning the Iran-Iraq conflict into a full scale war.

BIRTHS

Geronimo Cardano, Italian physician and mathematician, **1501**; Horace Walpole, English writer, **1717**; F. Scott Fitzgerald, US novelist, **1896**; Howard Walter Florey, pathologist, **1898**; Gerry Marsden, English rock musician, **1942**.

DEATHS

Pépin III (the Short), king of the Franks, **768**; Pope Innocent II, **1143**; Paracelsus, Swiss physician, alchemist, and scientist, **1541**.

NOTES

September 25

*"I believe that man will not merely endure, he will prevail.
He is immortal, not because he, alone among creatures, has
an inexhaustible voice but because he has a soul, a spirit
capable of compassion and sacrifice and endurance."*
—WILLIAM FAULKNER, *speech on receiving the Nobel Prize*

EVENTS

1513 Vasco Balboa, Spanish explorer, became the first European to sight the Pacific Ocean after crossing the Darien isthmus. **1818** The first blood transfusion using human blood took place at Guy's Hospital in London. **1909** The French battleship *Liberté* exploded in Toulon Harbor, killing 226 people. **1954** François Duvalier ("Papa Doc") was elected president of Haiti. **1956** The first transatlantic telephone cable began operation. **1979** After 111 years, Canada's *Montreal Star* newspaper ceased publication after a long strike over the introduction of new technology.

BIRTHS

William Faulkner, US novelist, **1897**; Mark Rothko, US painter, **1903**; Dmitri Shostakovich, Russian composer, **1906**; Colin Davis, British conductor, **1927**; Barbara Walters, US TV interviewer, **1931**; Michael Douglas, US film actor, **1944**; Christopher Reeve, US film actor, **1952**.

DEATHS

Johann Strauss the Elder, Austrian composer, **1849**; Emily Post, US writer on etiquette, **1960**; Erich Maria Remarque, German novelist, **1970**; Walter Pidgeon, US film actor, **1984**.

NOTES

September 26

"I will show you fear in a handful of dust."
—T.S. ELIOT, The Waste Land

EVENTS

1687 The Parthenon in Athens was severely damaged by mortar bombs fired by the Venetian army as it besieged the Turkish-held Acropolis. **1887** German-born US inventor Emile Berliner patented the gramophone, the first phonograph. **1961** Folk singer Bob Dylan made his debut in New York's Greenwich Village, at Gerdie's Folk City. **1978** Karol Wojtyla, archbishop of Krakow, became Pope John Paul II, the first non-Italian pope since 1522. **1983** Alan Bond's *Australia II* won the America's Cup, the first non-US winner ever for 132 years. **1984** Britain agreed to transfer full sovereignty of Hong Kong to China in 1997. **1988** Canadian sprinter Ben Johnson was stripped of his gold medal in the 100 meters at the Seoul Olympics after failing a drug test. **1994** President Bill Clinton's health-care legislation was defeated in Congress.

BIRTHS

Théodore Géricault, French painter, **1791**; Ivan Petrovich Pavlov, Russian physiologist, **1849**; T.S. Eliot, US-born British poet and playwright, **1888**; George Gershwin, US composer, **1898**; Bryan Ferry, English rock singer, **1945**; Olivia Newton-John, Australian pop singer, **1948**.

DEATHS

Daniel Boone, US frontiersman, **1820**; Béla Bartók, Hungarian composer, **1945**; Alberto Moravia, Italian writer, **1990**.

NOTES

September 27

"You'd be better off dead than in show business."
—CLARA BOW'S MOTHER, *waking her with a butcher's knife after young Clara had accepted a movie role*

EVENTS

1821 Mexico achieved independence through the efforts of General Hubride, who declared himself Emperor Augustin I. **1826** The Stockton and Darlington Railway, the first passenger rail service, opened, with its first steam locomotive traveling at 10 mph. **1922** Constantine I, king of Greece, abdicated following the Greek defeat in Turkey. **1939** Warsaw, the capital of Poland, surrendered to the German forces. **1964** The Warren Commission report was released on the Kennedy assassination and concluded that Lee Harvey Oswald was the sole assassin.

BIRTHS

Samuel Adams, US revolutionary leader, **1722**; George Cruikshank, English caricaturist and illustrator, **1792**; Louis Botha, South African politician, **1862**; Vincent Youmans, US composer, **1898**; Cheryl Tiegs, US model and actress, **1947**.

DEATHS

Ivan Alexandrovich Goncharov, Russian novelist, **1891**; Edgar Degas, French painter, **1917**; Engelbert Humperdinck, German composer, **1921**; Aimee Semple McPherson, US evangelist, **1944**; Aristide Maillol, French painter and sculptor, **1944**; Clara Bow, US silent-film actress, **1965**; Gracie Fields, English singer and comedian, **1979**.

NOTES

September 28

"A whale ship was my Yale College and my Harvard."
—HERMAN MELVILLE, Moby Dick

EVENTS

490 BC The Greeks defeated the Persians at the Battle of Marathon. **1745** At the Drury Lane Theatre, London, "God Save the King," the British national anthem, was sung for the first time. **1864** The First International was founded in London, when Karl Marx proposed the formation of an International Working Men's Association. **1904** Police arrested a woman for smoking in an open automobile on Fifth Avenue, New York—she had violated custom but had not broken any law. **1945** A weekly round-the-world air service, taking about six days to complete the trip, was inaugurated in Washington, DC. **1978** Pope John Paul I, pope for only 33 days, was found dead.

BIRTHS

Caravaggio, Italian painter, **1573**; Prosper Merimée, French writer, **1803**; Georges Clemenceau, French politician, **1841**; Peter Finch, British film actor, **1916**; Marcello Mastroianni, Italian film actor, **1924**; Brigitte Bardot, French film actress, **1934**.

DEATHS

Andrea del Sarto, Italian painter, **1530**; Herman Melville, US novelist, **1891**; Louis Pasteur, French chemist, **1895**; Émile Zola, French novelist, **1902**; Arthur "Harpo" Marx, US film comedian, **1964**; Gamal Abdel Nasser, Egyptian statesman, **1970**; W.H. Auden, English poet, **1973**.

NOTES

September 29

"Don't talk with your ear, nor listen with your mouth."
—SIGN, *1914 telephone instructions for US callers*

EVENTS

1399 The first English monarch to abdicate, Richard II, was replaced by Bolingbroke, who ascended the throne as Henry IV. **1911** Italy declared war on Turkey over possession of Tripoli, in Libya. **1916** John D. Rockefeller became the world's first billionaire during the share boom in the US. **1938** The Munich Agreement between Germany and France, Italy, and Britain was signed. **1944** Soviet troops entered Yugoslavia. **1950** The first automatic telephone answering machine was tested by the US Bell Telephone Company. **1991** Haiti's first freely elected president, Jean-Bertrand Aristide, was ousted in a military coup.

BIRTHS

Miguel de Cervantes, Spanish playwright and novelist, **1547**; Horatio Nelson, English admiral, **1758**; Enrico Fermi, Italian-born US physicist, **1901**; Gene Autry, US cowboy star and singer, **1907**; Stanley Kramer, US film director, **1913**; Cliff Robertson, US film actor, **1925**; Jerry Lee Lewis, US singer and pianist, **1935**; Lech Walesa, Polish leader, **1943**.

DEATHS

Winslow Homer, US painter, **1910**; Rudolf Diesel, German engineer, **1913**; Willem Einthoven, Dutch physiologist, **1927**; Winifred Holtby, English novelist, **1935**; Carson McCullers, US author, **1967**.

NOTES

September 30

The national day of Botswana.

EVENTS

1791 The first performance of Mozart's *The Magic Flute* took place in Vienna. **1902** Rayon, or artificial silk, was patented. **1928** Scotland's Alexander Fleming announced his discovery of penicillin. **1935** George Gershwin's opera *Porgy and Bess* was first performed, in Boston. **1939** The USSR and Germany agreed on the partition of Poland. **1952** Cinerama, invented by Fred Waller, was first exhibited in New York. **1983** Guion Bluford became the first black American to go into space.

BIRTHS

David Fyodorovich Oistrakh, Russian violinist, **1908**; Deborah Kerr, British actress, **1923**; Truman Capote, US author, **1924**; Angie Dickinson, US actress, **1931**; Johnny Mathis, US singer, **1935**.

DEATHS

James Dean, US film actor and cult figure, **1955**; Simone Signoret, French film actress, **1985**; Virgil Thomson, US composer, **1989**.

NOTES

October 1

*"We should live our lives as though
Christ were coming this afternoon."*
—JIMMY CARTER

The national days of China, Nigeria, and Cyprus.

EVENTS

1908 The first Model T, produced in Detroit, was introduced by Henry Ford; it cost $850. **1918** The Arab forces of Emir Faisal, with British officer T.E. Lawrence ("Lawrence of Arabia"), captured Damascus from the Turks. **1936** General Francisco Franco took office as head of Spain's Nationalist government. **1949** The People's Republic of China was proclaimed, with Mao Zedong as its chairman. **1962** James Meredith became the first black student at the University of Mississippi after 3,000 troops quelled disorder on campus. **1971** Disney World, the world's largest amusement park, was opened in Orlando, Florida.

BIRTHS

Vladimir Horowitz, Russian-born US pianist, **1904**; Walter Matthau, US comic film actor, **1920**; James Whitmore, US actor, **1921**; Jimmy Carter, 39th US president, **1924**; Richard Harris, British actor, **1933**; Julie Andrews, English actress and singer, **1935**.

DEATHS

Pierre Corneille, French dramatist, **1684**; Edwin Landseer, English painter, **1873**; Wilhelm Dilthey, German philosopher, **1911**; Louis Leakey, English anthropologist, **1972**; Roy Harris, US composer, **1979**.

NOTES

October 2

*"Our worst enemies here are not the ignorant and the simple,
however cruel; our worst enemies are the intelligent and corrupt."*
—GRAHAM GREENE, The Human Factor

EVENTS

1187 Saladin, the Muslim sultan, captured Jerusalem after its 88-year occupation by the Franks. **1608** The first telescope was demonstrated by the Dutch lensmaker Hans Lipperschey. **1835** The first significant battle in the Texas revolution took place when Texan leaders staged an armed uprising against the Mexican army at Gonzales. **1836** Charles Darwin returned from his five-year survey of South American waters aboard the HMS *Beagle*. **1871** Mormon leader Brigham Young was arrested for bigamy in Salt Lake City. **1950** Charles Schulz's comic strip *Peanuts* first appeared in the US. **1967** Thurgood Marshall became the first black Supreme Court associate justice.

BIRTHS

Mohandas Karamchand Gandhi, Indian leader, **1869**; Cordell Hull, US secretary of state and Nobel Peace Prize winner, **1871**; Julius "Groucho" Marx, US comedian, **1890**; Graham Greene, English novelist, **1904**; Rex Reed, US film critic, **1938**; Sting, English rock singer, **1951**.

DEATHS

Samuel Adams, US statesman, **1803**; Max Bruch, German composer, **1920**; Marcel Duchamp, French painter, **1968**; Rock Hudson, US film actor, **1985**.

NOTES

October 3

EVENTS

1906 SOS was established as an international distress signal, replacing the call sign CQD. **1929** The Kingdom of Serbs, Croats, and Slovenes was renamed Yugoslavia. **1990** East and West Germany were officially reunified, with Berlin as the capital. **1994** US Secretary of Agriculture Mike Espy resigned after the Office of Government Ethics alleged he accepted gifts from farming and food-processing companies. **1995** In America's most spectacular TV celebrity trial, O.J. Simpson, the actor, sports commentator, and former football star, was found not guilty of murdering his wife and her friend Ronald Goldman; the verdict polarized American opinion along racial lines.

BIRTHS

Pierre Bonnard, French painter, **1867**; Louis Aragon, French poet, **1897**; James Herriot, Scottish author, **1916**; Gore Vidal, US author, **1925**; Chubby Checker, US rock 'n' roll singer who popularized the Twist dance, **1941**.

DEATHS

St. Francis of Assisi, Italian founder of the Franciscan order, **1226**; Myles (or Miles) Standish, American military leader of Plymouth colony and treasurer of Massachusetts, **1656**; William Morris, English designer, socialist, and poet, **1896**; Woody Guthrie, US folk singer and composer, **1967**; Jean Anouilh, French dramatist, **1987**.

NOTES

October 4

The national day of Lesotho.

EVENTS

1905 Orville Wright became the first to fly an aircraft for over 33 minutes. **1910** Portugal was proclaimed a republic when King Manuel II was driven from the country by a revolution. **1957** The USSR's *Sputnik I*, the first space satellite, was launched. **1958** BOAC (now British Airways) began operating the first transatlantic passenger jet service. **1965** Pope Paul VI visited New York to address the UN, becoming the first pope to visit the US. **1983** A world record speed of 663.5 mph was achieved by Richard Noble in his jet-powered automobile *Thrust II*, in Nevada.

BIRTHS

Giambattista Piranesi, Italian architect, **1720**; Jean François Millet, French painter, **1814**; Rutherford B. Hayes, 19th US president, **1822**; Frederick Remington, US artist who depicted frontier life, **1861**; Damon Runyon, US short-story writer, **1880**; Engelbert Dollfuss, Austrian statesman, **1892**; Buster Keaton, US silent-film comedian, **1892**; Charlton Heston, US film actor, **1924**.

DEATHS

Benozzo Gozzoli, Italian painter, **1497**; Rembrandt (van Rijn), Dutch painter, **1669**; John Rennie, Scottish civil engineer, **1821**; Janis Joplin, US rock singer, overdosed, **1970**.

NOTES

October 5

EVENTS

1880 The earliest "ball pen," with its own ink supply and retractable tip, was patented by Alonzo T. Cross. **1911** Italian troops occupied Tripoli, in Libya, during its war with Turkey. **1914** The first air battle took place between French and German aircraft during World War I. **1930** The British airship *R101*, the world's largest dirigible at that time, crashed in France en route to India. **1970** Anwar Sadat succeeded Gamal Abdel Nasser as president of Egypt. **1994** Police found 53 members of a religious cult, the Order of the Solar Temple, dead at two locations in Switzerland; five more members were found dead in Quebec, Canada.

BIRTHS

Denis Diderot, French philosopher, **1713**; Chester A. Arthur, 21st US president, **1830**; Glynis Johns, British actress, **1923**; Václav Havel, Czech dramatist and president, **1936**; Bob Geldof, Irish musician, **1954**.

DEATHS

Philip III (the Bold), king of France, **1285**; Joachim Patinir, Dutch painter, **1524**; Jacques Offenbach, German-born French composer, **1880**; Jean Vigo, French film director, **1934**; Nelson Riddle, US composer and arranger, **1985**.

NOTES

October 6

"Wait a minute! Wait a minute! You ain't heard nothin' yet."
—AL JOLSON, *first words in* The Jazz Singer

EVENTS

1769 English naval explorer Captain James Cook, aboard the *Endeavour*, landed in New Zealand. **1883** The "Orient Express" completed its first run from Paris to Constantinople (now Istanbul) in nearly 78 hours. **1908** Austria annexed Bosnia and Herzegovina. **1927** Warner Brothers' *The Jazz Singer*, the first talking feature film (starring Al Jolson), premiered in New York. **1928** Nationalist General Chiang Kai-shek became president of China. **1981** One day after the 11th anniversary of his election to office, Egyptian President Anwar Sadat was assassinated by Muslim extremists.

BIRTHS

Jenny Lind (the "Swedish nightingale"), operatic soprano, **1820**; Le Corbusier, Swiss architect, **1887**; Helen Wills-Moody, US tennis champion, **1905**; Janet Gaynor, US film actress, **1906**; Thor Heyerdahl, Norwegian ethnologist, **1914**.

DEATHS

William Tyndale, English Bible translator, **1536**; Charles Stewart Parnell, Irish nationalist, **1891**; Alfred, Lord Tennyson, English poet, **1892**; George du Maurier, English novelist, **1896**; Anwar Sadat, Egyptian statesman, assassinated, **1981**.

NOTES

October 7

*"The chances of peaceful change in
South Africa are virtually nil."*
—BISHOP DESMOND TUTU, *Sept. 7, 1985*

EVENTS

1806 The first carbon paper was patented by its English inventor, Ralph Wedgwood. **1919** The Dutch airline KLM, the oldest existing airline, was established. **1949** Mrs. I. Toguri D'Aquino was sentenced to 10 years in prison for her wartime propaganda broadcasts as "Tokyo Rose"; she was released in 1956 and pardoned in 1977. **1949** The German Democratic Republic, or East Germany, was formed. **1958** The first photograph of the far side of the Moon was transmitted from the USSR's *Lunik I*. **1985** The Italian liner *Achille Lauro* was seized by Palestinian terrorists; they surrendered two days later, having killed one US passenger. **1988** Gray whales trapped under ice in Alaska became the focus of an international rescue effort.

BIRTHS

James Whitcombe Riley, US poet, **1849**; Niels Bohr, Danish physicist, **1885**; June Allison, US film actress, **1917**; Desmond Tutu, archbishop of Cape Town, **1931**; Oliver North, US lieutenant colonel involved in the Iran-Contra scandal, **1943**; Yo Yo Ma, Chinese cellist, **1955**.

DEATHS

Edgar Allan Poe, US writer, **1849**; Oliver Wendell Holmes, US writer, **1894**; Clarence Birdseye, US frozen-food inventor, **1967**; Bette Davis, US film actress, **1989**; Agnes De Mille, US choreographer, **1993**.

NOTES

October 8

"Nothing is surely a waste of time when one enjoys the day."
—ARTHUR KOESTLER, *reported on Oct. 8, 1972*

EVENTS

1085 St. Mark's Cathedral in Venice was consecrated. **1754** Britain forced the Acadian French from Nova Scotia, Canada, to resettle in Louisiana, where they became known as Cajuns. **1871** The great fire of Chicago started. It burned until October 11, killing over 250 people and making 95,000 homeless. **1905** A permanent waving machine was first used on a woman's hair, by Charles Nessler. **1939** Western Poland was incorporated in the Third Reich. **1993** The international community lifted sanctions against South Africa.

BIRTHS

John Milton Hay, US secretary of state, **1838**; Eddie Rickenbacker, US fighter pilot in World War I who shot down a record 69 enemy aircraft and later became chairman of Eastern Airlines, **1890**; Juan Perón, Argentine dictator, **1895**; David Carradine, US film actor, **1937**; Jesse Jackson, US politician and civil-rights campaigner, **1941**; Sigourney Weaver, US film actress, **1949**.

DEATHS

Jan Massys, Flemish painter, **1575**; Henry Fielding, English novelist, **1754**; Franklin Pierce, 14th US president, **1869**; Kathleen Ferrier, English operatic contralto, **1953**; Clement Attlee, British prime minister, **1967**; Willy Brandt, German chancellor, **1992**.

NOTES

October 9

The national day of Uganda.

EVENTS

1779 The first English Luddite riots, against the introduction of machinery for spinning cotton, began in Manchester. **1875** The Universal Postal Union was established, with headquarters in Berne, Switzerland. **1888** The massive marble Washington Monument, designed by Robert Mills, was opened. **1934** Alexander, king of Yugoslavia, and French Foreign Minister Louis Barthou were assassinated by Croatian terrorists in Marseilles. **1967** Ernesto "Che" Guevara, Argentinian-born guerrilla leader and revolutionary, was captured and executed in Bolivia.

BIRTHS

Camille Saint-Saëns, French composer, **1835**; Aimee Semple McPherson, US evangelist, **1890**; Jacques Tati, French comic actor and film director, **1908**; John Lennon, English singer-songwriter and member of the Beatles, **1940**.

DEATHS

Gabriel Fallopius, Italian anatomist, **1562**; Pope Pius XII, **1958**; André Maurois, French writer, **1967**; Clare Booth Luce, US writer and politician, **1987**.

NOTES

October 10

"This is the biggest electric train set any boy ever had!"
—ORSON WELLES, *of the RKO studio*

EVENTS

732 The Franks, under Charles Martel, defeated the Saracens at the Battle of Tours. **1845** The US Naval Academy opened. **1886** The dinner jacket was first worn in New York by its creator at the Tuxedo Park Country Club, after which it was named. **1903** Mrs. Emmeline Pankhurst formed the Women's Social and Political Union to fight for women's emancipation in Britain. **1911** China's imperial dynasty was forced to abdicate, and a republic was proclaimed, under Sun Yat-sen. **1935** George Gershwin's opera *Porgy and Bess* opened in New York City. **1973** US Vice President Spiro Agnew resigned after being fined $10,000 for income tax evasion.

BIRTHS

Jean Antoine Watteau, French painter, **1684**; Henry Cavendish, English physicist, **1731**; Giuseppe Verdi, Italian composer, **1813**; Thelonious Monk, US jazz pianist and composer, **1918**; Harold Pinter, British dramatist, **1930**; Chevy Chase, US comic actor, **1943**; Tanya Tucker, US country singer, **1958**.

DEATHS

Fra Filippo Lippi, Italian painter, **1469**; Edith Piaf, French singer, **1963**; Eddie Cantor, US actor and entertainer, **1964**; Ralph Richardson, English actor, **1983**; Orson Welles, US actor, director, and producer, **1985**; Yul Brynner, US film actor, **1985**.

NOTES

October 11

"Tact consists in knowing how far we may go too far."
—JEAN COCTEAU

EVENTS

1689 Peter the Great, czar of Russia, assumed control of the government. **1968** The US spacecraft *Apollo 7* was launched from Cape Kennedy, with a crew of three. **1980** The Soviet *Salyut 6* returned to Earth; its cosmonauts had been in space for a record 185 days. **1982** The *Mary Rose*, which had been the pride of Henry VIII's fleet until it sank in the Solent in 1545, was raised. **1984** Dr. Kathryn Sullivan became the first American woman to walk in space. **1994** The Colorado Supreme Court struck down the state's Amendment 2 (approved in 1992), which prohibited local governments from legally protecting homosexuals from discrimination.

BIRTHS

George Williams, founder of the YMCA, **1821**; Eleanor Roosevelt, wife of President Franklin D. Roosevelt and human-rights campaigner, **1884**; Richard Burton, Welsh-born Hollywood actor, **1925**; Elmore Leonard, US crime writer, **1925**.

DEATHS

Huldrych Zwingli, Swiss religious reformer, **1531**; Meriwether Lewis, US explorer, **1809**; James Joule, English physicist, **1889**; Anton Bruckner, Austrian composer, **1896**; Leonard "Chico" Marx, US film comedian, **1961**; Jean Cocteau, French poet, dramatist, and film director, **1963**; Jess Thomas, US operatic tenor, **1993**.

NOTES

October 12

"I have been up to see the Congress and they do not
seem to be able to do anything except to eat peanuts
and chew tobacco, while my army is starving."
—ROBERT E. LEE, *remark to his son about the*
Confederate Congress, 1865

EVENTS

1492 Columbus sighted land in the New World, calling it San Salvador. **1901** US President Theodore Roosevelt renamed the executive mansion "The White House." **1928** The first iron lung was used, at Boston Children's Hospital. **1968** The 19th Olympic Games opened in Mexico City. **1984** An IRA bomb exploded in an unsuccessful attempt to murder Prime Minister Margaret Thatcher and the British cabinet. **1992** Demonstrations were held in many Latin American countries against celebrations of the 500th anniversary of Columbus's arrival in the Americas.

BIRTHS

Edward VI, king of England, **1537**; Isaac Newton Lewis, US soldier and inventor of the machine gun named for him, **1858**; Elmer Ambrose Sperry, US inventor of the gyrocompass, **1860**; Luciano Pavarotti, Italian operatic tenor, **1935**.

DEATHS

Piero della Francesca, Italian painter, **1492**; Elizabeth Fry, English prison reformer, **1845**; Robert E. Lee, US Confederate general, **1870**; Anatole France, French author, **1924**; Tom Mix, US cowboy star, **1940**; Leon Ames, US film actor, **1993**.

NOTES

October 13

"No one would remember the Good Samaritan if he'd only had good intentions. He had money as well."
—MARGARET THATCHER

EVENTS

1307 On the orders of Philip IV of France, the arrest of the Templars on charges of heresy took place in Paris. **1792** The cornerstone of the White House, Washington, DC, was laid by President George Washington. **1884** Greenwich was adapted as the universal time meridian of longitude from which standard times throughout the world are calculated. **1904** Sigmund Freud's *The Interpretation of Dreams* was published. **1985** The world's largest atom smasher, the Fermi National Accelerator Laboratory at Batavia, Illinois, began operation. **1988** The Cardinal of Turin confirmed reports that the Shroud of Turin, believed to carry the imprint of Christ's face, had been scientifically dated to the Middle Ages.

BIRTHS

Lillie Langtry, British actress, **1853**; Yves Montand, French singer and actor, **1921**; Margaret Thatcher, British prime minister, **1925**; Paul Simon, US singer and songwriter, **1941**; Marie Osmond, US singer, **1959**.

DEATHS

Claudius I, Roman emperor, **54**; Nicholas de Malebranche, French philosopher, **1715**; Antonio Canova, Italian sculptor, **1822**; Henry Irving, English actor, **1905**; Clifton Webb, US actor, **1966**; Josef von Sternberg, Austrian-born Hollywood director, **1969**.

NOTES

October 14

---

*"I can't understand why a quiet, reserved fellow like
me should be involved in the news so much."*
—ERROL FLYNN

The national day of Madagascar.

EVENTS

1066 The Battle of Hastings was fought on Senlac Hill, where
King Harold was slain as William the Conqueror's troops routed
the English army. **1884** Photographic film was patented by US
entrepreneur and inventor George Eastman. **1920** Oxford
University degrees were conferred on women for the first time.
1947 The first supersonic flight (670 mph) was made in California
by Charles Yeagar in his *Bell XI* rocket plane. **1971** The US spacecraft *Mariner 9* transmitted the first close-up TV pictures of Mars
to Earth.

BIRTHS

William Penn, Quaker founder of Pennsylvania, **1644**; Éamon de
Valera, Irish statesman, **1882**; Dwight D. Eisenhower, 34th US
president, **1890**; e e cummings, US poet, **1894**; Lillian Gish, US
film actress, **1899**; Ralph Lauren, US fashion designer, **1939**; Cliff
Richard, English singer, **1940**; Anne Rice, US novelist, **1941**.

DEATHS

Erwin Rommel, German field-marshal, **1944**; Errol Flynn,
Australian-born US actor, **1959**; Edith Evans, English actress,
1976; Bing Crosby, US singer and film actor, **1977**; Leonard
Bernstein, US conductor and composer, **1990**.

NOTES

October 15

EVENTS

1581 The first major ballet was staged at the request of Catherine de' Medici at the palace in Paris. **1582** The Gregorian calendar was adopted in Italy, Spain, Portugal, and France; October 5 became October 15. **1858** The final Lincoln-Douglas debate occurred in Illinois, the series having begun on August 21; Stephen A. Douglas eventually defeated Lincoln for a US Senate seat. **1878** Thomas A. Edison established his Edison Electric Light Company. **1917** Mata Hari, Dutch spy, was shot in Paris, having been found guilty of espionage for the Germans. **1928** The German airship *Graf Zeppelin*, captained by Hugo Eckener, completed its first transatlantic flight. **1961** The human-rights organization Amnesty International was established in London.

BIRTHS

Virgil, Roman poet, **70 BC**; Evangelista Torricelli, Italian physicist, **1608**; Friedrich Wilhelm Nietzsche, German philosopher, **1844**; P.G. Wodehouse, English novelist, **1881**; C.P. Snow, English scientist and novelist, **1905**; Mario Puzo, US novelist, **1920**; Lee Iacocca, US automobile executive, **1924**.

DEATHS

Antoine de la Mothe Cadillac, French explorer, **1730**; Raymond Poincaré, French statesman, **1934**; Hermann Goering, Nazi leader, **1946**; Cole Porter, US composer and lyricist, **1964**.

NOTES

October 16

"We are all in the gutter, but some of us are looking at the stars."
—OSCAR WILDE, Lady Windermere's Fan

EVENTS

1815 Napoleon was exiled to the Atlantic island of St Helena. **1846** The first public surgical operation using ether as an anesthetic was performed at the Massachusetts General Hospital, Boston. **1859** The abolitionist John Brown and 21 followers raided and seized the US armory at Harpers Ferry, Virginia; it was retaken the next morning by Robert E. Lee. **1922** The Simplon II railroad tunnel, under the Alps, was completed. **1946** Nazi war criminals, including von Ribbentrop, Rosenberg, and Streicher, were hanged at Nuremberg. **1964** China exploded a nuclear device. **1978** Karol Cardinal Wojtyla was elected Pope John Paul II—the first non-Italian pope since 1542. **1995** The "Million Man March" civil-rights rally, organized by radical black leader Louis Farrakhan, took place in Washington, DC.

BIRTHS

Noah Webster, US lexicographer, **1758**; Oscar Wilde, Irish dramatist and author, **1854**; David Ben-Gurion, Israeli prime minister, **1886**; Eugene O'Neill, US dramatist, **1888**; Günter Grass, German novelist, **1927**.

DEATHS

Marie Antoinette, queen of France, **1793**; George Marshall, US general and diplomat, **1959**; Moshe Dayan, Israeli general and politician, **1981**; Cornel Wilde, US film actor, **1989**; Paolo Bortoluzzi, Italian dancer and choreographer, **1993**.

NOTES

October 17

EVENTS

1651 England's Charles II, defeated by Cromwell at Worcester, fled to France, destitute and friendless. **1777** General Horatio Gates won the Battle of Saratoga, a key victory for the American colonists. **1914** An earthquake struck Greece and Asia Minor, killing over 3,000 people. **1931** US gangster Al Capone was sentenced to 11 years in prison for income-tax evasion, the only charge that could be sustained against him. **1959** The South African De Beers diamond firm announced that synthetic industrial diamonds had been produced. **1977** A US Supreme Court ruling allowed the European supersonic airplane *Concorde* to use Kennedy Airport, New York. **1989** San Francisco experienced a severe earthquake that caused 59 deaths.

BIRTHS

Isak Dinesen (Karen Blixen), Danish author, **1885**; Nathaniel West, US novelist, **1903**; Arthur Miller, US dramatist, **1915**; Rita Hayworth, US film actress, **1918**; Montgomery Clift, US film actor, **1938**.

DEATHS

Philip Sidney, English poet and soldier, **1586**; Frédéric Chopin, Polish pianist and composer, **1849**; Gustav Robert Kirchoff, German physicist, **1887**; Julia Ward Howe, US author, **1910**; S.J. Perelman, US humorist, **1979**.

NOTES

October 18

---

*"Dictators have only become possible through
the invention of the microphone."*
—SIR THOMAS INSKIP, *reported on Oct. 18, 1936*

EVENTS

1873 Delegates from Columbia, Princeton, Rutgers, and Yale met in New York to formulate standard rules for football. **1887** Russia transferred Alaska to the US for $7.2 million. **1922** The British Broadcasting Company (later Corporation) was officially formed. **1977** Germany's antiterrorist squad stormed a hijacked Lufthansa aircraft at Mogadishu Airport, Somalia, killing three of the four Palestinian hijackers and freeing all of the hostages. **1989** Following a wave of pro-democracy demonstrations in East Germany, Erich Honecker was replaced as head of state by Egon Krenz. **1989** With the end of communist rule, Hungary was proclaimed a free republic.

BIRTHS

Canaletto, Italian painter, **1697**; Henri Bergson, French philosopher, **1859**; Pierre Trudeau, Canadian prime minister, **1919**; Chuck Berry, US rock singer, **1926**; George C. Scott, US film actor, **1927**; Martina Navratilova, Czech-born US tennis player, **1956**.

DEATHS

Lord Palmerston, British prime minister, **1865**; Charles Babbage, English mathematician, **1871**; Charles Gounod, French composer, **1893**; Thomas Edison, US inventor, **1931**; Elizabeth Arden, cosmetics company founder, **1966**; Pierre Mendès-France, French statesman, **1982**.

NOTES

October 19

EVENTS

1781 General Washington received the British surrender at Yorktown, Virginia, marking the end of the American Revolution. **1860** The first company to manufacture internal combustion engines was formed in Florence. **1864** In the Civil War, Union General Philip Sheridan was victorious over the Confederates at the Battle of Cedar Creek, Virginia. **1872** The Holtermann nugget was mined at Hill End, New South Wales; weighing 630 lbs, it was the largest gold-bearing nugget ever found. **1987** Wall Street was struck by "Black Monday," during which millions were wiped out on stock markets around the world.

BIRTHS

Alfred Dreyfus, French army officer, **1859**; Auguste Marie Lumière, French photographic pioneer, **1862**; Jack Anderson, US columnist, **1922**; John Le Carré, English spy novelist, **1931**; Peter Tosh, Jamaican reggae musician, **1944**.

DEATHS

Jonathan Swift, Irish author, **1745**; George Pullman, US engineer and sleeping-car manufacturer, **1897**; Ernest Rutherford, New Zealand physicist, **1937**; Martha Raye, US comedienne, **1994**.

NOTES

October 20

EVENTS

1818 The US and Britain established the 49th parallel as the boundary between Canada and the US. **1827** The Battle of Navarino, off the coast of Greece, ended with the combined British, French, and Russian fleets completely destroying the Egyptian and Turkish fleets. **1935** Mao Zedong's Long March ended in Yenan, north China. **1944** The Allies captured Aachen, Germany. **1968** Jacqueline Kennedy, widow of US President John Kennedy, married Greek millionaire Aristotle Onassis.

BIRTHS

Christopher Wren, English architect, **1632**; Lord Palmerston, British prime minister, **1784**; Arthur Rimbaud, French poet, **1854**; John Dewey, US philosopher who advocated progressive education, **1859**; Charles Ives, US composer, **1874**; Bela Lugosi, Hungarian-born US horror actor, **1884**; Art Buchwald, US humorist and columnist, **1925**; Tom Petty, US guitarist and singer, **1953**.

DEATHS

Richard Francis Burton, English explorer and scholar, **1890**; Herbert Hoover, 31st US president, **1964**.

NOTES

October 21

"I had nothing to offer except my own confusion."
—JACK KEROUAC

EVENTS

1805 The British defeated the Franco-Spanish fleet at the Battle of Trafalgar. **1858** Offenbach's opera *Orpheus in the Underworld* was first performed, in Paris. **1934** Mao Zedong's Long March, with his 100,000-strong Communist army, began. **1950** Tibet was occupied by Chinese forces. **1966** The Welsh mining village of Aberfan was engulfed by a collapsed slagheap, killing 144, including 116 children. **1967** Egyptian missiles sank the Israeli destroyer *Eilat*, with the loss of over 40 lives. **1991** Jesse Turner, an American who had been held hostage in Lebanon for just under five years, was freed by his captors. **1994** Congress canceled the Superconducting Supercollider (SSC) which would have permitted scientists to study colliding atomic particles; $2 billion had already been spent on the project at Waxahachie, Texas.

BIRTHS

Katsushika Hokusai, Japanese artist and printmaker, **1760**; Samuel Taylor Coleridge, English poet, **1772**; Alfred Nobel, Swedish industrialist, **1833**; Georg Solti, Hungarian-born British conductor, **1912**; John Birks "Dizzie" Gillespie, US jazz trumpeter, **1917**; Carrie Fisher, US film actress, **1956**.

DEATHS

Pietro Aretino, Italian writer, **1556**; Horatio, Viscount Nelson, English admiral, killed at Trafalgar, **1805**; Jack Kerouac, US poet and novelist, **1969**.

NOTES

October 22

EVENTS

1797 The first parachute jump was made by André-Jacques Garnerin from a balloon above the Parc Monceau, Paris. **1883** New York's Metropolitan Opera House opened. **1909** French aviator Elise Deroche became the first woman to make a solo flight. **1935** Haiti was struck by a hurricane, causing over 2,000 deaths. **1962** President Kennedy announced that Soviet missile bases had been installed in Cuba. **1987** The first volume of the Gutenberg Bible was sold at auction in New York for $5.39 million, a record price for a printed book.

BIRTHS

Franz Liszt, Hungarian pianist and composer, **1811**; Sarah Bernhardt, French actress, **1844**; Doris Lessing, English novelist, **1919**; Robert Rauschenberg, US artist, **1925**; Derek Jacobi, English actor, **1938**; Michael Crichton, US novelist, **1942**; Annette Funicello, US film actress, **1942**; Catherine Deneuve, French film actress, **1943**; Jeff Goldblum, US film actor, **1952**.

DEATHS

Charles Martel, leader of the Franks, **741**; Thomas Sheraton, English furniture maker, **1806**; Paul Cézanne, French painter, **1906**; Pablo Casals, Spanish cellist, **1973**; Arnold Joseph Toynbee, English historian, **1975**.

NOTES

October 23

EVENTS

1642 The Battle of Edgehill took place, the first major conflict of the English Civil War. **1942** In World War II, the Second Battle of El Alamein, in Egypt, began. **1946** The first meeting of the United Nations General Assembly took place in New York. **1956** The Hungarian revolt against Soviet leadership began, in which thousands of demonstrators called for the withdrawal of Soviet forces. **1970** Gary Gabelich achieved the world land speed record of 631.367 mph, in his rocket-engine automobile on Bonneville Salt Flats, Utah. **1983** A suicide terrorist bomber killed 241 US Marines with the UN peacekeeping force in Beirut, Lebanon; another Beirut bomb killed over 40 French paratroopers.

BIRTHS

Pierre Larousse, French lexicographer, **1817**; Louis Riel, French-Canadian rebel, **1844**; Johnny Carson, US TV talkshow host, **1925**; Pelé, Brazilian soccer star, **1940**.

DEATHS

Marcus Junius Brutus, Roman statesman and one of the assassins of Julius Caesar, **42 BC**; Théophile Gautier, French poet, **1872**; John Boyd Dunlop, Scottish inventor of the pneumatic rubber tire, **1921**; Zane Grey, US novelist, **1939**; Al Jolson, US singer and actor, **1950**.

NOTES

October 24

―――

"We cannot in any better manner glorify the Lord and Creator of the universe than that in all things ... we contemplate the display of his omnificence and perfections with the utmost admiration."
—ANTON VAN LEEUWENHOEK

―――

The national day of Zambia and United Nations Day.

EVENTS

1648 The Treaty of Westphalia was signed, ending the Thirty Years' War. **1861** The first US transcontinental telegraph line went into operation. **1901** Mrs. Ann Edson Taylor braved a descent over Niagara Falls in a padded barrel to help pay the mortgage. **1945** The United Nations charter came into force. **1989** US television evangelist Jim Bakker was sentenced to 45 years in prison and fined $500,000 for his multi-million-dollar scam. **1992** The Toronto Blue Jays became the first team from outside the US to win baseball's World Series.

BIRTHS

Anton van Leeuwenhoek, Dutch microscope pioneer, **1632**; Jacques Lafitte, French banker and politician, **1767**; Sarah Hale, US poet who wrote "Mary Had a Little Lamb," **1788**; Tito Gobbi, Italian operatic baritone, **1915**.

DEATHS

Tycho Brahe, Danish astronomer, **1601**; Vidkun Quisling, Norwegian politician and Nazi collaborator, **1945**; Christian Dior, French couturier, **1957**; Mary McCarthy, US author, **1989**; Jiri Hajek, Czech human-rights campaigner, **1993**.

NOTES

―――――――――――――――――――――

―――――――――――――――――――――

―――――――――――――――――――――

―――――――――――――――――――――

October 25

EVENTS

1415 The English army, led by King Henry V, defeated the French at the Battle of Agincourt, during the Hundred Years' War. **1854** Lord Cardigan led the Charge of the Light Brigade during the Battle of Balaclava in the Crimean War. **1881** The famous "Gunfight at the OK Corral" at Tombstone, Arizona, saw Marshal Wyatt Earp, his two brothers, and "Doc" Holliday out-shoot the Clantons and McLowerys. **1931** Opening of the George Washington Bridge between Manhattan and New Jersey, the longest suspension bridge yet built. **1944** General MacArthur returned to the Philippines, fulfilling the promise he had made when forced to retreat from the Japanese. **1983** Over 2,000 US troops invaded Grenada and ousted the Marxist regime.

BIRTHS

Thomas Babington Macaulay, English historian and essayist, **1800**; Johann Strauss the Younger, Austrian composer, **1825**; Georges Bizet, French composer, **1838**; Pablo Picasso, Spanish artist, **1881**; Richard Evelyn Byrd, US aviator and explorer, **1888**.

DEATHS

Geoffrey Chaucer, English poet, **1400**; Giorgione, Italian painter, **1510**; Evangelista Torricelli, Italian physicist and inventor of the barometer, **1647**; George II, king of England, **1760**; Frank Norris, US novelist, **1902**; Vincent Price, US film actor, **1993**.

NOTES

October 26

---

*"The Bible and the Church have been the greatest stumbling blocks
in the way of women's emancipation."*
—ELIZABETH CADY STANTON

The national days of Iran and of Austria.

EVENTS

1825 The Erie Canal, linking the Niagara River with the Hudson
River, was opened to traffic. **1860** Italian unification leader
Giuseppe Garibaldi proclaimed Victor Emmanuel king of Italy.
1905 Sweden and Norway ended their union and Oscar II, the
Norwegian king, abdicated. **1927** Duke Ellington and his orchestra recorded the jazz classic "Creole Love Song." **1929** T.W. Evans
of Miami became the first woman to give birth aboard an airplane. **1956** The UN's International Atomic Energy Agency was
formed. **1965** Queen Elizabeth II presented the Beatles with their
MBE (Member of the Order of the British Empire) titles at
Buckingham Palace. **1985** A US infant, known as Baby Fae, was
given a baboon's heart to replace her malformed one.

BIRTHS

Georges Danton, French revolutionary leader, **1759**; Leon
Trotsky, Russian Communist leader, **1879**; François Mitterand,
French statesman, **1916**; Hillary Clinton, US first lady, **1947**.

DEATHS

Gilles de Rais, French marshal, **1440**; William Hogarth, English
artist and engraver, **1764**; Elizabeth Cady Stanton, US feminist,
1902; Igor Sikorsky, US aeronautical engineer, **1972**.

NOTES

October 27

"There can be no fifty-fifty Americanism in this country. There is room here for only 100 percent Americanism, only for those who are Americans and nothing else."
—THEODORE ROOSEVELT

EVENTS

1775 The Continental Congress established the US Navy with a fleet of eight ships. **1901** In Paris, a "getaway car" was used for the first time, when thieves robbed a shop and sped away. **1904** The first section of New York City's subway system was opened. **1917** In World War I, US troops entered the fighting on the Western Front in France. **1936** Mrs. Wallis Simpson was granted a divorce from her second husband, leaving her free to marry Britain's King Edward VIII. **1971** The Republic of Congo changed its name to the Republic of Zaire.

BIRTHS

Captain James Cook, English naval explorer, **1728**; Niccolò Paganini, Italian violinist and composer, **1782**; Theodore Roosevelt, 26th US president, **1858**; Dylan Thomas, Welsh poet, **1905**; Roy Lichtenstein, US painter, **1923**; Sylvia Plath, US poet, **1932**; John Cleese, English actor, **1939**.

DEATHS

Ivan III (the Great), czar of Russia, **1505**; Lise Meitner, Austrian nuclear physicist, **1968**; James M. Cain, US novelist, **1977**.

NOTES

October 28

"France is the only place where you can make love in the afternoon without people hammering on your door."
—BARBARA CARTLAND, *reported on Oct. 28, 1984*

EVENTS

1636 Harvard College (now University), the first in the US, was founded. **1746** An earthquake demolished Lima and Callao, in Peru. **1831** English chemist and physicist Michael Faraday demonstrated the first dynamo. **1886** The Statue of Liberty was dedicated. **1914** George Eastman, of Eastman Kodak Company, announced the introduction of a color photographic process. **1982** Felipe González became Spain's first Socialist prime minister, with a sweeping electoral victory.

BIRTHS

Evelyn Waugh, English novelist, **1903**; Francis Bacon, British painter, **1909**; Jonas Salk, US microbiologist who developed the polio vaccine, **1914**; Carl Davis, US composer, **1936**.

DEATHS

John Locke, English philosopher, **1704**; Ottmar Mergenthaler, German inventor of the Linotype typesetting machine, **1899**; Georges Carpentier, French boxer, **1975**; Pietro Annigoni, Italian painter, **1988**.

NOTES

October 29

The national day of Turkey.

EVENTS

1618 Sir Walter Raleigh, English navigator, courtier, and once favorite of Elizabeth I, was beheaded at Whitehall for treason. **1863** The International Red Cross was founded by Swiss philanthropist Henri Dunant. **1929** The Wall Street crash known as "Black Tuesday" took place, leading to the Great Depression. **1967** Expo-67, an international exhibition, opened in Montreal. **1991** Vietnam formally approved a plan to forcibly repatriate tens of thousands of Vietnamese refugees living in camps in Hong Kong. **1994** Francisco Martin Duran, of Colorado Springs, fired up to 30 rounds from a semiautomatic rifle at the White House from Pennsylvania Avenue before members of the public disarmed him.

BIRTHS

James Boswell, Scottish diarist, **1740**; Jean Giraudoux, French author, **1882**; Fanny Brice, US singer and comedienne, **1891**; Joseph Goebbels, German Nazi propaganda chief, **1897**; Richard Dreyfuss, US actor, **1947**; Winona Ryder, US film actress, **1971**.

DEATHS

Joseph Pulitzer, US newspaper publisher, **1911**; Gustav V, king of Sweden, **1950**; Louis Burt Mayer, US film producer and distributor, **1957**; Woody Herman, US bandleader and clarinetist, **1987**.

NOTES

October 30

*"I have made my contribution to society.
I have no plans to work again."*
—JOHN LENNON, *reported on Oct. 30, 1977*

EVENTS

1650 "Quakers," the more common name for the Society of Friends, came into being during a court case in England, at which George Fox, the founder, told the magistrate to "quake and tremble at the word of God." **1911** P'u-yi, the boy emperor of China, aged five, granted a new constitution, officially ending three centuries of Manchu domination over China. **1918** The Republic of Czechoslovakia was proclaimed. **1925** The Scottish inventor John Baird made the first televised transmission of a moving object (a 15-year-old office boy). **1938** US actor Orson Welles' radio production of *The War of the Worlds* by H.G. Wells caused panic in the US. **1988** Sun Myung Moon, head of the Unification Church, conducted the marriage of 6,516 couples in a Seoul factory; the couples had first met the day before.

BIRTHS

John Adams, second US president, **1735**; Richard Brinsley Sheridan, Irish dramatist, **1751**; Alfred Sisley, French painter, **1840**; Ezra Pound, US poet, **1885**; Louis Malle, French film director, **1932**; Diego Maradona, Argentinian soccer player, **1960**.

DEATHS

Pio Baroja, Spanish novelist, **1956**; Barnes Neville Wallis, British aeronautical engineer who invented the "bouncing bomb," **1979**.

NOTES

October 31

All Hallows' Eve (Halloween).

EVENTS

1517 Martin Luther nailed his 95 theses against indulgences to
the church door at Wittenberg, Germany. **1864** Nevada became
the 36th state. **1902** The first telegraph cable across the Pacific
Ocean was completed. **1940** The Battle of Britain ended. **1952** At
Eniwetok Atoll, in the Pacific, the US detonated the first hydrogen bomb. **1956** British and French troops bombed Egyptian
airfields at Suez. **1995** Voters in the French-speaking province of
Quebec voted against separatism from Canada by a narrow mar-
gin of just over 1%.

BIRTHS

Jan Vermeer, Dutch painter, **1632**; John Keats, English poet, **1795**;
Chiang Kai-shek, Chinese leader, **1887**; Michael Collins, US
astronaut who circled the moon in the mother ship while Neil
Armstrong and "Buzz" Aldrin landed on the Moon, **1930**; Dan
Rather, US TV news anchorman, **1931**.

DEATHS

Harry Houdini, US magician and escape artist, **1926**; Augustus
John, Welsh painter, **1961**; Indira Gandhi, Indian prime minister,
assassinated, **1984**; Federico Fellini, Italian film director, **1993**;
River Phoenix, US film actor, **1993**.

NOTES

November 1

*"One of the pleasures of middle age is to find out
that one WAS right, and that one was much righter
than one knew at say 17 or 23."*
—EZRA POUND, ABC of Reading

The national day of Algeria.

EVENTS

1755 An earthquake reduced two-thirds of Lisbon to rubble and resulted, according to accounts, in the death of around 60,000 people. **1914** The British ships *Good Hope* and *Monmouth* were sunk by the Germans, at the Battle of Coronel. **1950** Two Puerto Rican nationalists attempted to assassinate President Harry Truman. **1972** Orissa, India, was struck by a tidal wave which killed some 10,000 people and left 5 million homeless. **1994** The European Union's new treaty, approved in Maastricht, the Netherlands, in December 1991, came into effect after a two-year ratification process.

BIRTHS

Benvenuto Cellini, Italian sculptor and goldsmith, **1500**; Antonio Canova, Italian sculptor, **1757**; Stephen Crane, US novelist, **1871**; L.S. Lowry, English painter, **1887**; Victoria de los Angeles, Spanish soprano, **1923**; Gary Player, South African golfer, **1935**.

DEATHS

Ezra Pound, US poet, **1972**; King Vidor, US film director, **1982**; Phil Silvers, US comedian and actor, **1985**; Louis Johnson, New Zealand poet, **1988**.

NOTES

November 2

"Aggression unopposed becomes a contagious disease."
—JIMMY CARTER

EVENTS

1871 The "Rogues Gallery" was started, when photographs of all prisoners in Britain were first taken. **1889** North Dakota became the 39th state and South Dakota the 40th. **1930** Ras Tafari, King of Ethiopia, was crowned Emperor Haile Selassie ("Might of the Trinity"). **1947** Howard Hughes, US millionaire film producer and aircraft designer, piloted the world's largest aircraft ever flown, his $18 million Hercules wooden seaplane known as *The Spruce Goose*; it barely took off and never flew again. **1960** A British jury acquitted Penguin Books of obscenity for publishing D.H. Lawrence's *Lady Chatterley's Lover*. **1962** President Kennedy announced that Soviet missiles in Cuba were being removed. **1976** James Earl (Jimmy) Carter was elected the 39th president of the US.

BIRTHS

Daniel Boone, US frontiersman, **1734**; Marie Antoinette, queen of King Louis XVI of France, **1755**; Joseph Radetzky, Austrian field-marshal, **1766**; James Knox Polk, 11th US president, **1795**; Warren G. Harding, 29th US president, **1865**; Luchino Visconti, Italian film director, **1906**; Burt Lancaster, US film actor, **1913**; Stefanie Powers, US film actress, **1942**.

DEATHS

Richard Hooker, English theologian, **1600**; Jenny Lind, Swedish operatic soprano, **1887**; George Bernard Shaw, Irish dramatist, **1950**; James Thurber, US humorous writer and cartoonist, **1961**.

NOTES

_____

_____

_____

_____

November 3

"I wouldn't mind turning into a vermilion goldfish."
—HENRI MATISSE

The national day of Panama.

EVENTS

1493 Christopher Columbus, on his second voyage of discovery, sighted Dominica, in the West Indies. **1706** A violent earthquake occurred in the Abruzzi, Italy, killing some 15,000 inhabitants. **1927** Turkey adopted the Roman alphabet, abolishing the use of Arabic. **1957** The Russian dog Laika became the first in space aboard *Sputnik 2*. **1975** The North Sea pipeline, the first to be built underwater, was officially opened. **1982** George Wallace won a fourth term as governor of Alabama. **1993** A mystery woman paid a record 5 million Swiss francs ($3.4 million) for an envelope with two stamps sent from Mauritius to a Bordeaux wine exporter in 1847.

BIRTHS

Vincenzo Bellini, Italian composer, **1801**; Karl Baedeker, German guide-book publisher, **1801**; Charles Bronson, US film actor, **1922**; Michael Dukakis, governor of Massachusetts and Democratic presidential candidate, **1933**; Roy Emerson, Australian tennis player, **1936**; Larry Holmes, US heavyweight boxing champion, **1949**; Roseanne Barr, US TV comic actress, **1953**.

DEATHS

Constantine II, Roman emperor of the East, **361**; Annie Oakley, US entertainer and markswoman, **1926**; Henri Matisse, French painter, **1954**; Leon Theremin, Russian inventor, **1993**.

NOTES

November 4

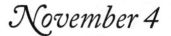

*"I don't make jokes—I just watch the
government and report the facts."*
—WILL ROGERS

EVENTS

1841 The first wagon train of settlers reached California, having left Independence, Missouri, on May 1. **1862** US inventor Richard Gatling patented the rapid-fire, or machine, gun. **1914** The first fashion show was organized by Edna Woodman Chase of *Vogue* magazine, held at the Ritz-Carlton Hotel, New York. **1922** British archeologist Howard Carter discovered the tomb of the Egyptian pharaoh Tutankhamen. **1946** UNESCO was established, with headquarters in Paris. **1979** Iranian students stormed the US embassy in Teheran and held over 60 staff and US Marines hostage. **1980** Ronald Reagan was elected 40th US president. **1991** Imelda Marcos returned to the Philippines after five years of exile in the US.

BIRTHS

William III, king of Britain and Ireland, **1650**; Will Rogers, US humorist and actor, **1879**; Walter Cronkite, US TV news anchorman, **1916**; Art Carney, US actor, **1918**.

DEATHS

Felix Mendelssohn, German composer, **1847**; Paul Delaroche, French painter, **1856**; Wilfred Owen, English poet, **1918**; Gabriel Fauré, French organist and composer, **1924**; Yitzhak Rabin, Israeli statesman, assassinated, **1995**.

NOTES

November 5

*"When my time comes, just skin me and
put me right up there on Trigger."*
—ROY ROGERS, *who had his horse Trigger stuffed and displayed*

EVENTS

1854 The combined British and French armies defeated the Russians at the Battle of Inkerman during the Crimean War. **1911** C.P. Rodgers arrived in Pasadena, California, after making the first transcontinental airplane flight; he had left New York on September 17 and made several stops. **1919** Rudolph Valentino, the archetypal romantic screen lover, married actress Jean Acker; the marriage lasted less than six hours. **1968** Richard Nixon was elected 37th US president. **1990** Rabbi Meir Kahane, founder of the militant Jewish Defense League and Israel's extremist anti-Arab Kach party, was assassinated in a New York City hotel.

BIRTHS

Roy Rogers, US cowboy star, **1912**; Vivien Leigh, British actress, **1913**; Elke Sommer, German actress, **1940**; Art Garfunkel, US singer and composer, **1941**; Sam Shepherd, US dramatist and actor, **1943**; Tatum O'Neal, US film actress, **1953**.

DEATHS

Maurice Utrillo, French painter, **1955**; Mack Sennett, US film producer, **1960**; Al Capp, US cartoonist, **1979**; Jacques Tati, French comic film actor and director, **1982**; Vladimir Horowitz, Russian-born US pianist, **1989**; Robert Maxwell, British publishing and newspaper proprietor, **1991**.

NOTES

November 6

"With malice toward none; with charity for all; with firmness in the right, as God gives us to see the right."
—ABRAHAM LINCOLN, *second Inaugural Address,*
March 4, 1865

EVENTS

1860 Abraham Lincoln was elected 16th US president. **1869** Diamonds were discovered at Kimberley, in Cape Province, South Africa. **1932** In general elections held in Germany, the Nazis emerged as the largest party. **1956** Construction of the Kariba High Dam, on the Zambezi River between Zambia and Zimbabwe, began. **1988** Six thousand US Defense Department computers were crippled by a virus; the culprit was the 23-year-old son of the head of the country's computer security agency. **1994** In a letter to the American people, former President Ronald Reagan said he had Alzheimer's disease.

BIRTHS

Alois Senefelder, Austrian inventor of lithography, **1771**; Adolphe Sax, Belgian inventor of the saxophone, **1814**; John Philip Sousa, US bandmaster and composer for whom the sousaphone is named, **1854**; Mike Nichols, US film director, **1931**; Sally Field, US film actress, **1946**.

DEATHS

Gustavus II, king of Sweden, **1632**; Heinrich Schütz, German composer, **1672**; Peter Ilyich Tchaikovsky, Russian composer, **1893**; Gene Eliza Tierney, US film actress, **1991**.

NOTES

November 7

*"You know what charm is: getting the answer yes
without having asked any clear question."*
—ALBERT CAMUS

EVENTS

1872 The *Marie Celeste*, the ill-fated brigantine, sailed from New York to be found mysteriously abandoned near the Azores some time later. **1916** Jeanette Rankin of Montana became the first woman member of the US Congress. **1917** The Bolshevik Revolution, led by Lenin, overthrew Prime Minister Alexander Kerensky's government. **1972** Richard Nixon was reelected US president. **1988** In Las Vegas, Sugar Ray Lewis knocked out Canadian Donny Londe, completing his collection of world titles at five different weights. **1990** Mary Robinson became the Irish Republic's first woman president.

BIRTHS

Marie Curie, Polish physicist, **1867**; Leon Trotsky, Russian Communist leader, **1879**; Chandrasekhara Venkata Raman, Indian physicist, **1888**; Billy Graham, US evangelist, **1918**; Albert Camus, French writer, **1913**; Joan Sutherland, Australian operatic soprano, **1926**; Joni Mitchell, Canadian singer-songwriter, **1943**.

DEATHS

Eleanor Roosevelt, US writer, first lady, and lecturer, **1962**; Gene Tunney, US heavyweight boxer, **1978**; Steve McQueen, US film actor, **1980**; Alexander Dubček, Czech statesman, **1992**; Adelaide Hall, US singer, dancer, and actress, **1993**.

NOTES

_____

_____

_____

_____

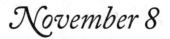

November 8

"Fame is no plant that grows on mortal soil."
—JOHN MILTON

EVENTS

1793 The Louvre art gallery in Paris was opened to the public. **1889** Montana became the 41st state. **1895** William Röntgen discovered X-rays during an experiment at the University of Wurzburg. **1932** Promising the American people a "New Deal," Franklin D. Roosevelt won a landslide presidential election victory against Herbert Hoover. **1942** Under Eisenhower's command, US and British forces invaded North Africa, in "Operation Torch." **1966** Republican Edward Brooke, the first black US senator in 85 years, was elected in Massachusetts. **1994** US mid-term elections gave Republicans control of the Senate and House for the first time, respectively, since 1986 and 1954.

BIRTHS

Edmond Halley, English astronomer who predicted the return of the comet that bears his name, **1656**; Bram Stoker, Irish writer who created Dracula, **1847**; Margaret Mitchell, US journalist whose only novel was *Gone with the Wind*, **1900**; June Havoc, US film actress, **1916**; Christiaan Barnard, South African heart transplant pioneer, **1922**; Patti Page, US singer, **1927**; Alain Delon, French film actor, **1935**.

DEATHS

John Milton, English poet, **1674**; Victorien Sardou, French dramatist, **1908**; Ivan Alexeyevich Bunin, Russian poet, **1953**; Edgard Varèse, French composer, **1965**; Norman Rockwell, US illustrator, **1978**.

NOTES

November 9

*"How can you govern a country which has
246 varieties of cheese?"*
—CHARLES DE GAULLE

The national day of Cambodia.

EVENTS

1799 Napoleon Bonaparte overthrew the Directory to become France's new ruler. **1858** The New York Symphony Orchestra gave its first concert. **1924** The first two women governors were elected in the US: Nellie Tayloe Ross was installed January 5, 1925, in Wyoming, and Miriam "Ma" Ferguson on January 20, 1925, in Texas. **1925** The SS (Schutzstaffel or "Protection Squad") was formed in Germany. **1965** An electric power failure lasting until November 10 blacked out New York City, the northeastern US, and parts of Canada. **1988** Gary Kasparov became world chess champion after beating Anatoly Karpov, who had held the title for ten years, in Moscow.

BIRTHS

Ivan Turgenev, Russian novelist, **1818**; Edward VII, king of Britain, **1841**; Katharine Hepburn, US film actress, **1909**; Hedy Lamarr, US film actress, **1913**; Carl Sagan, US astronomer, **1934**.

DEATHS

Guillaume Apollinaire, French poet, **1918**; James Ramsay MacDonald, Britain's first Labour prime minister, **1937**; Neville Chamberlain, British prime minister, **1940**; Dylan Thomas, Welsh poet, **1953**; Charles de Gaulle, French general and president, **1970**; Yves Montand, French singer and actor, **1991**.

NOTES

November 10

"Dr. Livingstone, I presume?"
—HENRY MORTON STANLEY, How I Found Livingstone

EVENTS

1775 The Continental Congress authorized the creation of the "Continental Marines," now the US Marines. **1862** The first performance of Giuseppe Verdi's opera *La Forza del Destino* was held in St. Petersburg. **1871** Henry Morton Stanley found missing explorer David Livingstone at Ujiji, on Lake Tanganyika. **1926** Hirohito was crowned Emperor of Japan. **1938** Kristallnacht, or "night of (broken) glass", took place when Nazis burned 267 synagogues and destroyed thousands of Jewish homes and businesses in Germany. **1989** Bulldozers began demolishing the 28-year-old Berlin Wall.

BIRTHS

Martin Luther, German Protestant reformer, **1483**; François Couperin, French composer, **1668**; William Hogarth, English painter and engraver, **1697**; Johann Christoph Friedrich von Schiller, German poet and dramatist, **1759**; Richard Burton, Welsh actor, **1925**; Roy Scheider, US film actor, **1932**.

DEATHS

Pope Leo I (the Great), **461**; Arthur Rimbaud, French poet, **1891**; Mustapha Kemal Atatürk, Turkish statesman, **1938**; Leonid Brezhnev, Soviet political leader, **1982**; Carmen McRae, US singer, **1994**; Ken Saro-Wiwa, Nigerian author and civil-rights activist, executed, **1995**.

NOTES

_____

_____

_____

_____

November 11

"Men reject their prophets and slay them, but they love their martyrs and honor those whom they have slain."
—FYODOR DOSTOEVSKY, The Brothers Karamazov

EVENTS

1889 Washington became the 42nd state. **1918** The armistice was signed between the Allies and Germany in Compiègne, France, effectively ending World War I. **1940** The Willys-Overland Company launched a four-wheel drive vehicle for the US Army, named "Jeep" after GP (general purpose). **1952** The first video recorder was demonstrated in Beverly Hills, California, by its inventors, John Mullin and Wayne Johnson. **1965** Ian Smith, prime minister of Rhodesia, unilaterally declared his country's independence from Britain. **1984** The New Orleans World's Fair, which opened May 12, closed as a financial flop; up to 12 million visitors had been expected, but only 7 million came.

BIRTHS

Fyodor Dostoevsky, Russian author, **1821**; Edouard Vuillard, French painter, **1868**; George Patton, US general in World War II, known as "Blood and Guts," **1885**; Kurt Vonnegut, US novelist, **1922**; Demi Moore, US film actress, **1962**.

DEATHS

Nat Turner, US slave and radical preacher, hanged, **1831**; Sören Kierkegaard, Danish philosopher, **1855**; Jerome Kern, US composer, **1945**; Dimitri Tiomkin, US composer, **1979**; Vyacheslav Mikhailovich Molotov, Soviet politician, **1986**.

NOTES

November 12

*"I'll not listen to reason ... Reason always
means what someone else has got to say."*
—ELIZABETH GASKELL

EVENTS

1660 English author John Bunyan was arrested for preaching without a license; refusing to give up preaching, he remained in jail for 12 years. **1847** The first public demonstration of the use of chloroform as an anesthetic took place in Edinburgh. **1859** Jules Léotard, the daring young man on the flying trapeze, made his debut at the Cirque Napoléon, in Paris. **1918** The Republic of Austria was declared, thus ending the Hapsburg dynasty. **1981** The US shuttle *Columbia* became the first reusable crewed spacecraft, by making its second trip.

BIRTHS

Alexander Borodin, Russian composer, **1833**; Auguste Rodin, French sculptor, **1840**; Sun Yat-sen, Chinese nationalist politician, **1866**; Jo Stafford, US singer, **1918**; Grace Kelly (Princess Grace of Monaco), **1929**; Neil Young, Canadian rock singer and guitarist, **1946**; Nadia Comaneci, Romanian gymnast, **1961**.

DEATHS

John Sylvan, French astronomer, **1793**; Elizabeth Gaskell, English novelist, **1865**; Percival Lowell, US astronomer, **1916**; Rudolf Friml, Czech-born US composer, **1972**; H.R. Haldeman, US political aide involved in Watergate **1993**.

NOTES

November 13

*"An actress can only play a woman. I'm an actor,
I can play anything."*
—WHOOPI GOLDBERG

EVENTS

1002 The Massacre of the Danes in the southern counties of England took place by order of Ethelred II. **1851** The telegraph service between London and Paris began operating. **1907** The first helicopter rose 6.5 ft/2 m above ground in Normandy. **1914** US heiress Mary Phelps Jacob patented a new female undergarment, known as the "backless brassiere." **1916** In World War I, the Battle of the Somme ended, having caused the deaths of some 60,000 Allied soldiers. **1970** A cyclone and tidal waves struck East Pakistan, killing over 500,000 people. **1985** The Colombian volcano Nevado del Ruiz, dormant since 1845, erupted, killing over 20,000 people.

BIRTHS

Charles Frederick Worth, English couturier, **1825**; Robert Louis Stevenson, Scottish writer, **1850**; Eugene Ionesco, Romanian-born French author and dramatist, **1912**; George Carey, British archbishop of Canterbury, **1935**; Whoopi Goldberg, US film actress, **1949**.

DEATHS

Gioacchino Rossini, Italian composer, **1868**; Camille Pissarro, French painter, **1903**; Elsa Schiaparelli, Italian couturière, **1973**; Vittorio de Sica, Italian film director, **1974**.

NOTES

November 14

*"No Southern woman with proper self-respect would
now accept an invitation to the White House."*
—MEMPHIS NEWSPAPER, *after black educator
Booker T. Washington was invited to dinner on
Oct. 16, 1901, by President Theodore Roosevelt*

EVENTS

1925 An exhibition of Surrealist art opened in Paris, including works by Max Ernst, Man Ray, Joan Miró, and Pablo Picasso. **1940** Enemy bombing destroyed the medieval cathedral in Coventry, England. **1963** The island of Surtsey off Iceland was "born" by the eruption of an underwater volcano. **1991** Prince Sihanouk, Cambodia's former head of state, returned to Phnom Penh after nearly 13 years in exile to head the country's interim government. **1993** Puerto Ricans turned down US statehood by 48% to 46%; Puerto Rico remained a US commonwealth.

BIRTHS

Robert Fulton, US engineer and inventor, **1765**; Claude Monet, French painter, **1840**; Jawaharlal Nehru, Indian statesman, **1889**; Joseph McCarthy, US senator, **1909**; Hussein, king of Jordan, **1935**; Charles, the British Prince of Wales, **1948**.

DEATHS

Nell Gwyn, actress, mistress of Charles II of England, **1687**; Gottfried Leibniz, German philosopher, **1716**; Georg Wilhelm Friedrich Hegel, German philosopher, **1831**; Booker T. Washington, US educator, **1915**; Manuel de Falla, Spanish composer, **1946**.

NOTES

November 15

"Human beings do not carry civilization in their genes."
—MARGARET MEAD

EVENTS

1777 The Continental Congress adopted the Articles of Confederation. **1837** Pitman's system of shorthand was published, under the title *Stenographic Sound-Hand*. **1889** Dom Pedro was overthrown, and Brazil was proclaimed a republic. **1969** A demonstration march against the Vietnam War drew some 250,000 protesters to Washington, DC. **1983** An independent Turkish Republic of Northern Cyprus was unilaterally proclaimed, recognized only by Turkey.

BIRTHS

William Pitt the Elder, British statesman, **1708**; William Herschel, English astronomer, **1738**; Marianne Moore, US poet, **1887**; Erwin Rommel, German field-marshal, **1891**; Averell Harriman, US diplomat, **1891**; Petula Clark, British pop singer, **1934**; Daniel Barenboim, Israeli pianist and conductor, **1942**.

DEATHS

George Romney, English painter, **1802**; Henryk Sienkiewicz, Polish novelist, **1916**; Lionel Barrymore, US actor, **1954**; Tyrone Power, US film actor, **1958**; Jean Gabin, French actor, **1976**; Margaret Mead, US anthropologist, **1978**; Luciano Liggio, Italian racketeer, **1993**.

NOTES

November 16

"His ears make him look like a taxi-cab with both doors open."
—HOWARD HUGHES, *on turning down Clark Gable for
Hughes' 1931 movie* The Front Page

EVENTS

1869 The Suez Canal, which had taken 10 years to build, was formally opened. **1907** Oklahoma became the 46th state. **1913** The first volume of *Remembrance of Things Past*, the classic autobiographical novel by Marcel Proust, was published in Paris. **1918** Hungary achieved independence from the Austro-Hungarian empire and was proclaimed a republic. **1965** The USSR launched *Venus III*, an unmanned spacecraft that successfully landed on Venus. **1982** The US space shuttle *Columbia* landed after its first operational flight. **1993** Amid the tears of employees and sympathizers, Vladimir Lenin's mausoleum was closed by the Russian authorities; it was the first site in Moscow linked to Lenin to be shut down.

BIRTHS

Tiberius, Roman emperor, **42 BC**; W.C. Handy, blues composer who wrote "St. Louis Blues," **1873**; George S. Kaufman, US dramatist, **1889**; Burgess Meredith, US film actor, **1909**; Frank Bruno, British heavyweight boxing champion, **1961**.

DEATHS

Louis Riel, Canadian leader of the Métis rebellion, **1885**; Clark Gable, US film actor, **1960**; William Holden, US film actor, **1981**.

NOTES

_____

_____

_____

_____

November 17

*"I find that the three major administrative problems on
a campus are sex for the students, athletics for the
alumni and parking for the faculty."*
—CLARK KERR, *president of the University of
California in* Time, *Nov. 17, 1958*

EVENTS

1800 The US Congress met for the first time in Washington, DC, the new capital of the US. **1922** The last sultan of Turkey was deposed by Kemal Atatürk. **1922** Siberia voted for union with the USSR. **1970** The USSR's *Luna 17* landed on the Sea of Rains on the moon and released the first moonwalker vehicle. **1987** Columbia University's football team set a record by losing its 40th straight game. **1988** Benazir Bhutto was elected prime minister of Pakistan, becoming the first female leader of a Muslim state.

BIRTHS

Louis XVIII, king of France, **1755**; Bernard Law Montgomery, British field marshal, **1887**; Lee Strasberg, US director who taught "method" acting at his Actors' Studio in New York, **1901**; Martin Scorsese, US film director, **1942**; Danny DeVito, US comic film actor and director, **1944**.

DEATHS

Pico della Mirandola, Italian philosopher, **1497**; Mary I, queen of England, **1558**; Robert Owen, British socialist, **1856**; Auguste Rodin, French sculptor, **1917**; Heitor Villa-Lobos, Brazilian composer, **1959**.

NOTES

November 18

"Happiness is salutary for the body but sorrow develops the powers of the spirit."
—MARCEL PROUST

EVENTS

1477 William Caxton's *The Dictes or Sayinges of the Philosophres* was published, the first printed book in England bearing a date. **1626** St. Peter's in Rome was consecrated. **1903** The US and Panama signed the Panama Canal treaty, which gave the land "in perpetuity" to the US. **1928** The first experimental sound cartoon, *Steamboat Willie*, starring Mickey Mouse, was screened in the US. **1977** President Anwar Sadat became the first Egyptian leader to visit Israel and to address the Knesset (parliament). **1991** The Shi'ite Muslim faction Islamic Jihad freed US university professor Thomas Sutherland (held since June 1985) and Church of England envoy Terry Waite (held since January 1987).

BIRTHS

Carl Maria von Weber, German composer, **1786**; Ignacy Jan Paderewski, Polish musician and statesman, **1860**; George Gallup, US journalist, **1901**; Imogene Coca, US TV comedienne, **1908**; Alan Shepard, US astronaut, **1923**; Linda Evans, US actress, **1942**.

DEATHS

Chester Alan Arthur, 21st US president, **1886**; Marcel Proust, French author, **1922**; Niels Henrik Bohr, Danish physicist, **1962**; Man Ray, US photographer and artist, **1976**; Gustáv Husák, Czech politician, **1991**; Cab Calloway, US bandleader and singer, **1994**.

NOTES

November 19

"Fourscore and seven years ago our fathers brought forth upon this continent a new nation, conceived in liberty, and dedicated to the proposition that all men are created equal."
—ABRAHAM LINCOLN, *Gettysburg Address*

EVENTS

1493 On his second voyage to the New World, Columbus discovered Puerto Rico. **1863** President Lincoln delivered his famous Gettysburg Address, during the American Civil War. **1942** The Red Army counterattacked and surrounded the German army at Stalingrad. **1969** Brazilian soccer player Pelé scored his 1,000th goal in his 909th first-class match. **1987** A record price for an automobile was reached when a 1931 Bugatti Royale was sold at auction for $8.5 million.

BIRTHS

Charles I, king of England and Scotland, **1600**; Ferdinand de Lesseps, French engineer, **1805**; James A. Garfield, 20th US president, **1831**; Anton Walbrook, German actor, **1900**; Indira Gandhi, Indian prime minister, **1917**; Dick Cavett, US TV talkshow host, **1936**; Ted Turner, US media owner, **1938**; Calvin Klein, US fashion designer, **1942**; Jodie Foster, US film actress, **1963**; Meg Ryan, US film actress, **1963**.

DEATHS

Nicolas Poussin, French painter, **1665**; Franz Schubert, Austrian composer, **1828**; William Siemens, German metallurgist, **1883**.

NOTES

_____

_____

_____

_____

November 20

EVENTS

1759 The British fleet under Admiral Hawke defeated the French at the Battle of Quiberon Bay, thwarting an invasion of England. **1818** Simón Bolívar, known as "the Liberator," declared Venezuela to be independent of Spain. **1945** The Nuremberg trials of 24 chief Nazi war criminals by an international military tribunal began. **1980** The *Solar Challenger* was flown for the first time, entirely under solar power. **1993** Congress approved the North American Free Trade Agreement (NAFTA), which went into effect on January 1, 1994.

BIRTHS

Edwin Powell Hubble, US astronomer, **1889**; Alexandra Danilova, Russian ballerina and choreographer, **1906**; Alistair Cooke, English-born journalist and broadcaster, **1908**; Nadine Gordimer, South African novelist, **1923**; Robert Kennedy, US attorney general and brother of John F. Kennedy, **1925**; Dick Smothers, US comedian and musician, **1939**; Bo Derek, US film actress, **1956**.

DEATHS

Anton Rubinstein, Russian pianist and composer, **1894**; Leo Tolstoy, Russian novelist, **1910**; John Rushworth Jellicoe, British admiral, **1935**; Francisco Franco, Spanish dictator, **1975**.

NOTES

November 21

EVENTS

1783 François de Rozier and the Marquis d'Arlandres made the first human flight when they lifted off from the Bois de Boulogne, Paris, in a hot-air balloon built by the Montgolfier brothers. **1789** North Carolina became the 12th state. **1918** The German High Seas Fleet surrendered to the Allies. **1934** Cole Porter's *Anything Goes* was first performed in New York. **1953** The discovery of the Piltdown Man skull by Charles Dawson in Sussex, England, in 1912 was finally revealed as a hoax. **1990** Leaders of NATO and Warsaw Pact member states signed the Charter of Paris and a treaty on conventional forces in Europe, bringing an end to the Cold War.

BIRTHS

Voltaire, French philosopher and writer, **1694**; Adolph "Harpo" Marx, US film comedian, **1888**; René Magritte, Belgian painter, **1898**; Coleman "Hawk" Hawkins, US jazz saxophonist, **1904**; Natalia Makarova, Russian ballerina, **1940**; Goldie Hawn, US comic actress, **1945**.

DEATHS

Henry Purcell, English composer, **1695**; Franz Josef I, emperor of Austria, **1916**; James Hertzog, South African premier, **1942**; Venkata Raman, Indian physicist, **1970**.

NOTES

November 22

"The real 1960s began on the afternoon of November 22, 1963 ...
It came to seem that Kennedy's murder opened some malign trap
door in American culture, and the wild bats flapped out."
—LANCE MORROW, *in* Time, *Nov. 14, 1983*

EVENTS

1497 Portuguese navigator Vasco da Gama rounded the Cape of Good Hope in his search for a route to India. **1938** The first coelacanth, a prehistoric fish believed to be extinct, was caught off the South African coast. **1956** The 16th Olympic Games opened in Melbourne. **1963** John F. Kennedy, 35th US president, was assassinated in Dallas, Texas, allegedly by Lee Harvey Oswald. **1975** Two days after the death of General Franco, Juan Carlos I was sworn in as king of Spain. **1990** British Prime Minister Margaret Thatcher announced her resignation.

BIRTHS

Wassily Kandinsky, Russian painter, **1866**; André Gide, French author, **1869**; Wiley Post, US aviator, **1889**; Charles de Gaulle, French general and president, **1890**; Hoagy Carmichael, US songwriter who wrote "Stardust," **1899**; Billie Jean King, US tennis champion, **1943**; Jamie Lee Curtis, US film actress, **1958**; Boris Becker, German tennis champion, **1967**.

DEATHS

Robert Clive, British general, **1774**; Arthur Sullivan, English composer, **1900**; Jack London, US novelist, **1916**; Mae West, US film actress, **1980**; Sterling Holloway, US film actor, **1992**.

NOTES

November 23

"America's present need is not heroics, but healing; not nostrums, but normalcy; not revolution, but restoration."
—WARREN G. HARDING, *speech, May 14, 1920*

EVENTS

1670 Molière's *Le Bourgeois Gentilhomme* was performed for the first time in Paris. **1889** The first juke box was installed in the Palais Royal Saloon in San Francisco. **1903** Italian operatic tenor Enrico Caruso made his American debut, singing the role of the Duke in Verdi's *Rigoletto* at the Metropolitan Opera House. **1921** US President Warren Harding banned doctors from prescribing beer, eliminating a loophole in the prohibition law. **1980** A violent earthquake struck southern Italy, killing over 4,000 people.

BIRTHS

Franklin Pierce, 14th US president, **1804**; William Bonney, US outlaw known as "Billy the Kid," **1859**; Manuel de Falla, Spanish composer, **1876**; Boris Karloff, English-born US film actor, **1887**; Lew Hoad, Australian tennis player, **1934**; Shane Gould, Australian swimmer, **1956**.

DEATHS

Abbé Prévost, French author, **1763**; Arthur Wing Pinero, British dramatist, **1934**; André Malraux, French novelist, **1976**; Merle Oberon, British-born Hollywood actress, **1979**.

NOTES

_____

_____

_____

_____

November 24

"Gaiety is the most outstanding feature of the Soviet Union."
—JOSEF STALIN, *reported on Nov. 24, 1935*

EVENTS

1642 Dutch navigator Abel Tasman discovered Van Diemen's Land, which he named for his captain; it was later renamed Tasmania. **1859** Darwin's controversial evolutionary theories were published in *On the Origin of Species*. **1963** Lee Harvey Oswald, charged with the assassination of John F. Kennedy, was shot while in police custody by Jack Ruby, a nightclub owner. **1989** Czech politician Alexander Dubček made his first public appearance in over 20 years, speaking at a prodemocracy rally in Prague.

BIRTHS

Baruch Spinoza, Dutch philosopher, **1632**; Laurence Sterne, Irish novelist, **1713**; Zachary Taylor, 12th US president, **1784**; Henri de Toulouse-Lautrec, French painter, **1864**; Scott Joplin, US ragtime pianist and composer, **1868**; William Buckley, US writer and conservative advocate, **1925**.

DEATHS

John Knox, Scottish religious reformer, **1572**; Georges Clemenceau, French statesman, **1929**; George Raft, US film actor, **1980**; Anthony Burgess, British novelist and critic, **1993**.

NOTES

November 25

EVENTS

1884 Evaporated milk was patented by John Mayenberg of St. Louis. **1952** The world's longest-running play, *The Mousetrap* by Agatha Christie, opened in London. **1963** President John F. Kennedy was buried in Arlington National Cemetery with full military honors. **1975** Suriname, formerly called Dutch Guiana, became a fully independent republic.

BIRTHS

Andrew Carnegie, Scottish-born US industrialist and philanthropist, **1835**; Carl Benz, German engineer and automobile manufacturer, **1844**; Joe DiMaggio, New York Yankee baseball star who married Marilyn Monroe, **1914**; Augusto Pinochet, Chilean dictator, **1915**; Ricardo Montalban, US film actor, **1920**.

DEATHS

Bojangles (Bill Robinson), US tapdancer and entertainer, **1949**; Myra Hess, British pianist, **1965**; Upton Sinclair, US novelist, **1968**; Yukio Mishima, Japanese novelist, **1970**; U Thant, Burmese diplomat and secretary general of the UN, **1974**.

NOTES

November 26

"God made the country, and man made the town."
—WILLIAM COWPER, The Task

EVENTS

1789 Thanksgiving was celebrated nationally for the first time.
1906 President Theodore Roosevelt returned to Washington after a trip to Central America, having been the first US president to travel abroad while in office. **1942** Soviet forces counterattacked the Germans at Stalingrad, ending the siege and forcing General von Paulus's Sixth Army to retreat. **1949** India became a republic. **1966** French President Charles de Gaulle opened the world's first tidal power station in Brittany. **1990** Lee Kuan Yew, Singapore's prime minister for 31 years, announced that he was stepping down.

BIRTHS

William Cowper, English poet, **1731**; Charles Schultz, US cartoonist, **1922**; Tina Turner, US rock singer, **1938**.

DEATHS

Isabella I, queen of Castile and Aragon, **1504**; John McAdam, Scottish engineer, **1836**; Nicolas Soult, French general, **1851**; Leander Jameson, British colonial administrator, **1917**; Tommy Dorsey, US trombonist and bandleader, **1956**; Arnold Zweig, German novelist, **1968**.

NOTES

November 27

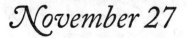

"Dare to be wise."
—HORACE

EVENTS

1095 Pope Urban began to preach the First Crusade at Clermont, France. **1582** William Shakespeare, aged 18, married Anne Hathaway. **1919** A massive meteor landed in Lake Michigan. **1940** In Romania, the profascist group Iron Guard murdered 64 people, including former Prime Minister Jorga. **1967** French President Charles de Gaulle rejected Britain's entry into the Common Market.

BIRTHS

Anders Celsius, Swedish astronomer and thermometer inventor, **1701**; Fanny Kemble, English actress, **1809**; Chaim Weizmann, chemist and first president of Israel, **1874**; Konosuke Matsushita, Japanese industrialist, **1894**; David Merrick, US stage producer, **1912**; Alexander Dubček, Czech statesman, **1920**; Jimi Hendrix, US guitarist and singer, **1942**.

DEATHS

Horace, Roman poet, **8 BC**; Black Kettle, Cheyenne chief, during an attack on his village by troops led by George Armstrong Custer; **1868**; Alexandre Dumas *fils*, French novelist and dramatist, **1895**; Eugene O'Neill, US dramatist, **1953**; Arthur Honegger, Swiss composer, **1955**.

NOTES

November 28

"I am always at a loss to know how much to believe of my own stories."
—WASHINGTON IRVING, Tales of a Traveller

EVENTS

1520 Portuguese navigator Ferdinand Magellan sailed through the straits at the tip of South America, which now bear his name, and reached an ocean which he named the Pacific. **1905** The Irish political party Sinn Fein was founded by Arthur Griffith in Dublin. **1909** In France, a law was passed allowing women eight weeks' maternity leave. **1948** Edwin Land's first Polaroid cameras went on sale in Boston. **1960** Mauritania gained independence. **1978** Amid growing fundamentalist opposition, the Iranian government banned religious rallies.

BIRTHS

Jean Baptiste Lully, Italian-born French composer, **1632**; William Blake, English poet and artist, **1757**; Friedrich Engels, German socialist, **1820**; Alberto Moravia, Italian writer, **1907**; Claude Lévi-Strauss, French anthropologist, **1908**; Hope Lange, US film actress, **1931**; Randy Newman, US singer and songwriter, **1943**.

DEATHS

Giovanni Lorenzo Bernini, Italian sculptor, **1680**; Washington Irving, US author, **1859**; Enrico Fermi, Italian-born US physicist, **1954**; Jerry Rubin, US radical of the 1960s, **1994**.

NOTES

November 29

EVENTS

1864 The Sand Creek massacre took place when over 150 Cheyenne and Arapaho Indians who had surrendered and were disarmed were killed by US cavalry. **1929** US Admiral Richard Byrd became the first man to fly over the South Pole, with his pilot Bernt Balchen. **1932** Cole Porter's *The Gay Divorcee*, starring Fred Astaire, was first performed in New York. **1945** Yugoslavia was proclaimed a Federal People's Republic, under Tito's leadership. **1990** The UN Security Council, at the urging of the US, authorized the use of force against Iraq if it did not withdraw totally from Kuwait by January 15, 1991.

BIRTHS

Gaetano Donizetti, Italian composer, **1797**; Christian Johann Doppler, Austrian physicist, **1803**; Louisa May Alcott, US author, **1832**; C.S. Lewis, English scholar and writer, **1898**; Jacques Chirac, French statesman, **1932**; John Mayall, British vocalist and blues guitarist, **1949**.

DEATHS

Horace Greeley, who founded the *New York Tribune* and advised "Go west, young man," **1872**; Giacomo Puccini, Italian composer, **1924**; Graham Hill, English racing driver, **1975**; Natalie Wood, US film actress, drowned, **1981**; Ralph Bellamy, US film actor, **1991**.

NOTES

November 30

The national day of Scotland.

EVENTS

1914 Charlie Chaplin made his film debut in *Making a Living,* a Mack Sennett one-reeler. **1939** The USSR invaded Finland. **1988** PLO leader Yassir Arafat attempted to enter the US to address the UN General Assembly, but was refused a visa. **1993** President Clinton signed the "Brady Bill" (named for White House Press Secretary James Brady, who was wounded during the 1981 assassination attempt on President Reagan), which requires gun purchasers to wait five days while their backgrounds are checked. **1994** Congress passed a stricter gun law requiring the registration of all firearms and a ban on most automatic and semiautomatic weapons.

BIRTHS

Andrea Palladio, Italian architect, **1508**; Philip Sidney, English poet and soldier, **1554**; Jonathan Swift, Irish author, **1667**; Mark Twain (Samuel Clemens), US author and humorist, **1835**; Winston Churchill, British statesman, **1874**; Dick Clark, US TV rock 'n' roll host, **1929**.

DEATHS

Oscar Wilde, Irish dramatist, **1900**; Beniamino Gigli, Italian operatic tenor, **1957**; Herbert "Zeppo" Marx, US actor and comedian, **1979**; Cary Grant, US film actor, **1986**; James Baldwin, US writer, **1987**.

NOTES

December 1

"When it's three o'clock in New York, it's still 1938 in London."
—BETTE MIDLER

World AIDS day.

EVENTS

1640 The Spanish were driven out of Portugal and the country regained its independence. **1919** US-born Lady Nancy Astor became the first woman to take her seat in Britain's House of Commons. **1925** The Locarno Pact was signed, guaranteeing peace and frontiers in Europe. **1953** The first issue of Hugh Heffner's *Playboy* magazine was published; the center-spread nude featured Marilyn Monroe. **1989** Pope John Paul II and Mikhail Gorbachev met in Rome, ending 70 years of hostility between the Vatican and the USSR. **1991** France won its first Davis Cup tennis title in 59 years by defeating the US at the finals in Lyons, France.

BIRTHS

Madame Tussaud, French wax-modeler, **1761**; Woody Allen, US film actor, writer, and director, **1935**; Lee Trevino, US golfer, **1939**; Richard Pryor, US comedian and actor, **1940**; Bette Midler, US singer and actress, **1945**.

DEATHS

Henry I, king of England, **1135**; Lorenzo Ghiberti, Italian sculptor and goldsmith, **1455**; Vincent d'Indy, French composer, **1931**; David Ben-Gurion, Israeli prime minister, **1973**; James Baldwin, US writer, **1987**.

NOTES

_____

_____

_____

_____

December 2

"They are leading old John Brown to execution. This is sowing the wind to reap the whirlwind, which will soon come."
—HENRY WADSWORTH LONGFELLOW,
reported on Dec. 2, 1859

EVENTS

1823 US President James Monroe proclaimed the Monroe Doctrine. **1859** Abolitionist John Brown was hanged for treason at Charlestown, Virginia. **1901** King Camp Gillette patented a safety razor with a double-edged disposable blade. **1942** The first nuclear chain reaction took place at the University of Chicago, directed by physicists Enrico Fermi and Arthur Compton. **1982** Dr. Barney Clark became the first recipient of a permanent artificial heart, in Salt Lake City. **1988** In Bangladesh, a cyclone killed thousands of people and left 5 million homeless. **1990** West German Chancellor Helmut Kohl was elected chancellor of a united Germany.

BIRTHS

Georges Seurat, French painter, **1859**; Ruth Draper, US entertainer, **1884**; Peter Carl Goldmark, US inventor of the LP record, **1906**; Maria Callas, US operatic soprano, **1923**; Alexander Haig, US general and secretary of state, **1924**; Julie Harris, US actress, **1925**.

DEATHS

Hernándo Cortés, Spanish conquistador, **1547**; Gerhardt Mercator, Belgian cartographer, **1594**; Marquis de Sade, French writer and philosopher, **1814**; Aaron Copland, US composer, **1990**.

NOTES

December 3

"A belief in the supernatural source of evil is not necessary;
men alone are quite capable of every wickedness."
—JOSEPH CONRAD

EVENTS

1818 Illinois became the 21st state. **1910** Neon lighting was displayed for the first time at the Paris Motor Show. **1917** The Quebec Bridge, the world's longest cantilever, over the St. Lawrence River, was opened; 87 lives were lost during its construction. **1967** At Groote Schurr Hospital, Capetown, South Africa, Dr. Christiaan Barnard carried out the world's first heart transplant. **1984** A chemical leakage at a pesticide factory in Bhopal, India, caused the deaths of over 2,500 people and blinded many thousands.

BIRTHS

Nicolò Amati, Italian violin-maker, **1596**; Joseph Conrad, Polish-born British novelist, **1857**; Anton von Webern, Austrian composer, **1883**; Andy Williams, US singer, **1930**; Jean-Luc Godard, French film director, **1930**; Franz Klammer, Austrian skier, **1953**.

DEATHS

Frederick VI, king of Denmark, **1839**; Robert Louis Stevenson, Scottish novelist, **1894**; Mary Baker Eddy, US founder of Christian Science, **1910**; Pierre Auguste Renoir, French painter, **1919**; Lewis Thomas, US physician, biologist, and writer, **1993**; Frank Zappa, US composer and rock guitarist, **1993**.

NOTES

_____

_____

_____

_____

December 4

"The history of the world is but the biography of great men."
—THOMAS CARLYLE

EVENTS

1808 Napoleon abolished the Inquisition in Spain. **1867** The Grange was founded in the US by farmers to represent their interests. **1947** The first performance of Tennessee Williams' *A Streetcar Named Desire*, starring Marlon Brando and Jessica Tandy, opened in New York. **1991** News correspondent Terry Anderson, the longest-held Western hostage in Lebanon (2,454 days in captivity), was freed by Islamic Jihad. **1991** PanAm, founded in 1927, was closed down with massive debts.

BIRTHS

Thomas Carlyle, Scottish essayist and historian, **1795**; Rainer Maria Rilke, German poet, **1875**; Francisco Franco, Spanish dictator, **1892**; Deanna Durbin, Canadian film actress, **1921**; Jeff Bridges, US film actor, **1949**.

DEATHS

Cardinal Richelieu, French politician, **1642**; John Gay, English poet and dramatist, **1732**; Luigi Galvani, Italian physiologist, **1798**; Benjamin Britten, English composer, **1976**.

NOTES

December 5

The national day of Thailand.

EVENTS

1766 James Christie, founder of the famous auctioneers, held his first sale in London. **1908** The first American football game in which players were numbered was played at Pittsburgh. **1933** Prohibition was repealed in the US after more than 13 years. **1955** America's two largest labor groups, the American Federation of Labor and the Congress of Industrial Organizations, merged as the AFL-CIO.

BIRTHS

Martin Van Buren, 8th US president, **1782**; Christina Rossetti, English poet, **1830**; Fritz Lang, Austrian-born US film director, **1890**; Walt Disney, US filmmaker and animator, **1901**; Otto Preminger, Austrian-born US film director, **1906**; Little Richard, US rock 'n' roll pioneer, **1932**; José Carreras, Spanish operatic tenor, **1946**.

DEATHS

Wolfgang Amadeus Mozart, Austrian composer, **1791**; Alexandre Dumas *père*, French novelist, **1870**; Claude Monet, French painter, **1926**; Jan Kubelik, Czech violinist, **1940**; Robert Aldrich, US film director, **1983**.

NOTES

_____

_____

_____

_____

December 6

"Those who have courage to love should have courage to suffer."
—ANTHONY TROLLOPE, The Bertrams

The national day of Finland.

EVENTS

1492 Columbus discovered Hispaniola, now Haiti and the Dominican Republic. **1790** Congress met in its temporary capital of Philadelphia. **1865** The US officially abolished slavery with the ratification of the 13th Amendment. **1877** With a recording of himself reciting "Mary Had a Little Lamb," Thomas Edison demonstrated the first gramophone, in New Jersey. **1907** In Monongah, West Virginia, 361 people were killed in America's worst mine disaster. **1917** Finland proclaimed independence from Russia. **1921** The Irish Free State was formally created. **1990** Saddam Hussein announced that he would free 2,000 foreign hostages held in Iraq and occupied Kuwait. **1994** Orange County, California, became the largest US municipality to file for bankruptcy.

BIRTHS

Henry VI, king of England, **1421**; **1608**; Warren Hastings, British administrator, **1732**; Ira Gershwin, US lyricist, **1896**; Dave Brubeck, US jazz musician, **1920**.

DEATHS

Jean-Baptiste-Siméon Chardin, French painter, **1779**; Madame du Barry, mistress of King Louis XV of France, **1793**; Anthony Trollope, English novelist, **1882**; Ernst Werner von Siemens, German inventor, **1892**.

NOTES

December 7

"Most plays—certainly mine—are like blank checks. The actors and directors put their own signatures on them."
—THORNTON WILDER

EVENTS

1431 In Paris, Henry VI of England was crowned king of France. **1787** Delaware became the first state to ratify the US Constitution. **1941** The Japanese attacked the US fleet in Pearl Harbor, Hawaii, killing 2,300. **1982** The first execution by lethal injection took place at Fort Worth Prison, Texas. **1988** An earthquake in Armenia killed thousands and caused widespread destruction. **1990** A week-long succession of violent clashes between Hindus and Muslims in several Indian cities began, resulting in about 300 deaths and 3,000 arrests.

BIRTHS

Giovanni Lorenzo Bernini, Italian sculptor, **1598**; Pietro Mascagni, Italian composer, **1863**; Willa Cather, US novelist, **1876**; Eli Wallach, US actor, **1915**; Mario Soares, Portuguese politician, **1924**; Ellen Burstyn, US actress, **1932**.

DEATHS

Cicero, Roman orator, **43 BC**; William Bligh, English sea captain of the *Bounty*, **1817**; Ferdinand de Lesseps, French engineer, **1894**; Kirsten Flagstad, Norwegian operatic soprano, **1962**; Thornton Wilder, US playwright and novelist, **1975**; Robert Graves, English poet and author, **1985**; Wolfgang Paul, German nuclear physicist, **1993**.

NOTES

December 8

"Then, with that faint fleeting smile playing about his lips, he faced the firing squad; erect and motionless, proud and disdainful, Walter Mitty, the undefeated, inscrutable to the last."
—JAMES THURBER, *"The Secret Life of Walter Mitty"*

EVENTS

1863 Tom King of England defeated American John Heenan, becoming the first world heavyweight boxing champion. **1886** The American Federation of Labor (AFL) was founded by 25 unions. **1941** The US, Britain, and Australia declared war on Japan, one day after the attack on Pearl Harbor. **1980** John Lennon, British rock singer, songwriter, and former member of the Beatles, was shot and killed in New York. **1987** US President Reagan and Soviet President Gorbachev signed the Intermediate Nuclear Forces treaty in Washington, DC, the first nuclear arms reduction agreement. **1991** The leaders of Russia, Byelorussia, and the Ukraine signed an agreement forming a "Commonwealth of Independent States" to replace the USSR; President Gorbachev said the decision was unconstitutional.

BIRTHS

Horace, Roman poet, 65 BC; Mary Stuart, Queen of Scots, 1542; James Thurber, US humorous writer and cartoonist, 1894; Sammy Davis, Jr., US singer, actor, and dancer, 1925; Jim Morrison, US singer, 1943; Kim Basinger, US film actress, 1953.

DEATHS

Herbert Spencer, British philosopher, 1903; Simon Marks, English retailer, 1964; Golda Meir, Israeli prime minister, 1978.

NOTES

December 9

"Good taste is the worst vice ever invented."
—DAME EDITH SITWELL

The national day of Tanzania.

EVENTS

1868 William Gladstone was elected prime minister of Britain, beginning the first of his four terms. **1955** America's Sugar Ray Robinson knocked out Carl Olson, regaining his world middleweight boxing title. **1987** The first martyrs of the "intifada" in the Gaza Strip were created when an Israeli patrol attacked the Jabaliya refugee camp. **1990** Lech Walesa, leader of the once-outlawed Solidarity labor movement, was elected president of Poland. **1992** US troops arrived in Somalia, under UN mandate, to protect humanitarian food deliveries.

BIRTHS

John Milton, English poet, **1608**; Joel Chandler Harris, US writer who created "Uncle Remus" and "Br'er Rabbit," **1848**; Clarence Birdseye, US inventor of the deep-freezing process, **1886**; Douglas Fairbanks, Jr., US film actor, **1909**; Kirk Douglas, US film actor, **1918**; Michael Douglas, US film actor, **1944**; Donny Osmond, US pop singer, **1957**.

DEATHS

Anthony Van Dyck, Flemish painter, **1641**; Joseph Bramah, English inventor of the hydraulic press, **1814**; Edith Sitwell, English poet and author, **1964**; Karl Barth, Swiss theologian, **1968**; Bernice Abbott, US photographer, **1991**.

NOTES

December 10

"Success is counted sweetest
By those who ne'er succeed."
—EMILY DICKINSON

EVENTS

1817 Mississippi became the 20th state. **1845** Pneumatic tires were patented by Scottish civil engineer Robert Thompson. **1869** The Territory of Wyoming gave women the right to vote. **1898** Cuba became independent of Spain following the Spanish-American War. **1901** Nobel Prizes were first awarded. **1941** The Royal Naval battleships *Prince of Wales* and *Repulse* were sunk by Japanese aircraft in the Battle of Malaya. **1958** National Airlines began the first domestic jet passenger service in the US, between New York and Miami.

BIRTHS

César Franck, Belgian composer, **1822**; Emily Dickinson, US poet, **1830**; Melvil Dewey, US inventor of the library decimal classification system for books, **1851**; William Plomer, South African author, **1903**; Olivier Messiaen, French composer and organist, **1908**; Dorothy Lamour, US film actress, **1914**; Kenneth Branagh, British actor and director, **1960**.

DEATHS

Paolo Uccello, Italian painter, **1475**; Leopold I, king of the Belgians, **1865**; Alfred Nobel, Swedish industrialist and philanthropist, **1896**; Damon Runyon, US writer, **1946**; Otis Redding, US soul singer and songwriter, **1967**; Jascha Heifetz, Russian-born US violinist, **1987**.

NOTES

December 11

---

*"One of the extraordinary things about human events
is that the unthinkable becomes thinkable."*
—SALMAN RUSHDIE

EVENTS

1769 Edward Beran of London patented Venetian blinds. **1816** Indiana became the 19th state. **1844** Nitrous oxide, or laughing gas, was first used for a tooth extraction. **1894** The first motor show opened in Paris, with nine exhibitors. **1941** The US declared war on Germany and Italy. **1987** Charlie Chaplin's trademark cane and bowler hat were sold at Christie's, London for £82,500 (over $125,000). **1991** Salman Rushdie, under an Islamic death sentence for blasphemy, made his first public appearance since 1989 in New York, at a dinner marking the 200th anniversary of the First Amendment.

BIRTHS

Pope Leo X, **1475**; Hector Berlioz, French composer, **1803**; Carlo Ponti, Italian film director and producer, **1913**; Alexander Solzhenitsyn, Russian author, **1918**; Kenneth MacMillan, Scottish choreographer, **1929**; Brenda Lee, US country singer, **1944**.

DEATHS

Llewlyn ap Gruffydd, last native prince of Wales, **1282**; Bernardino Pinturicchio, Italian painter, **1513**; Olive Schreiner, South African novelist, **1920**; Edward R. Murrow, US journalist and broadcaster, **1965**.

NOTES

December 12

The national day of Kenya.

EVENTS

1787 Pennsylvania became the 2nd state. **1896** Guglielmo Marconi gave the first public demonstration of radio. **1915** The first all-metal aircraft, the German *Junkers J1*, made its first flight. **1925** The world's first motel, in San Luis Obispo, California, opened. **1955** British engineer Christopher Cockerell patented the first hovercraft. **1989** US billionairess Leona Helmsley, dubbed the "Queen of Greed," was fined $7 million and sentenced to four years in prison for tax evasion.

BIRTHS

Gustave Flaubert, French novelist, **1821**; Edvard Munch, Norwegian painter, **1863**; Edward G. Robinson, US film actor, **1893**; Frank Sinatra, US singer and film actor, **1915**; Edward Koch, mayor of New York City, **1924**; Connie Francis, US singer, **1938**; Dionne Warwick, US singer, **1941**.

DEATHS

Robert Browning, English poet, **1889**; Douglas Fairbanks, Sr., US film actor, **1939**; Peter Fraser, New Zealand politician, **1950**; Tallulah Bankhead, US actress, **1968**; Anne Baxter, US film actress, **1985**.

NOTES

December 13

EVENTS

1577 Francis Drake began his journey in the *Golden Hind* that was to take him around the world. **1642** Dutch navigator Abel Tasman discovered New Zealand. **1862** Robert E. Lee's Confederate troops inflicted a severe defeat on Ambrose Burnside's army at the Battle of Fredericksburg. **1903** Molds for ice cream cones were patented by Italo Marcione of New York. **1967** A military coup replaced the monarchy in Greece, sending King Constantine II into exile.

BIRTHS

Heinrich Heine, German poet, **1797**; Alvin York, US hero as a sergeant in World War I, **1887**; Laurens van der Post, South African writer and explorer, **1906**; Balthazar Johannes Vorster, South African politician, **1915**; Dick Van Dyke, US comic actor, singer, and dancer, **1925**; Christopher Plummer, Canadian actor, **1929**.

DEATHS

Moses Maimonides, Jewish philosopher, **1204**; Donatello, Italian sculptor, **1466**; Samuel Johnson, English lexicographer, **1784**; Wassily Kandinsky, Russian painter, **1944**; Grandma Moses, US primitive painter (aged 101), **1961**; Mary Renault, English novelist, **1983**.

NOTES

December 14

EVENTS

1819 Alabama became the 22nd state. **1900** Max Planck of Berlin University revealed his revolutionary quantum theory. **1911** A Norwegian expedition led by Roald Amundsen became the first to reach the South Pole, 35 days ahead of Britain's Captain Robert Scott. **1959** Archbishop Makarios was elected Cyprus' first president. **1962** US *Mariner II* sent the first close-up pictures of the planet Venus back to Earth. **1990** After 30 years in exile, ANC president Oliver Tambo returned to South Africa.

BIRTHS

Nostradamus, French physician and astrologer, **1503**; Tycho Brahe, Danish astronomer and mathematician, **1546**; George VI, king of Britain, **1895**; Charlie Rich, US country singer, **1932**; Lee Remick, US actress, **1935**; Stan Smith, US tennis player, **1946**; Patty Duke, US film actress, **1946**.

DEATHS

George Washington, 1st US president, **1799**; Prince Albert, consort of Queen Victoria of Britain, **1861**; Stanley Baldwin, British politician, **1947**; Andrei Sakharov, Russian physicist and human-rights campaigner, **1989**.

NOTES

December 15

"What an artist dies with me!"
—NERO, *on his deathbed*

EVENTS

1654 A meteorological office established in Tuscany began recording daily temperature readings. **1791** The Bill of Rights' ten amendments became part of the US Constitution. **1916** In World War I, the first Battle of Verdun ended; over 700,000 German and Allied soldiers died in the action. **1939** Nylon was first produced commercially in Delaware. **1961** Nazi official Adolph Eichmann was found guilty of crimes against the Jewish people and sentenced to death, after a trial in Jerusalem. **1982** Gibraltar's frontier with Spain was opened to pedestrian use after 13 years.

BIRTHS

Nero, Roman emperor, **37**; Gustave Eiffel, French engineer, **1832**; Jean Paul Getty, US oil billionaire, **1892**; Edna O'Brien, Irish novelist, **1936**.

DEATHS

Jan Vermeer, Dutch painter, **1675**; Izaak Walton, English author of *The Compleat Angler*, **1683**; Sitting Bull, chief of the Sioux Indians, **1890**; "Fats" Waller, US jazz pianist, **1943**; Charles Laughton, English actor, **1962**; Walt Disney, US filmmaker and animator, **1966**.

NOTES

December 16

"Lastly, I make this vow, that mine eyes desire you above all things. Farewell."
—CATHERINE OF ARAGON, *letter to Henry VIII, written on her deathbed*

EVENTS

1773 The Boston Tea Party, a protest against British taxation, took place off Griffin's Wharf in Boston harbor. **1809** Napoleon divorced his wife Josephine because she had not produced children. **1850** The first immigrant ship, the *Charlotte Jane*, arrived at Lyttleton, New Zealand. **1944** The Battle of the Bulge, in the Ardennes, began with a strong counteroffensive by the Germans under General von Rundstedt. **1990** Jean-Bertrand Aristide, a leftist priest, was elected president in Haiti's first democratic elections. **1991** The UN General Assembly voted to repeal its 1975 resolution equating Zionism with racism.

BIRTHS

Catherine of Aragon, first wife of Henry VIII of England, **1485**; Ludwig van Beethoven, German composer, **1770**; Jane Austen, English novelist, **1775**; Noël Coward, English dramatist, actor, and composer, **1889**; Margaret Mead, US anthropologist, **1901**.

DEATHS

Wilhelm Grimm, German philologist and folklorist, **1859**; Camille Saint-Saëns, French composer, **1921**; Glenn Miller, US trombonist and bandleader, **1944**; Somerset Maugham, British novelist, **1965**; Kakuei Tanaka, Japanese politician, **1993**.

NOTES

_____

_____

_____

_____

December 17

*"For all sad words of tongue or pen,
The saddest are these: 'It might have been!'"*
—JOHN GREENLEAF WHITTIER

EVENTS

1777 France formally recognized US independence. **1843** *A Christmas Carol* by Charles Dickens was published. **1892** Tchaikovsky's *The Nutcracker* was first performed, in St. Petersburg. **1903** Orville Wright made the first successful controlled flight in a powered aircraft, at Kill Devil Hill, near Kitty Hawk, North Carolina. **1939** The German battleship *Graf Spee* was scuttled off Montvideo, Uruguay, after the Battle of the River Plate. **1973** Thirty-one people were killed at Rome airport after Arab guerillas hijacked a German airliner. **1986** Davina Thompson became the world's first recipient of a heart, lungs, and liver transplant. **1992** Israel deported over 400 Palestinians to Lebanese territory in an unprecedented mass expulsion of suspected militants.

BIRTHS

Domenico Cimarosa, Italian composer, **1749**; Joseph Henry, US scientist, **1797**; John Greenleaf Whittier, US poet, **1807**; William Lyon MacKenzie King, Canadian prime minister, **1874**; Erskine Caldwell, US novelist, **1903**.

DEATHS

Simón Bolívar, South American revolutionary leader, **1830**; Alphonse Daudet, French novelist, **1897**; Harold Holt, Australian politician, **1967**; Sy Oliver, US composer, **1988**.

NOTES

December 18

*"It is a gentleman's first duty to remember in the
morning who it was he took to bed with him"*
—DOROTHY L. SAYERS, Busman's Honeymoon

EVENTS

1787 New Jersey became the 3rd state. **1865** The ratification of the 13th Amendment made slavery illegal in the US. **1912** The immigration of illiterate persons to the US was prohibited by Congress. **1912** The discovery of the Piltdown Man in East Sussex was announced; it was proved to be a hoax in 1953. **1969** The death penalty for murder was abolished in Britain. **1970** Divorce became legal in Italy. **1979** The sound barrier on land was broken for the first time by Stanley Barrett, driving at 739.6 mph, in California.

BIRTHS

Paul Klee, Swiss painter, **1879**; Willy Brandt, German statesman, **1913**; Betty Grable, US film actress, **1916**; Keith Richards, British guitarist, **1943**; Steven Spielberg, US film director, **1947**.

DEATHS

Antonio Stradivari, Italian violin maker, **1737**; Dorothy L. Sayers, English author, **1957**; Bobby Jones, US golfer, **1971**; Paul Tortelier, French cellist, **1990**.

NOTES

December 19

EVENTS

1154 Henry II became king of England. **1562** The Battle of Dreux was fought between the Huguenots and the Catholics, beginning the French Wars of Religion. **1842** Hawaii's independence was recognized by the US. **1955** "Blue Suede Shoes" was recorded by Carl Perkins in Memphis. **1984** Britain and China signed an agreement in Beijing, in which Britain agreed to transfer full sovereignty of Hong Kong to China in 1997.

BIRTHS

Albert Abraham Michelson, the first US scientist to be awarded a Nobel Prize, **1852**; Ralph Richardson, English actor, **1902**; Leonid Brezhnev, Soviet leader, **1906**; Jean Genet, French dramatist and essayist, **1910**; Edith Piaf, French singer, **1915**.

DEATHS

Vitus Bering, Danish navigator, **1741**; Emily Brontë, English novelist, **1848**; Joseph Turner, English painter, **1851**; Robert Andrews Millikan, US physicist, **1953**; Alexei Nikolaievich Kosygin, Soviet politician, **1980**.

NOTES

December 20

"Time is the only critic without ambition."
—JOHN STEINBECK

EVENTS

1803 The US officially became the owner of the Louisiana Territory and New Orleans, which it had purchased for $15 million from France in April 1803. **1835** Cherokees were forced to cede land in Georgia after gold was discovered. **1860** South Carolina seceded from the Union. **1933** *Flying Down to Rio*, the first film to feature Fred Astaire and Ginger Rogers, opened in New York. **1957** Elvis Presley, at the height of his stardom, received his draft papers. **1989** General Manuel Noriega, Panama's dictator, was overthrown by a US invasion force invited by the new civilian government; he took refuge in the Vatican mission until January 3, 1990. **1990** Soviet foreign minister Edvard Shevardnadze resigned, complaining of conservative attacks on his policies.

BIRTHS

Robert Menzies, Australian politician, **1894**; George Roy Hill, US film director, **1922**; Bo Diddley, US rock 'n' roll pioneer, **1928**; Uri Geller, Israeli psychic/illusionist, **1946**; Kiefer Sutherland, US film actor, **1966**.

DEATHS

Erich Ludendorff, German general, **1937**; John Steinbeck, US novelist, **1968**; Artur Rubinstein, Polish-born US pianist, **1982**; Dean Rusk, US secretary of state, **1994**.

NOTES

December 21

*"A big man has no time really to do
anything but just sit and be big."*
—F. SCOTT FITZGERALD, This Side of Paradise

EVENTS

1879 Ibsen's *A Doll's House* was first performed in Copenhagen, with a revised happy ending. **1925** Eisenstein's film *Battleship Potemkin* was first shown in Moscow. **1937** Walt Disney's *Snow White and the Seven Dwarfs* was shown in Los Angeles, the first full-length animated talking picture. **1958** Charles de Gaulle became president of France. **1988** A PanAm jet blew up in mid-flight and crashed in Lockerbie, Scotland, killing all 259 passengers aboard and 11 people on the ground; the terrorist bomb had been concealed within a radio. **1990** In a German television interview, Saddam Hussein declared that he would not withdraw from Kuwait by the UN deadline.

BIRTHS

Benjamin Disraeli, British prime minister and novelist, **1804**; Joseph Stalin, Soviet leader, **1879**; Heinrich Böll, German author, **1917**; Jane Fonda, US film actress, **1937**; Frank Zappa, US rock singer and composer, **1940**; Chris Evert, US tennis player, **1954**.

DEATHS

Giovanni Boccaccio, Italian author, **1375**; James Parkinson, British neurologist, **1824**; F. Scott Fitzgerald, US novelist, **1940**; Gen. George Patton, US military leader, **1945**.

NOTES

December 22

"Waiting for Godot."
—SAMUEL BECKETT, *title of play*

EVENTS

1894 Alfred Dreyfus, the French officer who was falsely convicted for selling military secrets, was sent to Devil's Island. **1895** German physicist Wilhelm Röntgen made the first X-ray, of his wife's hand. **1961** James Davis became the first US soldier to die in Vietnam, while US involvement was still limited to the provision of military advisers. **1988** In the US, Drexel Burnham Lambert agreed to pay a record $650 million fine for six federal violations in stock dealings. **1989** Romanian dictator Nicolae Ceaușçescu was overthrown in a bloody revolutionary coup. **1991** Eleven of the 12 Soviet republics (excluding Georgia) agreed, in Alma Ata, Kazakhstan, on the creation of a Commonwealth of Independent States.

BIRTHS

John Crome, English painter, **1768**; Frank Billings Kellogg, US secretary of state, **1856**; Giacomo Puccini, Italian composer, **1858**; Peggy Ashcroft, English actress, **1907**; Maurice and Robin Gibb, Australian pop musicians, **1949**.

DEATHS

George Eliot (Mary Ann Evans), English novelist, **1880**; Beatrix Potter, English author and artist, **1943**; Harry Langdon, US silent-film comedian, **1944**; Samuel Beckett, Irish author and dramatist, **1989**.

NOTES

_____

_____

_____

_____

December 23

"Art is either plagiarism or revolution."
—PAUL GAUGUIN

EVENTS

1888 Following a quarrel with Paul Gauguin, Dutch painter Vincent Van Gogh cut off part of his own earlobe. **1913** The US Federal Reserve system was authorized to bring about banking reforms. **1948** General Tojo and six other Japanese military leaders were executed, having been found guilty of crimes against humanity. **1953** Soviet secret police chief Lavrenti Beria and six of his associates were shot for treason following a secret trial. **1986** Dick Rutan and Jeana Yeager made the first nonstop flight around the world without refueling, piloting the US plane *Voyager*. **1990** Elections in Yugoslavia ended, leaving four of its six republics with non-Communist governments.

BIRTHS

Richard Arkwright, English inventor, **1732**; Alexander I, czar of Russia, **1777**; Joseph Smith, US founder of the Mormon Church, **1805**; J. Arthur Rank, British film magnate, **1888**; Helmut Schmidt, German statesman, **1918**.

DEATHS

Thomas Robert Malthus, English economist, **1834**; George Catlin, US painter and explorer, **1872**; Charles Dana Gibson, US artist and illustrator, **1944**; Ernst Krenek, US composer, **1991**.

NOTES

December 24

"Twas the night before Christmas, when all through the house
Not a creature was stirring, not even a mouse;
The stockings were hung by the chimney with care,
In hopes that St. Nicholas soon would be there."
—CLEMENT MOORE, *"A Visit from St. Nicholas"*

Christmas Eve.

EVENTS

1814 The War of 1812 between the US and Britain ended with the signing of the Treaty of Ghent. **1871** Verdi's opera *Aida* was first performed, in Cairo. **1951** Libya achieved independence as the United Kingdom of Libya, under King Idris. **1979** Afghanistan was invaded by Soviet troops as the Kabul government fell.

BIRTHS

John, king of England, **1167**; Ignatius of Loyola, Spanish founder of the Jesuits, **1491**; Matthew Arnold, English poet and critic, **1822**; Howard Hughes, US tycoon, **1905**; Ava Gardner, US film actress, **1922**.

DEATHS

Vasco da Gama, Portuguese explorer and navigator, **1524**; William Makepeace Thackeray, English novelist, **1863**; Leon Bakst, Russian painter and stage designer, **1924**; Alban Berg, Austrian composer, **1935**; Karl Doenitz, German naval commander, **1980**.

NOTES

December 25

*"A lovely thing about Christmas is that it's compulsory, like a
thunderstorm, and we all go through it together."*
—GARRISON KEILLOR, Leaving Home, *"Exiles"*

Christmas Day.

EVENTS

800 Charlemagne was crowned first Holy Roman Emperor in
Rome by Pope Leo III. **1914** During World War I, British and
German troops observed an unofficial truce, even playing soccer
together on the Western front's "no man's land." **1926** Hirohito
succeeded his father Yoshihito as emperor of Japan. **1941** Hong
Kong surrendered to the Japanese. **1972** The Nicaraguan capital
Managua was devastated by an earthquake which killed over
10,000 people. **1989** Dissident playwright Vaclav Havel was
elected president of Czechoslovakia. **1991** Unable to maintain
control over a disintegrating Soviet Union, Mikhail Gorbachev
announced his resignation as president.

BIRTHS

Maurice Utrillo, French painter, **1883**; Humphrey Bogart, US film
actor, **1899**; Cab Calloway, US jazz musician, **1909**; Tony Martin,
US singer, **1913**; Anwar Sadat, Egyptian president, **1918**; Sissy
Spacek, US film actress, **1949**.

DEATHS

W.C. Fields, US comic actor, **1946**; Charlie Chaplin, English actor
and director, **1977**; Joan Miró, Spanish artist, **1983**; Nicolae
Ceausçescu, Romanian politician, executed, **1989**.

NOTES

December 26

EVENTS

1620 The Pilgrims landed at Plymouth, Massachusetts; 103 passengers disembarked from the *Mayflower*. **1776** General Washington captured some 1,000 of Britain's Hessian troops at Trenton, New Jersey, during the American Revolution. **1898** Marie and Pierre Curie discovered radium. **1908** Texan boxer "Galveston Jack" Johnson knocked out Tommy Burns in Sydney, Australia, to become the first black boxer to win the world heavyweight title. **1956** Fidel Castro attempted a secret landing in Cuba to overthrow the Batista regime; all but 11 of his supporters were killed. **1991** The Soviet Union's parliament formally voted the country out of existence.

BIRTHS

Charles Babbage, English mathematician, **1792**; George Dewey, US admiral in the Spanish-American War, **1837**; Henry Miller, US novelist, **1891**; Mao Zedong, Chinese Communist leader, **1893**; Richard Widmark, US film actor, **1914**.

DEATHS

John Wilkes, British politician and journalist who defended the American colonies, **1797**; Heinrich Schliemann, German archeologist, who discovered and excavated the site of ancient Troy, **1890**; Charles Pathé, French film pioneer, **1957**; Harry S. Truman, 33rd US president, **1972**; Jack Benny, US comedian, **1974**.

NOTES

_____

_____

_____

_____

December 27

---

*"At 20 you have many desires that hide the truth,
but beyond 40 there are only real and fragile
truths—your abilities and your failings."*
—GERARD DEPARDIEU

EVENTS

1831 Charles Darwin set sail in the *Beagle* on his voyage of scientific discovery. **1904** James Barrie's *Peter Pan* premiered in London. **1927** Defeated in his struggle for power against Stalin, Leon Trotsky was expelled from the Communist party. **1978** With the adoption of a new constitution, Spain became a democracy after 40 years of dictatorship.

BIRTHS

Johannes Kepler, German astronomer, **1571**; Louis Pasteur, French chemist and microbiologist, **1822**; Sydney Greenstreet, English-born US film actor, **1878**; Marlene Dietrich, German-born Hollywood singer and actress, **1901**; Gerard Depardieu, French film actor, **1948**.

DEATHS

Charles Lamb, English essayist and critic, **1834**; Max Beckmann, German painter, **1950**; Lester Pearson, Canadian statesman, **1972**; Houari Boumédienne, Algerian politician, **1978**; Hoagy Carmichael, US composer, singer, and pianist, **1981**; Hervé Guibert, French novelist and photographer, **1992**.

NOTES

December 28

"The world must be made safe for democracy."
—PRESIDENT WOODROW WILSON, *address to Congress*

EVENTS

1836 Mexico's independence was recognized by Spain. **1846** Iowa became the 29th state. **1908** An earthquake killed over 75,000 at Messina in Sicily. **1937** The Irish Free State became the Republic of Ireland when a new constitution established the country as a sovereign state under the name of Eire. **1989** Alexander Dubček, who had been expelled from the Communist party in 1970, was elected speaker of the Czech parliament. **1993** The US Department of Energy said government experiments in the 1940s and 1950s had exposed some 800 Americans to radiation.

BIRTHS

Woodrow Wilson, 28th US president, **1856**; Earl Hines, US jazz pianist, **1905**; Lew Ayres, US film actor, **1908**, Maggie Smith, English actress, **1934**; Denzel Washington, US film actor, **1954**.

DEATHS

Mary II, queen of England, Scotland and Ireland, **1694**; Rob Roy, Scottish clan chief, **1734**; Gustave Eiffel, French engineer, **1923**; Maurice Ravel, French composer, **1937**; Max Steiner, US film music composer, **1971**; Sam Peckinpah, US film director, **1984**.

NOTES

December 29

EVENTS

1170 English priest and politician St. Thomas à Becket, the 40th archbishop of Canterbury, was murdered in his own cathedral by four knights supposedly acting on Henry II's orders. **1845** Texas became the 28th state. **1890** The massacre at Wounded Knee, the last major battle between Native Americans and US troops, took place. **1895** The Jameson Raid from Mafikeng into Transvaal, which attempted to overthrow Kruger's Boer government, started. **1911** Sun Yat-sen became the first president of a republican China, following the Revolution. **1989** Following Hong Kong's decision to forcibly repatriate some Vietnamese refugees, thousands of Vietnamese "boat people" battled with riot police.

BIRTHS

Charles Goodyear, US inventor of vulcanized rubber, **1800**; Andrew Johnson, 17th US president, **1808**; William Gladstone, English prime minister, **1809**; Pablo Casals, Spanish cellist, **1876**; Mary Tyler Moore, US TV comedienne and actress, **1937**; Jon Voight, US film actor, **1938**; Ted Danson, US actor, **1947**.

DEATHS

Jacques Louis David, French painter, **1825**; Christina Rossetti, English poet, **1894**; Rainer Maria Rilke, German poet, **1926**; James Fletcher Henderson, US jazz pianist and composer, **1952**; Harold Macmillan, British prime minister, **1986**.

NOTES

December 30

―――――

"The idiot who praises with enthusiastic tone
All centuries but this and every country but his own."
—W.S. GILBERT

―――――

EVENTS

1460 At the Battle of Wakefield, in England's Wars of the Roses, the duke of York was defeated and killed by the Lancastrians. **1879** Gilbert and Sullivan's *The Pirates of Penzance* was first performed. **1880** The Transvaal was declared a republic by Paul Kruger, who became its first president. **1922** The Union of Soviet Socialist Republics was formed. **1947** King Michael of Romania abdicated in favor of a Communist republic.

BIRTHS

André Messager, French composer, **1853**; Rudyard Kipling, English author and poet, **1865**; Bo Diddley, US rhythm and blues singer, **1928**; Tracey Ullman, English comedienne, **1959**; Ben Johnson, Canadian track athlete, **1961**.

DEATHS

Robert Boyle, Irish physicist and chemist, **1691**; Amelia Bloomer, US social reformer, **1894**; Grigori Efimovich Rasputin, Siberian mystic, **1916**; Trygve Lie, Norwegian government minister and first secretary general of the UN, **1968**; Richard Rodgers, US composer, **1979**.

NOTES

―――――

―――――

―――――

―――――

December 31

---

*"Time has no divisions to mark its passage, there is never
a thunderstorm or blare of trumpets to announce the beginning
of a new month or year. Even when a new century begins it
is only we mortals who ring bells and fire off pistols."*
—THOMAS MANN, The Magic Mountain

New Year's Eve.

EVENTS

1891 New York's new immigration depot was opened at Ellis
Island. **1943** Frank Sinatra started a singing engagement at New
York's Paramount Theater and became the idol of the nation's
"bobby soxers." **1970** The National Air Quality Control Act was
signed by President Nixon. **1990** Titleholder Gary Kasparov of
the USSR won the world chess championship match against his
countryman Anatoly Karpov.

BIRTHS

George Meade, US Union general. 1815; John Thompson, US soldier who invented the tommy gun, 1860; Henri Matisse, French
painter, 1869; George Marshall, US general and statesman, 1880;
Anthony Hopkins, Welsh actor, 1937; John Denver, US folk
singer, 1943; Val Kilmer, US film actor, 1959.

DEATHS

Gustave Courbet, French painter, 1877; Miguel de Unamuno,
Spanish writer, 1936; Marshall McLuhan, Canadian theorist of
communication, 1980; Rick Nelson, US rock 'n' roll singer, 1985.

NOTES

Appendices

Months

The names of the months were probably derived as follows:

January	Janus, Roman god	July	Julius Caesar, Roman general
February	Februar, Roman festival of purification	August	Augustus, Roman emperor
March	Mars, Roman god	September	Latin *septem*, "seven"
April	Latin *aperire*, "to open"	October	Latin *octo*, "eight"
May	Maia, Roman goddess	November	Latin *novem*, "nine"
June	Juno, Roman goddess	December	Latin *decem*, "ten"

September, October, November, December were originally the seventh, eighth, ninth and tenth months of the Roman year.

Days of the Week

The names of the days are derived as follows:

English	*Latin*	*Saxon*
Sunday	Dies Solis	Sun's Day
Monday	Dies Lunae	Moon's Day
Tuesday	Dies Martis	Tiu's Day
Wednesday	Dies Mercurii	Woden's Day
Thursday	Dies Jovis	Thor's Day
Friday	Dies Veneris	Frigg's Day
Saturday	Dies Saturni	Saeternes' Day

Movable Christian Feasts 1996–2016

	Ash Wednesday	Easter Day	Ascension Day	Pentecost (Whit Sunday)	Advent Sunday
1996	Feb. 21	Apr. 7	May 16	May 26	Dec. 1
1997	Feb. 12	Mar. 30	May 8	May 18	Nov. 30
1998	Feb. 25	Apr. 12	May 21	May 31	Nov. 29
1999	Feb. 17	Apr. 4	May 13	May 23	Nov. 28
2000	Mar. 8	Apr. 23	Jun. 1	Jun. 11	Dec. 3
2001	Feb. 28	Apr. 15	May 24	Jun. 3	Dec. 2
2002	Feb. 13	Mar. 31	May 9	May 19	Dec. 1
2003	Mar. 5	Apr. 20	May 29	Jun. 8	Nov. 30
2004	Feb. 25	Apr. 11	May 20	May 30	Nov. 28
2005	Feb. 9	Mar. 27	May 5	May 15	Nov. 27
2006	Mar. 1	Apr. 16	May 25	Jun. 4	Dec. 3
2007	Feb. 21	Apr. 8	May 17	May 27	Dec. 2
2008	Feb. 6	Mar. 23	May 1	May 11	Nov. 30
2009	Feb. 25	Apr. 12	May 21	May 31	Nov. 29
2010	Feb. 17	Apr. 4	May 13	May 23	Nov. 28
2011	Mar. 9	Apr. 24	Jun. 2	Jun. 12	Nov. 27
2012	Feb. 22	Apr. 8	May 17	May 27	Dec. 2
2013	Feb. 13	Mar. 31	May 9	May 19	Dec. 1
2014	Mar. 5	Apr. 20	May 29	Jun. 8	Nov. 30
2015	Feb. 18	Apr. 5	May 14	May 24	Nov. 29
2016	Mar. 10	Mar. 27	May 5	May 15	Nov. 27

Advent Sunday is the fourth Sunday before Christmas Day.
Ash Wednesday is the first day of Lent, and falls in the seventh week before Easter.
Holy Week is the week before Easter Day, and includes Palm Sunday, Maundy Thursday, Good Friday, and Easter Eve.
Ascension Day is 40 days after Easter Day.
Pentecost (Whit Sunday) is seven weeks after Easter Day.
Trinity Sunday is eight weeks after Easter Day.

Christian Festivals and Holy Days

January 1	The naming of Jesus. The Circumcision of Christ. The Solemnity of Mary Mother of God
January 6	Epiphany
January 25	The Conversion of St. Paul
February 2	The Presentation of Christ in the Temple
March 19	St. Joseph of Nazareth, Husband of the Blessed Virgin Mary
March 25	The Annunciation of Our Lord to the Blessed Virgin Mary
April 25	St. Mark the Evangelist
May 1	St. Philip and St. James, Apostles
May 14	St. Matthias the Apostle
May 31	The Visitation of the Blessed Virgin Mary
June 11	St. Barnabas the Apostle
June 24	The Birth of St. John the Baptist
June 29	St. Peter the Apostle
July 3	St. Thomas the Apostle
July 22	St. Mary Magdalen
July 25	St. James the Apostle
August 6	The Transfiguration of our Lord
August 24	St. Bartholomew the Apostle
September 1	New Year (Eastern Orthodox Church)
September 8	The Nativity of the Blessed Virgin Mary
September 14	The Exaltation of the Holy Cross
September 21	St. Matthew the Apostle
September 29	St. Michael and All Angels (Michaelmas)
October 18	St. Luke the Evangelist
October 28	St. Simon and St. Jude, Apostles
November 1	All Saints
November 21	Presentation of the Blessed Virgin Mary in the Temple
November 30	St. Andrew the Apostle
December 8	The Immaculate Conception of the Blessed Virgin Mary
December 25	Christmas
December 26	St. Stephen the first Martyr
December 27	St. John the Evangelist
December 28	The Holy Innocents

Buddhist Festivals

Burma (Myanmar)

April 16–17	New Year
May–June	The Buddha's Birth ● Enlightenment & Death
July	The Buddha's First Sermon ● Beginning of the Rains Retreat
October	End of the Rains Retreat
November	Kathina Ceremony

China

June–August	Summer Retreat
August	Festival of Hungry Ghosts ● Gautama Buddha's Birth ● Kuan-Yin

Sri Lanka

April 13	New Year
May–June	The Buddha's Birth ● Enlightenment & Death
June–July	Establishment of Buddhism in Sri Lanka
July	The Buddha's First Sermon
July–August	Procession of the Month of Asala
September	The Buddha's First Visit to Sri Lanka
December–January	Arrival of Sanghamitta

Thailand

April 13–16	New Year
May	The Buddha's Enlightenment
May–June	The Buddha's Cremation
July–October	Rains Retreat
October	End of the Rains Retreat
November	Kathina Ceremony ● Festival of Lights
February	All Saints' Day

Tibet

February	New Year
May	The Buddha's Birth, Enlightenment & Death
June	Dzamling Chisang
June–July	The Buddha's First Sermon
October	The Buddha's Descent from Tushita
November	Death of Tsongkhapa
January	The Conjunction of Nine Evils and the Conjunction of Ten Virtues

Hindu Festivals

January	Makar Sankranti/Til Sankranti/Lohri, Pongal, Kumbha Mela at Prayag (every 12 years)
January–February	Vasanta Panchami/Shri Panchami/Saraswati Puja, Bhogali Bihu, Mahashivratri
February 20	Ramakrishna Utsav
February–March	Holi
March–April	Ugadi, Basora, Rama Navami, Hanuman Jayanti
April	Vaisakhi
April–May	Akshaya Tritiya, Chittrai
May–June	Ganga Dasa-hara, Nirjala Ekadashi, Snan-yatra
June–July	Ratha-yatra/Jagannatha, Ashadhi Ekadashi/Toli Ekadashi
July–August	Teej, Naga Panchami, Raksha Bandhan/Shravana Purnima/Salono/Rakhi Purnima
August–September	Onam, Ganesha Chaturthi, Janamashtami/Krishna Jayanti
September–October	Mahalaya/Shraddha/Pitri Paksha/Kanagat, Navaratri/Durga Puja/Dassehra, Lakshmi Puja
October 2	Gandhi Jayanti
October–November	Divali/Deepavali Chhath, Karttika Ekadashi/Devuthna Ekadashi/Tulsi Ekadashi, Karttika Purnima/Tripuri Purnima, Hoi, Skanda Shasti
November–December	Vaikuntha Ekadashi, Lakshmi Puja (Orissa)

Islamic Calendar

The Islamic calendar is reckoned from the year of the Hegira, or flight of Mohammed from Mecca to Medina. The corresponding date in the Julian calendar is July 16 AD 622. The years are purely lunar, and consist of 12 months with alternately 29 or 30 days, plus one extra day at the end of the 12th month (Dhul-Hijjah) in leap years, which occur at stated intervals in each cycle of 30 years.

Islamic Calendar 1417 AH

The beginning of the month in the Islamic calendar depends on the visibility of the new moon; therefore dates may differ from those stated here

Hijrah month	*1417 AH*
Muharram	May 19 1996
Safar	June 18 1996
Rabi'a I	Jul. 16 1996
Rabi'a II	Aug. 16 1996
Jumada I	Sept. 13 1996
Jumada II	Oct. 13 1996
Rajab	Nov. 12 1996
Sha'ban	Dec. 11 1996
Ramadan	Jan. 9 1997
Shawwal	Feb. 8 1997
Dhul-Qi'da	March 9 1997
Dhul-Hijja	April 8 1997

Important days	*1417 AH*
Hijrah New Year	May 19 1996
Ashura'	May 28 1996
Birthday of the prophet Mohammed	July 27 1996
Lailat-Ul-Isra'walmi'raj	Dec. 7 1995
Lailat-ul-Bara'ah	Dec. 25 1997
Ramadan	Jan. 9 1997
Lailat-ul-Qadr	Feb. 2 1997
Eid-ul-Fitr	Feb. 7 1997
Arafat	Apr. 16 1997
Eid-ul-Adha	Apr. 17 1997

AH—*anno Hejirae* (since the year of the Hegira, the beginning of the Muslim era)

Jewish Holy Days 1996–1999

Festival details		1996	1997	1998	1999
PASSOVER					
Pesach	1st day	Apr. 4	Apr. 22	Apr. 11	Apr. 1
	2nd day	Apr. 5	Apr. 23	Apr. 12	Apr. 2
	7th day	Apr. 10	Apr. 28	Apr. 17	Apr. 7
	8th day	Apr. 11	Apr. 29	Apr. 18	Apr. 8
PENTECOST					
Sharuot	1st day	May 24	Jun. 11	May 31	May 21
	2nd day	May 25	Jun. 12	Jun. 1	May 22
NEW YEAR					
Rosh Hashanah	1st day	Sept. 14	Oct. 2	Sept. 21	Sept. 11
	2nd day	Sept. 15	Oct. 3	Sept. 22	Sept. 12
DATE OF ATONEMENT					
Yom Kippur		Sept. 23	Oct. 11	Sept. 30	Sept. 20
TABERNACLES					
Succot	1st day	Sept. 28	Oct. 16	Oct. 5	Sept. 25
	2nd day	Sept. 29	Oct. 17	Oct. 6	Sept. 26
Shemini Atzeret	8th day	Oct. 5	Oct. 23	Oct. 12	Oct. 2
Simchat Torah	9th day	Oct. 6	Oct. 24	Oct. 13	Oct. 3

*Solar and Lunar Eclipses until 2001**

date	type of eclipse	time of maxi. eclipse	main area of visibility
1996			
April 3/4	Moon total	00 hr 10 min	E North America, Central and South America, Europe, Africa, W Asia
April 17	Sun partial	22 hr 38 min	New Zealand, Southern Pacific Ocean
September 27	Moon total	02 hr 54 min	The Americas, Europe, Africa, W Asia
October 12	Sun partial	14 hr 03 min	NE Canada, Greenland, W Europe, N Africa
1997			
March 9	Sun total	01 hr 25 min	E Asia, Japan
September 1/2	Sun partial	00 hr 05 min	Australia, New Zealand
September 16	Moon total	18 hr 47 min	Europe, Africa, Asia, Australasia
1998			
February 26	Sun total	17 hr 29 min	S and E US, Central America, N South America
August 22	Sun annular	02 hr 07 min	SE Asia, Oceania, Australasia
1999			
February 16	Sun annular	06 hr 35 min	Indian Ocean, Antarctica, Australia
August 11	Sun total	11 hr 04 min	Europe, N Africa, Arabia, W Asia
2000			
January 21	Moon total	04 hr 44 min	The Americas, Europe, Africa, W Asia
February 5	Sun partial	12 hr 50 min	Antarctica
July 1	Sun partial	19 hr 34 min	SE Pacific Ocean
July 16	Moon total	13 hr 56 min	SE Asia, Australasia
July 31	Sun partial	02 hr 14 min	Arctic regions
December 25	Sun partial	17 hr 36 min	US, E Canada, Central America, Caribbean
2001			
January 9	Moon total	20 hr 21 min	Africa, Europe, Asia
June 21	Sun total	12 hr 04 min	Central and S Africa
December 14	Sun annular	20 hr 52 min	Pacific Ocean

*except partial eclipses of the Moon

Wedding Anniversaries

In many Western countries, different wedding anniversaries have become associated with gifts of different materials. There is variation between countries.

anniversary	material	anniversary	material
1st	paper	14th	ivory
2nd	cotton	15th	crystal
3rd	leather	20th	china
4th	linen	25th	silver
5th	wood	30th	pearl
6th	iron	35th	coral
7th	copper, wool	40th	ruby
8th	bronze	45th	sapphire
9th	pottery, china	50th	gold
10th	tin, aluminum	55th	emerald
11th	steel	60th	diamond
12th	silk, linen	70th	platinum
13th	lace		

Birthstones

month	stone	quality
January	garnet	constancy
February	amethyst	sincerity
March	bloodstone	courage
April	diamond	innocence & lasting love
May	emerald	success & hope
June	pearl	health & purity
July	ruby	love & contentment
August	agate	married happiness
September	sapphire	wisdom
October	opal	hope
November	topaz	fidelity
December	turquoise	harmony

Signs of the Zodiac

Spring

Aries	The Ram	Mar. 21–Apr. 20
Taurus	The Bull	Apr. 21–May 21
Gemini	The Twins	May 22–June 21

Summer

Cancer	The Crab	June 22–July 23
Leo	The Lion	July 24–Aug. 23
Virgo	The Virgin	Aug. 24–Sept. 23

Autumn

Libra	The Balance	Sept. 24–Oct. 23
Scorpio	The Scorpion	Oct. 24–Nov. 22
Sagittarius	The Archer	Nov. 23–Dec. 21

Winter

Capricorn	The Goat	Dec. 22–Jan. 20
Aquarius	The Water Bearer	Jan. 21–Feb. 19
Pisces	The Fishes	Feb. 20–Mar. 20